LISTEN UP !

LISTEN UP!

RECORDING MUSIC WITH

BOB DYLAN, NEIL YOUNG, U2, R.E.M., THE TRAGICALLY HIP, RED HOT CHILI PEPPERS, TOM WAITS . . .

MARK HOWARD with CHRIS HOWARD

Published by ECW Press
665 Gerrard Street East
Toronto, Ontario, Canada M4M 1Y2
416-694-3348 / info@ecwpress.com

Editor for the press: Michael Holmes
Cover design: David A. Gee
Front cover photos: Mark Howard at console, Tom Waits, Neil Young, Rickie Lee Jones, and Feist courtesy Mark Howard; Bob Dylan © Bob Lanois; Willie Nelson © Donata Wenders; Robert Plant © Trixie Whitley; Teatro interior © Bob Lanois
Interior photos: Unless otherwise specified photos and Polaroids by Mark Howard
Author photo: Lisa Macintosh

LIBRARY AND ARCHIVES CANADA CATALOGUING IN PUBLICATION

Howard, Mark, 1964–, author
    Listen up! : recording music with Bob Dylan, Neil Young, U2, R.E.M., the Tragically Hip, Red Hot Chili Peppers, Tom Waits... / Mark Howard with Chris Howard.

Issued in print and electronic formats.
ISBN 978-1-77041-482-2 (softcover)
ISBN 978-1-77305-348-6 (PDF)
ISBN 978-1-77305-347-9 (EPUB)

    1. Howard, Mark, 1964–. 2. Sound recording executives and producers—Canada—Biography. 3. Sound engineers—Canada—Biography. 4. Sound—Recording and reproducing—Handbooks, manuals, etc. I. Howard, Chris, 1955–. author II. Title.

ML429.H852A3 2019   782.42164092
C2018-905296-1   C2018-905297-X

The publication of *Listen Up!* has been generously supported by the Canada Council for the Arts which last year invested $153 million to bring the arts to Canadians throughout the country and is funded in part by the Government of Canada. *Nous remercions le Conseil des arts du Canada de son soutien. L'an dernier, le Conseil a investi 153 millions de dollars pour mettre de l'art dans la vie des Canadiennes et des Canadiens de tout le pays. Ce livre est financé en partie par le gouvernement du Canada.* We acknowledge the support of the Ontario Arts Council (OAC), an agency of the Government of Ontario, which last year funded 1,737 individual artists and 1,095 organizations in 223 communities across Ontario for a total of $52.1 million. We also acknowledge the contribution of the Government of Ontario through the Ontario Book Publishing Tax Credit, and through Ontario Creates for the marketing of this book.

PRINTED AND BOUND IN CANADA
PRINTING: FRIESENS   5 4 3 2 1

For my daughters, Fiana and Thea,
the greatest inspirations in my life.

CONTENTS

PROLOGUE

THIS IS A BACKSTAGE PASS INTO THE lives of some of the planet's most iconic musicians. Moreover, it's a rare glimpse into the normally invisible, almost secretive, side of the music story: that of the producer and recording engineer. These pages will take you to a star-studded world of recording and producing Grammy Award winners in which Iggy Pop shows up to record clad in see-through plastic pants, no underwear, and Bob Dylan will only record at night. You'll learn about Tom Waits's strange vocabulary — and what "put a little hair on it" really means — and discover that because Neil Young will only work on the three days before a full moon, it takes six months to make his record.

This is also a production guide for anyone interested in music, providing an understanding of the equipment used in making the world's most unforgettable records and explaining the methods needed to get the very best sound. Each chapter gives recording and producing information and tips, including inside stories about the making of great albums.

Upon accepting his Grammy Award for Album of the Year, Bob Dylan thanked me, saying, "We got a particular type of sound on this record which you don't get every day."

For the first time, readers can learn how.

INTRODUCTION

I LEFT WESTDALE SECONDARY SCHOOL IN HAMILTON, Ontario, Canada, in grade nine. My guidance counselor told me that if I dropped out, I'd end up in prison. All these years later, I *am* embarrassed to tell people where I ended up. I can't have a conversation about my occupation or latest projects without it sounding like I'm name dropping, because I ended up working with some of the most famous people on the planet, in amazing locations around the world.

Leaving school at a young age didn't limit my education; instead, I got my English degree from Bob Dylan, who didn't have notes, so I'd sit at the console and transcribe his lyrics while he sang in front of me. Many musicians read the classics and draw on them for lyrical content, like Robert Plant, who carried the poetry of William Blake into the studio. I've been exposed to a lot of literature despite leaving school. My education occurred in other ways, too, as I developed math skills managing both enormous and limited budgets.

I was born in Manchester, England, but in 1967 my family moved to Hamilton — sometimes referred to as "Steeltown" — when my father found work as an electrician as part of an incentive program for skilled workers. My dad was extremely athletic. A boxer during the war, he was the featherweight champion in England in the late 1940s and early 1950s. After moving to Canada, he became the coach for the Canadian wrestling team and then an official at the Olympics. Although

I grew up surrounded by sports, I wanted nothing to do with them — I thought they were boring. I know my dad was upset that I didn't choose sports, and he definitely didn't approve of a job in music. I once asked him to come down to a grungy bar on Locke Street in Hamilton to see what I did for a living. Unfortunately, a punk band was playing, and with the racket, the fighting, and the blood, he wasn't impressed. He told me to get a real job. It wasn't until years later when he had my Grammy on his shelf that he finally accepted my career.

I did try to hold down conventional jobs. From a young age, I was interested in architecture and design and had filled a notebook with sketches. After dropping out of school at sixteen, I walked into an architect's office and showed him my drawings. He was impressed and told me to go back to finish grade twelve and then he'd hire me. I had no intention of going back to school, so I found a job as a layout artist for gravestones.

Yet I was always drawn to music. I studied the conservatory program for drums as a teenager. When I was fifteen I took over our basement, and after turning the pool table into a drum riser, I filled the room with amps, posters, and black lights, and it looked like a club. Although perhaps unusual for a teenage boy, I added rugs and lighting, focusing on a design aesthetic. Looking back, I realize that was actually my first studio installation, where I realized the gear and sound are only half the equation — that the look and energy of a room mattered, too. To this day, no matter who I work with, I set up the gear so it isn't intimidating or the most obvious thing in the room. I never have cables lying all over the floor like they do in so many other studios.

In my late teens, I worked in the local Hamilton music scene, mixing and doing live sound, but by age twenty I'd had a serious motorcycle accident on my 1971 Norton 750, which left me unable to continue due to back injuries. Adversity equals opportunity, and with the brashness of youth, I marched into Grant Avenue Studio, a local recording studio.

"The government will pay half my wages if you pay the other half," I told them. I was hired.

Because I'd had so much experience on the road doing quick setups and sound checks for live shows, I was able to transfer those skills to the studio, and I was faster than a lot of studio guys, who are usually laid-back because they feel there is no time crunch.

In the years that followed there were only a few times I was tied down by a studio, such as Kingsway or the Teatro, but I simply don't work like other people, so a typical studio wasn't enough. I like high ceilings and interesting locations, and that's more difficult than ever to finance. Essentially, the bottom has dropped out of the music industry. CDs no longer sell much, and many young people expect music for free or as part of an online subscription. Everyone in the music industry needs to be more inventive now, and we're all being pushed to break new ground.

Luckily, I worked on timeless records. People who focused on making hits in the '80s were riding high, but it's hard to have longevity. The last record gets you to the next job by word of mouth.

The installations I set up to record individual albums are ideal, without the overhead needed to maintain a studio long term. Instead, I find a cool space, create the atmosphere, load it with fantastic gear, and then focus on the art. Sometimes I'll take everyone who is working on an album to a cottage — everyone has their own room, and I hire a chef — and the musicians live, sleep, and eat in the same place. Something about everyone being in close proximity for a period of time encourages the creative flow. I find that creating an installation studio — setting up an entire studio in a chosen location to record an artist, then dismantling it and moving on to the next location and the next artist — is ideal for maximum collaboration and creativity for both me and them.

I often think that rules that have been set out for making music — the ones taught in recording programs — were all made by people who simply couldn't figure anything else out. Whatever recording technique is taught in a college program, I generally do the opposite. I record drums in the control room; I don't isolate artists. The truth is anyone can record in their bedroom these days and make it sound good. That said, I'm anti-computers and programs like Pro Tools and GarageBand. I don't like the sounds and I don't find them musical. I want to push Record and begin, not mess around with drop-down menus or with a computer crashing — otherwise magic is lost. Essentially, you wipe out the performance with the technology and it actually makes things slower. Everything is being compressed these days, with no dynamics, but I think it's better if I am the human compressor. Everything in my mix is me.

I tell young people to get off the computer and get an old 4- or 8-track cassette recorder. Often, I hook up some of the older iconic singers with cassettes, and then I put them on my iZ Radar (multitrack recorder) to play with. Tom Waits recorded mouth rhythms in his bathroom. I've had a million dollars' worth of gear, but nothing can touch the punchy sound of a cheap cassette recorder.

I discovered when we're limited we're pushed to find new ways forward. For my first records, like with Bob Dylan and the Neville Brothers, I didn't have a compressor or extra gear and plugins. Good sounds come from the source: good guitars and amps. If things need to be tweaked for twenty minutes to make them sound better, then something is wrong.

This is why I don't think schools can teach recording. Perhaps you can learn engineering, but true creativity is about exploration, not rules. And no school teaches people to deal with a guy loaded on heroin. Recording is a mental game, and you need to learn how to handle musicians and artists.

Although breaking the rules has been key to my success, timing has also been important — being in the right room at the right time, taking the opportunity when it's presented. Instead of wasting my time crafting an image, I let my creative work speak for itself, and jobs came to me through word of mouth. Bob Dylan told Marianne Faithfull about me, advising her that I knew what to do with unusual vocalists. Being able to work with demanding, highly creative people, many considered to be geniuses, is not something at which everyone excels. Reading people is instinctive, and you need to gain musicians' trust before they're willing to be vulnerable with their art. To get the best out of a musician you need to play a bit of a game, know how far you can push them outside of their comfort zone to get what you need. It's an interesting aspect of working in the music business that isn't often talked about: how to motivate, challenge, and inspire creative minds, with all their individual quirks and eccentricities, so they can produce a work of art in which everyone takes pride. I've been lucky enough to work with some of the best.

CHAPTER 1

THE NEVILLE BROTHERS AT EMLAH COURT

THE RECORDING ENGINEER, SUPERVISED BY A PRODUCER, operates the recording console and other equipment. The engineer also sets up the studio and recording equipment. I started as a recording engineer and worked my way up to the producer's chair.

In 1988 I was asked to work on an album with the Neville Brothers. Before leaving Canada for New Orleans, I was asked to bring a couple of microphones with me. I picked up a Neumann U47 and a Sony C-37A, both vintage tube mics. Customs at the U.S. border hassled me about why I was carrying them, and I said I was a big fan of jazz music and was taking them so I could record at a jazz festival. They let me go: I passed my first importing test.

Once I arrived in New Orleans, I met Dan — Daniel Lanois — the producer, in the enormous apartment he had rented in the French Quarter, at 626 Royal Street.

"I got you a nice place to stay over on St. Ann Street," he told me, adding that he was only staying a couple more days and that once he left, I would move over to his place. He gave me the address of my accommodations on St. Ann and asked me to meet him back at his apartment in the morning.

Walking through the French Quarter, passing Bourbon Street, the swarms of drunken people and even a brass band made the experience a bit surreal. I grew up in a steel city that was a tough place full of blue-collar workers, and I'd never met anyone openly gay in my life. Suddenly, I found myself in the midst of men in assless chaps, and large hairy guys kissing young white boys in their underwear.

Still reeling from the antics of the French Quarter, once inside the house on St. Ann, I rang the bell and was greeted by a nice, old British man named John; he and his friendly wife were a welcome sight. He showed me my beautiful guesthouse, where I spent my first night alone in a strange city full of the most bizarre people I'd ever met, wondering what I'd just fallen into.

The next day Royal Street was blocked off and full of street musicians and tarot card readers. Dan and I went out for breakfast to a cool English place called The Cheshire Cat. He told me that he was leaving the next day for England to work with Brian Eno in a place called Woodbridge, a beautiful market town in the county of Suffolk. He informed me that I was responsible for finding a place to make the Neville Brothers' record, and that I'd need to buy and import all the gear from Canada, England, and New York. I'd have to set up the studio, buy a car, and furnish the place so we could sleep there. I also had to open a bank account. I basically had to be a real-estate agent, an international gear importer, and an accountant — all in an age with no cell phones or computers. To top it off, I looked really young for my age, more like a fifteen-year-old than a twenty-two-year-old; I still didn't even need to shave.

I met with Lucy Burnett, a New Orleans socialite with old money from a southern family — a real southern belle. She had the corner balcony apartment at Royal and St. Philip Streets, the best location for Mardi Gras parties. She was likely in her forties at the time and loved any reason to throw a party.

I explained my situation and she said, "I have just the guy for you, a real-estate guy who knows all the best properties."

First, I had to find a car so I could start looking for locations, and I bought a black 1965 Cadillac Calais — a huge boat in amazing shape, with low miles, electric windows, and white-wall tires. It could fit four people on the front bench seat and was the perfect people mover.

Dan had given me a ridiculous budget of only $1,200 per month to find a place to make the record. I met with the agent uptown at the Columns Hotel. The first location he showed me was an old children's asylum, and frankly, it was

THE NEVILLE BROTHERS AT EMLAH COURT

A Neville Brothers' *Yellow Moon* session in New Orleans (July 1988).

scary. It still had old beds and cribs in which the children used to sleep, and the vibe made it feel as though the kids had been prisoners.

He then showed me an old Mardi Gras float hanger. In one of the buildings I opened a janitor's closet, and through the darkness I could see a sink that was moving. I flicked on the light and discovered the sink was overflowing with huge cockroaches that immediately flew at me.

After not having much luck finding a place, I remembered a building beside the Columns Hotel, on St. Charles Avenue, that was for sale. I asked the agent if we could see the building, and he arranged an appointment. It was a five-story place called Emlah Court. A Louisianan oil baron had built it for his five daughters, each one getting a floor, and he'd used the first letter of each of their names to create the name *Emlah*. The entrance was two large glass doors framed with wrought iron, and inside was a cage elevator with mirrors on the walls. Each floor had a single huge apartment — each with three large bedrooms, three bathrooms, and a huge living area and separate dining room — and all the rooms had fifteen-foot ceilings and beautiful French windows from floor to ceiling. The place was perfect for making the record.

One of the most important things to think about when choosing a place to record is something called "magnetic field." If a person has a single coil pickup in their guitar running through a tube amp, it causes a problematic hum. Often, a quiet spot can be found by facing the guitar in a different direction, but if there is a big power transformer outside the building or somewhere close by, you might not get a clean signal. I had developed a test for this and carried a Lawrence pickup for an acoustic guitar and a little Peavey battery powered amp. I trolled the pickup along the floors to see if there was any noise. Occasionally, fluorescent light fixtures would cause a huge noise even though they were on the ceiling below.

An old man owned Emlah Court. He had bought it cheap and thought he could flip it for a high price, however the real-estate market was at an all-time low and he'd had it up for sale for two years with no offers. I told the agent to offer the owner six months' rent at $1,500 a month, a total of $9,000, all up front if he'd let me have it. I didn't think anyone would buy the building in the next six months, and the rental would make the owner a bit of money. The owner considered the idea but countered with $10,000 for six months. I agreed.

With the location and car in place, I still had the task of getting all the gear and installing it at Emlah Court. I bought an Amek Matchless 32-channel console from England, a console known for its ruggedness. We chose this console because U2 had used an Amek Angela console on their last record and Dan and I liked the sound of it. I discovered I could import it into the United States without paying duties and tax if I brought it in on a temporary import bond.

We already had a high-quality Studer A80 mk2 24-track tape recorder to be used as a master tape recorder, although it was the size of a huge industrial fridge and was sitting in Canada. I got the same temporary import bond I'd used in England to have it shipped down, but I had to have road cases made to ship it in. I also needed to have racks made for holding all the outboard gear, as well as cases for them, so I called one of my old bosses, Lou Furlanetto from the Guitar Clinic in Hamilton. Because they made guitars there, they made me wooden racks with a sunburst finish, like on a Fender Stratocaster.

The Studer tape recorder had to be broken down into two cases; they removed the huge meter bridge and put that in one case, and the body went in another. I hired Rock-it Cargo to ship it all to New Orleans.

A lot of the remaining gear came from New York. I bought a Dolby A XP24 noise reduction rack because Peter Gabriel's *So* album was recorded with one, and he'd used it as an effect on his vocals. When the Dolby is turned off on a vocal, it hypes the sound. For effects, I got an AMS (Advanced Music Systems) DMX 15 delay that had a computer-controlled digital delay with a truly unique sound. It was used by Stewart Copeland of the Police. I also bought two Lexicon PCM 70s, which boast a digital effects processor with chorus, flange, reverb, multiband delays, and resonant chords. Known for its classic sound, it was employed on every Pink Floyd album and tour.

The speakers I chose were a set of Tannoy Monitor Golds. Tannoy is an English speaker maker. The speakers were intended for radio and recording studios, yet many people installed them in their homes because of their fantastic sound. I shipped them from England and had speaker cabinets made for them based on the Lockwood speaker-cabinet design.

The rest of the gear was bought from a local music shop in New Orleans called Sound Chek. The owner cut me some great deals on cables, microphone stands, and amps.

I was still living on Royal Street when the first shipment came from Canada, so I had to store the cases in the horse carriageway of the apartment building. Once I took possession of Emlah Court, the console arrived. The console was shipped in a huge brown road case that was twelve feet long and four feet wide, along with a huge case that held two power supplies and the console stand. I hired a mammoth guy named Jimmy Mac to help me move the gear inside Emlah court. The studio was on the second floor and there was no way the console would fit in the elevator. Jimmy ran the crews at Jazz Fest, so he had a gang of guys who knew how to move gear. We had to remove the console from the case and carry it in; however, the stairs we had to take it up had three landings. The console was so long it couldn't be carried flat and had to be tilted vertically and then balanced on its end. It took six guys to get it upstairs, and we warned the crew they'd have to lose a finger before damaging or dropping the console. Luckily, neither the crew nor the console was hurt.

Jimmy's guys also carried the Studer tape recorder up, along with the rest of the cases.

With the gear in, it was time to install it. I set up the main control room in one of the bedrooms, leaving the living room for the performance room. I planned to sleep in the back bedroom. The top-floor apartment I set up for Dan. I used the console road case as his bed base and bought him a futon for the mattress. I had contacted an electrician, Mike Montero, to construct an electrical box that could be tied into the main panel, so I could have clean power to run the studio. Most of Emlah Court was clean in terms of the magnetic field, but there was a bad hum once you got close to the windows. On St. Charles Avenue streetcars on electrical lines ran down the center of the boulevard, and that proved to be where the noise was coming from. I needed to find a way to knock out that noise, so I ended up covering the windows with sheets of lead. When I found some Rubbertex I used that on the windows instead: it's a black foam material normally used to line the hulls of boats to drown out the sound of the motors. Finally, I put sheets of three-quarter inch plywood over it all. This knocked out all of the street noise and solved the magnetic field problems; the single coil pickups were quiet. Over top of the plywood-covered windows, I hung beautiful Indian tapestries.

I was alone in this big building for a couple of weeks, wiring and working out any issues. Once I had the studio set up and running, Bob Lanois paid me a visit. Bob had built Hamilton's Grant Avenue Studio and was an expert. He seemed impressed by Emlah Court, although he did notice that the cables coming out of the back of the Dolby rack didn't have any strain release. He helped me come up with a way to rectify that situation so the cables couldn't pull on the connectors.

It was Bob who encouraged me to finally try the seafood in New Orleans. I'd grown up in a blue-collar town and had never been exposed to anything other than meat and potatoes and fish and chips, and I'd certainly never eaten any international cuisine. Because of Bob, I tried crawfish, gumbo, and all the local dishes — he even had me eating broccoli. Bob had once told me the only reason I'd been hired was because I was small, agile, and I had the ability to walk into a room without attracting anyone's attention. He felt that if I was big or clumsy it would steal 60 percent of people's mental energy, which would disturb the creative process.

I created a swamp vibe in the studio by literally going to the swamp and bringing back Spanish moss to hang all over the place. I also found an old stuffed bobcat and some alligator heads, which I sat on top of the tape recorder.

The studio looked psychedelic. The Neville Brothers had been the backup band for the Grateful Dead for years, so they were into tie-dye. Charles Neville turned me on to the Grateful Dead's tie-dye guy, Dirty Bart. Pigpen was the first and best keyboard player for the Dead, and Bart was his friend. Bart got me some huge tie-dyed tapestries that I used to cover the studio walls. I also got some huge kilim rugs to cover the windows. Living in the French Quarter, I'd made friends with a guy who owned an Indian boutique. His name was Kruz, and he imported beautiful tapestries from India. He gave me incredible deals, and I used the tapestries to cover all the ugly road cases in the studio that I was using as stands for gear like the Dolby rack and the Studer 24-track tape recorder. Most of the furniture I got from thrift shops on Magazine Street, and I lit the studio like a film set. I'd found an old film house, Pan American Films, in the French Quarter that was going out of business. It had been the soundstage where some '60s and '70s TV shows like *Morgus the Magnificent* had been filmed. The old security guy said I could fill a shopping cart for a hundred dollars, and I found lots of film lights that reminded me of the ones from the opening of *Looney Tunes*. I also found some cool amps at the studio that I thought could be used for guitars.

In April 1987 Dan came back from Brian Eno's place in England. This was the first time he had seen the building and the studio, and he couldn't believe the amount of work that I had done in the month he'd been gone. The stage was now set for making the Nevilles' record. We had one more month to prep, and we spent that time gathering instruments and finding cool keyboard sounds. This was also the time when Dan began working on his first solo record.

We had a housecleaner, Miss Alberta, who was always disturbing the recording sessions. She would constantly yell my name through the building, "Mr. Mark! Mr. Mark! Where's my rags?" because I'd use her rags to clean the motorcycle collection we had so far assembled.

I slept on the floor of my room on a futon, but I was freaked out by all of the giant cockroaches getting on my bed. I'd heard that putting powdered boric acid on the floor would make a barrier cockroaches wouldn't cross, so I made a circle around my bed. Suddenly, Miss Alberta would not go in my room.

"I ain't going in Mr. Mark's room 'cos he into that voodoo."

She assumed the circle around my bed was some kind of voodoo ritual.

The Jazz Fest was on and we were invited to see Stevie Ray Vaughn perform on the *President*, a huge paddleboat like the one in the *Adventures of Huckleberry Finn*. It had an impressive ballroom in the middle of the boat, where the show was. We sat on the balcony behind the stage. Stevie was intensely loud: he had a row of double-stacked Marshall amps with clear Plexiglas sheets in front of them because they were so loud that he needed to be shielded from the immense volume. It may have been the closest thing to seeing Jimi Hendrix live. The band was nowhere near as talented as Stevie was, but they held up their end, and Stevie was sweating like no performer I'd seen before.

After the show we went backstage to a little room that had been set up as a dressing room. Stevie was a little shy and it was all a bit uncomfortable because he didn't really know Dan. No one quite knew what to say to each other. Then Stevie noticed I was wearing an Albert King shirt, and his face lit up. He told me Albert was one of his heroes and how nervous he'd been meeting him — that he'd felt like a kid meeting a superhero, he was in such awe. I told Stevie that I'd worked for Albert mixing one of his shows and that Albert had told a similar story about meeting his own hero, who'd inspired him to play guitar.

"It's funny how we all look up to someone, and it's silly to be nervous because we are all in the same place at the end of the day," Stevie said.

Through the years I've discovered backstage can be an uncomfortable scene for artists — there's something awkward about being forced to talk to people — and I think Stevie appreciated having a conversation with me, talking about things he was into and not having to deal with people who only wanted to blow smoke up his ass.

Malcolm Burn, a musician from Toronto, came down to engineer the Neville Brothers' *Yellow Moon* sessions. Malcolm had been in a Toronto band called the Boys Brigade but had left to start a solo career. He had come down months before to cut some demos with the Nevilles at Dan's apartment in the French Quarter. He also came to New Orleans a couple of weeks before we started the Nevilles' record in order to get settled in, and we ended up spending a lot of time working on Dan's own record. I engineered a couple of songs because Malcolm was busy playing on Dan's record.

Recording the Nevilles' album began in July 1988. The band room was set up with Willie Green's huge drum set and Tony Hall's Peavey bass rig. Cyril Neville had his whole percussion rig in there, too.

Once the Nevilles came in to record, things took a pretty interesting turn. We would huddle all the brothers up in the control room behind the console so they could hear the speakers; Tony and Brian would sit on the side couch and Willie would be in front of the console with a hand drum. The rhythms for the record were made with hand percussion, using whatever percussion was available to us. We used a Perrier bottle on the song "Yellow Moon," and we found the best eight bars and then looped it. The band played on top of the loop while the brothers sang live.

The record really took on a swamp-like energy, while songs like "Voodoo" and "With God on Our Side" were almost otherworldly. During a visit to Aaron Neville's house on Valence Street, I'd noticed some aluminum wind chimes hanging on his porch. I asked Aaron if we could borrow them. He asked me why, and I told him they might sound cool on a track. I ended up using them on "With God on Our Side," recording them at double speed so that when they were played back at normal speed they sounded like low-chiming church bells.

I recorded five versions of "With God on Our Side," and Dan told me to pick one that would be the master. How could I choose — every take was incredible. I'd developed a method for making decisions that I called my "barometer"; I didn't pick takes based on how perfectly they were played, but on how they made me *feel*. When you work with musicians of the Nevilles' caliber, sometimes the subtle difference is purely the magic a particular take makes you feel.

Funnily enough, one of the hardest things about making a record is getting the right food to sustain everyone. I hired the Upperline Restaurant to do the catering. It is a family-owned place that specializes in New Orleans food like red beans and rice, gumbo, shrimp, and crawfish. The owner's daughter, Morgan, was the one who would come in to set out the spread.

All of the brothers ate the food, but Willie Green and Tony Hall refused. They came to me and said, "We aren't eating that shit! Now go get us some Popeyes chicken."

The Nevilles were an amazing live band, but once you got them in the studio, they often came off like a bar band. This is often a problem with bands — they are amazing live, but their records never seem to capture that same excitement.

Although we had a whole band setup in the living room, we basically made the whole record in the control room. By building interesting percussion loops and having the guys overdub on top, the record found its way. We gave each band member a percussion instrument and sometimes we had to improvise, like when we used the little green-glass Perrier bottles. Recording loops at 30 inches per second (IPS) and then playing them back at 15 IPS (the two most common speeds for professional recording) gave the album a swamp groove, which can really be heard on "Voodoo."

There were only a few tracks that used a drum kit, "Wild Injuns" being one. I had recorded a Neville Brothers live show at Tipitina's (named after the 1953 song "Tipitina," by the famous Professor Longhair) uptown on Tchoupitoulas Street on an Akai 12-track. There was one song that stood out during their live show that had amazing drumming on it. Willie Green, who the locals called "Mean Willie Green," was the funkiest drummer I'd ever seen. His foot was amazing. The groove of the bass drum could make you move like never before.

The bass playing on the record stood out, too; Tony Hall really came to the table and made the record groove. Most of the album was recorded using a Peavey Dyna-Bass and a Peavey Max Head and only used the direct out. The Max Head had a crazy equalizer (EQ) on it and we ended up using the EQ as an effect on other instruments. Brian Stoltz was an awesome guitarist. We'd dial up a haunting sound for him, like the slide part on "Voodoo" that still gives me the shivers.

Charles Neville was between houses at the time and needed a place to stay, so I fixed up the first-floor apartment for him. Charles had had a rough life, just like the other brothers; he was the storyteller of the family and had lots of prison stories. Charles had been busted at the border coming back from a show in Toronto because someone had thrown a joint in his sax case. Because he was a Black man and it was the early '70s, they really threw the book at him and he was sentenced to ten years in Angola, the Louisiana State penitentiary. Right away he'd been put into the fields to pick cotton. Charles had never picked cotton before and he didn't know he was supposed to pull the cotton out from the middle of the plant very carefully, as the sharp thorns could rip hands open. Instead, he grabbed the top of each plant and threw it in the bag. The guards on horseback carried bats to hit the inmates with when they got out of line, and when they spotted Charles picking the cotton wrong, a guard rode over and beat him. Charles only spent a couple of days in the field; he was picked as the leader of the prison band because he knew all the songs.

During our time recording, Charles recounted some of his prison stories and we recorded him over swampy-sounding tracks. I thought that they should have gone on the record; perhaps one day they'll be released.

All of the Nevilles lived close to death. Art Neville had tragically just lost his wife to a drug overdose. Art suffered from narcolepsy, so he would fall asleep midsentence. My job was to give him a nudge when he stopped being awake. Art was always surrounded by some scary characters. One night "Dr. Death," who I suspected was a drug dealer, came by the studio to see him. Aaron Neville was all muscle, with a huge dagger tattoo on his face that he'd gotten while in prison. He'd do arm curls while sitting in the chair beside me. I'd do curls with him, and my arm looked like a toothpick compared to his, which was the size of my waist. Aaron told stories about when the brothers were kids, explaining they were so poor they would go into the graveyard and break into the tombs to steal the jewelry off the bodies.

Aaron recorded "Tell It Like It Is" in 1966, and he was given one hundred dollars for his vocal performance. He said he'd never seen a hundred-dollar bill before, so he took it home to show his mom. Aaron was in prison in 1967 for armed robbery when "Tell It Like It Is" hit number one on the U.S. R&B charts.

Cyril Neville reminded me of Bob Marley; he stood for freedom. He played percussion in the band and sang, and his hands were so calloused they looked like alligator skin. I was riding a 1936 Harley-Davidson Knucklehead at the time and wanted to show it to Cyril, so I took him out to the garage. Suddenly, Cyril wasn't interested in my bike.

"What is that on the wall?"

"That's a rebel flag," I said.

"Take it down right now," he demanded.

"Why?" I asked. "It's a biker flag."

"You really don't know anything," he said. He explained that the Confederate flag was a racist symbol.

I had no idea. In Canada, I hadn't learned a lot about American history. I pulled it down and threw it in the trash can in front of him.

CHAPTER 2

BOB DYLAN

IN 1989 I WAS STILL IN NEW ORLEANS, along with Dan, with whom I worked. After producing U2's *The Joshua Tree*, Dan had made a record with Robbie Robertson (who'd been a member of the famous group the Band) and it was Robertson who had told Dan to go to New Orleans, which is how we ended up there.

Dan mentioned to me one morning that he had two offers on the table for his next project: one was David Bowie (for what would become the *Tin Machine* record), and the other was Bob Dylan.

He asked, "Which one do you think I should do?"

Without blinking an eye, I responded, "Dylan — without a doubt."

It was Bono who told Bob Dylan that he should consider working with Dan, playing a show at Audubon Park, next to the zoo, and we were all given an invitation to attend. G.E. Smith, the guitar player from the Saturday Night Live Band, was the leader of Dylan's road band. G.E. was a real showman and could be a bit corny at times with his playing and his stage moves. After the show, we were ushered onto Dylan's bus by his manager, Elliot Roberts. Dylan was wearing a grey hoodie, something I would see him wearing often in the years ahead.

"What are you doing in New Orleans?" Dylan asked us.

"We're here making a record with the Neville Brothers," Dan told him and

Looking over lyrics with Bob Dylan.

then mentioned that we'd cut a couple of his songs, "Ballad of Hollis Brown" and "With God on Our Side."

Dylan was surprised. "What does that sound like?"

We suggested he drop by the studio the next day to check it out, and he agreed. The following day, Dylan arrived with Jeff Kramer, his road manager. I seated them behind the console, the location for the best sound. First I played them "Hollis Brown," a song Dylan had written back in the '60s. Dylan didn't say anything, just nodded his head. Then I played them "With God on Our Side," which was about seven minutes long.

"Now that's something I never expected," Dylan said as the song ended.

Aaron Neville's haunting vocal had blown him away. This was perhaps the game changer, the thing that made Dylan really think about making a record with us. Dan and Dylan walked into the kitchen to talk. A short while later, Dan walked Dylan outside and then returned, saying, "It looks like we are making a record with Bob Dylan."

CHAPTER 3

NEW ORLEANS WITH BRIAN ENO

AS THE NEVILLES' RECORD NEARED COMPLETION, WITH all the songs tracked and the mixing underway, Daniel said, "I need you to go to the airport today to pick up Brian Eno."

Eno would be contributing to the album. Brian Eno is a world-famous English producer of artists like Roxy Music, David Bowie, Talking Heads, Devo, U2, Coldplay, Genesis, and many others, but despite this, I didn't actually know what he looked like. I was told to just hold up a sign with his name on it.

Eno was a legend, and I was far too embarrassed to hold up a sign, so I went right to the gate. This was back in the days when you actually could go right to the gate to meet people arriving. I stood with the large crowd waiting and, under my breath, started to whisper, "Brian?" Eventually I saw a small bald man, and as we made eye contact, he smiled.

"Mark?"

We headed to the French Quarter. Brian was excited to finally go there after all he'd read, and he didn't want to step foot in the studio until he had seen Storyville.

Storyville was the red-light district of New Orleans, Louisiana, from 1897 to 1917. It was established in order to put some kind of control on prostitution and drugs. The city of New Orleans didn't actually legalize prostitution but instead designated a sixteen-block area where it was merely not illegal. The district was

Emlah Court, St. Charles Avenue, New Orleans. On the right is the Columns Hotel.

located by a train station, making it a popular destination for travelers through-out the city, and it became a central attraction in the heart of New Orleans. It was tradition in the better Storyville establishments to hire a piano player, sometimes even small bands. Famous musicians who got their start in Storyville include Buddy Bolden, Jelly Roll Morton, and Pops Foster. I didn't know how to tell Brian Eno that Storyville had been abolished in 1917.

I told Eno that we would drive by on our way to the studio, so I drove him to the French Quarter and drove him down Bourbon Street, which was as close to Storyville as I figured you could get.

The strip joints along Bourbon Street had the girls out front, clad in fishnet stockings, swinging in and out of the windows on swings. One girl had a huge python wrapped around her. I could see Eno's face break into a boyish grin. We stopped and asked one of the girls where Storyville was and I let her break the news to Eno.

LISTEN UP!

"Where is Storyville?" She laughed. "You guys are crazy! That place is gone, but if you guys come in, I will show you all that Storyville experience that you'll never forget."

We both smiled and I said, "Maybe later."

I drove though the French Quarter on a hot and sticky summer day and finally made it to St. Charles Avenue, which felt almost like a movie set — the street was lined with weeping trees, and the center island held the famous streetcar, just like the one in *A Streetcar Named Desire*.

I told Eno that he was going to be staying at the Columns Hotel, right next to the studio. The Columns was once an antebellum mansion, with a huge front porch with columns — a great spot for dining. Eno wanted to check in before heading to the studio, and I walked him up to his room, a huge southern style suite with a large wooden bed with a canopy, high ceilings, and a balcony that looked out over St. Charles Avenue.

The next day, I worked with Eno in the morning. He tried some treatments on "With God on Our Side." I had brought in a Yamaha DX7 keyboard, of which Eno was the master, reprogramming it so the sounds would be his own. While working, I suddenly thought that Eno's distinctive sound perfectly matched the cicada bugs I could hear outside the open window.

"Can you play that melody again, then stop?" I asked Eno.

He did, and we heard the cicadas repeat the melody. We looked at each other.

"Try a different melody," I told him, so he changed what he was playing and the insects copied him again. It was incredible — Eno was communicating with insects!

I learned a lot from Brian Eno, and I used his techniques to develop my own sound. The way he could take a simple, dry piano sound and turn it into something unrecognizable is what makes him so unique. He'd send the piano through different effect processors, like the Lexicon PCM 70. The original sound of the piano would be removed and the effects fed back into each other, creating unique sounds performing on top of each other and leaving the listener with only effects, the end result being a beautiful texture drone that makes you feel something that the original piano didn't.

Eno had been the one to create ambient music, a sound that no one had heard before, and I was lucky to be exposed to it so early in my career.

LISTEN UP!

CHAPTER 4

SONIAT STREET

I WAS SENT TO SANTA FE, NEW MEXICO, to scout locations for Bob Dylan's new record, and I used a video camera to film everything so I could show Daniel and Bob when I got back. I met with Darren Vigil Gray and Jill Momaday there, and they wanted me to stay with them. Darren is an amazing Appalachian artist, and he'd often tell stories of how Indigenous people would do mushrooms to talk to the gods. Darren set me up with a real-estate agent who showed me quite a few adobe-style houses and abandoned saloons. One of these houses was Burl Ives's former home. The agent felt a real selling feature of the house was the huge bathtub with a hoist so you could be lowered into the tub. Burl was a large man, and I guess he needed that.

The agent then showed me the Georgia O'Keeffe estate, an incredible adobe house with high ceilings. Georgia had moved there in 1984 but died just two years later, and the house had remained empty since her death. It had a magical energy and felt very musical and inspiring. I was excited by the possibility of living and recording there. I filmed all the rooms of the house to show Daniel.

I arrived back in New Orleans late, and although I was excited to show Daniel the O'Keeffe house, I had to wait until the next morning. Once he saw how amazing it was, he promised to call Dylan right away, which he did. I overheard him telling Dylan how perfect it was, but Dylan didn't agree. He said that he didn't want to work in Santa Fe. He believed the altitude would cause him problems singing; he'd toured extensively and knew how easy it was to lose his breath. Instead, Dylan loved the idea of recording in New Orleans. I was excited about Santa Fe, yet I found myself looking for another place in New Orleans.

The Neville Brothers' *Yellow Moon* record was complete and just needed to be mastered, and I flew to San Francisco to work on it at Fantasy Studios in Berkeley. It was my first time in California, and I stayed in North Beach at the Washington Square Inn, overlooking a beautiful park. Every morning, a group of women did tai chi on the lawn. There was an incredible vibe in San Francisco, and it was as if I could still feel the hippie presence. On Haight Street, I expected to meet the Grateful Dead at every turn.

The master for the record was a vinyl pressing, known as a lacquer cutting, and I had never seen this done before. Blank acetate is placed on a mastering lathe, which is a sort of a turntable with a cutting head. It was all done on the fly: the mastering engineer went through all the songs and made note of which songs sounded better with EQ and how much compression to add. Once he started the cutting, he had to dial up the next song's notes and, once the song ended, cross fade to the next song. The sequence and spacing between songs was assembled on a half-inch tape recorder, with side A and side B, each side being no more than eighteen minutes long.

The song "Hollis Brown" was mixed to cassette. I never bettered the rough mix of it, so I used that mix and transferred it to a half-inch. Once the mastering was done, I left with a test pressing of the vinyl and a cassette. I rented a Lincoln Town Car because it had a great stereo, checked out of the inn, and drove to L.A. All the way down the Pacific Coast Highway, I listened to the record: it was the perfect sound-track.

I stopped in Big Sur for the night and stayed at the Deetjen's Big Sur Inn. It was famous for attracting great writers like Henry Miller, Hunter S. Thompson, and Jack Kerouac. I stayed in one of the creek cottages overlooking the forest and stream.

The next day, I continued my drive along the coast and imagined how I would one day ride the same route on one of my bikes. I arrived in Malibu at night and kept driving until I saw a sign that said Sunset Boulevard.

When I returned to New Orleans, the Neville Brothers invited us to a show they were opening for the Grateful Dead. It was the birthday of one of the Dead's drummers, so the Nevilles wanted to throw him a New Orleans–style party the day before the show, at a fishing camp on the lake. At the end of a long dock to the lake, people were boiling shrimp and crawfish and drinking lots of booze. I was sitting out front of the house when I spotted Jerry Garcia walking down the dock, his wife carrying their baby beside him, all three were dressed in tie-dye. Behind them followed two huge bodyguards in black three-piece suits, one carrying a teddy bear and the other a stroller. Jerry and his wife were friendly, and they said hello right away with big smiles. Jerry asked me to keep an eye out for his biker friend, who was lost and couldn't find the camp, and I told him I would.

The Dead show the next day was incredible, and I had never heard sound like that at a concert before. The PA consisted of two towers that reached from the floor to the ceiling on each side of the stage. John Meyer had built the wall of sound for the Dead in the '60s, and he had designed this system back then; it's still the standard for concert PA arrays. The Grateful Dead had their larger drums behind the drum kit, and I could feel my pant legs move with every hit, as though a wind was blowing them. The backstage area may have been the coolest ever, and each band member had their own tent. Jerry's was all couches, lamps, Indian rugs, and tie-dyes. The other members also had their own little worlds. By accident, I walked into Mickey Hart's tent, in which he was sitting at a table being shot up with something when the table collapsed and he fell on the floor. I quickly turned and ran.

The Bangles opened the show, and then it was the Nevilles' turn. The Dead's engineer let me take a mix off his desk, so I was able to get a great recording of the show.

With the Neville's record complete, we jumped right back to Daniel's solo record while I simultaneously went on the hunt for a location to record what would become Dylan's *Oh Mercy* album. I followed the same plan as before and looked for mansions that were for sale. I found a house on Soniat Street in the Garden District of New Orleans. It was a big, blue Victorian mansion with high ceilings, stained-glass windows, and a pool and a carriage house in the back. I offered the same deal, where I'd pay six months' rent up front, and the sellers went for it. I rented the property without telling the seller it was Bob Dylan who would record there.

I took possession of the Soniat mansion while we were still in Emlah Court. Bono and Adam Clayton from U2 were driving across America and stopped in to say hello. I had bought futon beds for all the rooms in the Soniat mansion, so Dan suggested they stay there, even though the house was mainly empty, except for a Hammond B3 organ I'd bought.

One night, we took Bono and Adam out to a club called Storyville, a music venue in the French Quarter where a lot of people played. We found a table and sat down. A man nearby wouldn't stop staring at us. U2's *Joshua Tree* record was huge at the time, and the videos for it were playing nonstop on MTV. The guy came over to the table and with a drunken slur asked, "Hey, are are Bono from U2?"

Bono was wearing a beret and some round Lennon glasses, and in a French accent he replied, "No, I am not."

The drunk guy stumbled off, but when we left later that night, he noticed us and came over. "It *is* you!" he told Bono. "I knew it was you with those fake glasses and that fake nose."

We all laughed because it was Bono's real nose.

The Soniat house needed some soundproofing because it sat in the middle of the quiet Garden District, a residential area, and the neighbors might complain. The house had a huge parlor with fifteen-foot ceilings and a unique round glass room that opened onto a huge porch. The kitchen and dining room were open concept, with a counter separating them. I decided to make the dining area the control room and leave the parlor for the band recording area. In the parlor I constructed a drum room made out of sandbags and double-glass sliding doors, in the hopes this would keep the drums quiet and not disturb the neighborhood. I used the same Rubbertex to fill all the windows of the parlor and again covered them all with three-quarter-inch plywood, which I painted blue to match the house. Once again, I hired Jimmy Mac to help me move, as well as do all the construction.

The electrical of the house was not in very good shape and had no grounding. I got Mike Montero to install a new electrical panel and he put in a special five copper rod star grounding process — six-foot-long copper rods were driven

The Soniat Street mansion where *Oh Mercy* was recorded.

into the ground and then tied together, creating an isolated ground. It worked well and there was no humming.

I invented a system so that when the doorbell rang outside, a light I'd installed on the wall above the console would blink on and off, so that our recordings weren't ruined. I also did this for the phone so that a fast-blinking light meant it was ringing. The only problem with creating this system was that after using it for years, whenever I saw a blinking light I'd get up to answer the door.

In the control room / kitchen / dining room, I hung heavy salmon-colored curtains. It was not my color of choice, but they were theatrical curtains I got dirt cheap from the Pan American Film building. It was pretty cramped in there once all the recording gear was set up. I always put the Studer A80 mk2 24-track tape recorder in front of the console so that I could see the meter bridge. I had developed what I called "the horseshoe setup," with all the gear in a horseshoe shape. This allowed for easy access behind the gear. As an engineer, you learn that you spend very little time actually sitting at the console, that a lot of your time is just plugging things in, so you really need space behind the gear. In most big studios it's difficult to plug in things because all of the gear is against a wall or enclosed in a rack.

With the studio up and running, it was time to start building the instrument arsenal, and guitars and amps were first on the agenda.

CHAPTER 5

DYLAN'S *OH MERCY*

I CALLED GRUHN GUITARS IN NASHVILLE TO see what they had in stock. The list of what they ended up shipping down read:

1930s National all-metal Dobro (a resonator guitar painted a greenish brown)

1955 Butterscotch Fender Telecaster (one of the best-sounding, best-playing guitars)

1956 Guild M-20 (a small acoustic with a dark-mahogany finish)

1960s Martin 12-string (a superbly crafted acoustic)

1963 Fender Brown-era 4x10 Concert amp (a classic!)

1960 Vox AC30 top boost (a guitar amplifier made by Vox)

1957 Tweed Champ (an amp used by Buddy Holly and the Crickets)

I bought a Yamaha Maple drum kit from Sound Chek Music in Metairie because it was the same kit that Manu Katché (Peter Gabriel's drummer) played on the *So* record. I had already brought in a Hammond B3 organ but still needed a piano. Johnny O'Brien was a piano tuner at the Jazz Fest and had a company called U.S. Caribbean Piano, and he helped me find a couple of instruments. Werlein's was an old music store on Canal Street in the French Quarter. They had a Baldwin seven-foot grand piano there, so I had them bring it over to see how it sounded. John also found us a seven-foot Steinway Model B grand piano from the 1980s, which was a rental for the Jazz Fest. We had that sent over, too, so we could A/B it against the Baldwin. Then an 1800s Steinway seven-foot grand popped up that Johnny was selling for one of his customers, and we had that shipped in, too. There were three grand pianos sitting beside each other in the parlor, and it was still a couple of months before Dylan would be in.

In the weeks before recording, I kept asking Daniel if he'd heard from Dylan or heard any of the songs. A week before we were due to start, we received a cassette and I was relieved we would finally hear some of the material we'd be working on. Attached was a note that read, "This'll give you a good idea."

I sat down with Dan and our friend Malcolm Burn to listen, but we were surprised to hear Al Jolson's music. We fast-forwarded, but it was a whole tape of Al Jolson! We looked back at Dylan's note, which also read, "Listen to this. You can learn a lot." We didn't know what to make of it.

By the time Dylan arrived, I'd forgotten all of this. Then one evening we were discussing our favorite singers and who had been influences, especially when it came to phrasing. Dylan was adamant that phrasing was everything.

"My two favorite singers are Frank Sinatra and Al Jolson," he said.

I suddenly understood why he'd sent us that tape.

I asked who his favorite songwriters were and he told me, "Gordon Lightfoot and Kris Kristofferson, those are the guys."

I'm not sure if Dylan had an actual sound in his head to begin with when we started recording. He'd actually recorded the whole record already, with Ron Wood from the Rolling Stones, but for whatever reason he was starting over, and we came up with a completely different animal.

Bob Dylan had a rule — we only recorded at night. I think he's right about that. The body is ready to accommodate a certain tempo at night. I think it's something to do with the pushing and pulling of the moon. We're ready to be more mysterious and dark. *Oh Mercy* reflected that.

Dylan never really spoke to the other musicians. He'd chat with the people he knew, but he wasn't there to make friends — he was there to make music.

He always wore his grey hoodie. During the first few days of recording, we had

LISTEN UP!

the Neville Brothers' rhythm section there. After the second night of recording, the drummer, Willie Green, came up to me as I was sitting at the mixing board, with Dylan near me.

"Man, I've been here two or three days. When the fuck's Bob Dylan showing up?" Willie complained.

"Willie, he's sitting right next to you," I told him, and he gasped.

Then the bass player, Tony Hall, came in and said, "Man, that Bob Dylan is some weird motherfucker."

Dylan looked up and raised an eyebrow, and then he and I went right back to working on his lyrics.

The sessions were supposed to start at around four in the afternoon, but Dylan didn't show up until dark.

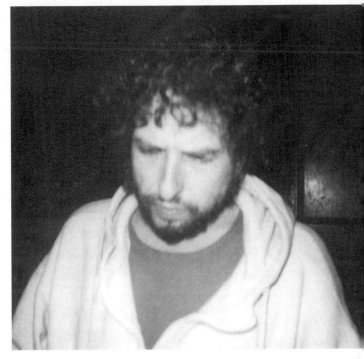

Polaroid of Bob Dylan — *Oh Mercy* session.

We would prepare some sounds for him to hear when he arrived. We had Dylan play the Telecaster through the Fender concert amp, but he wasn't that impressed with the sound. Dan showed him the Martin 12-string and asked, "What do you think of this guitar?"

"It's okay," Dylan said. "But if you want to get yourself a great guitar, you need to get yourself a Stella."

Stella guitars were played by notable artists like Lead Belly, Charley Patton, and Doc Watson. Kurt Cobain of Nirvana played an acoustic Stella on the recording of the song "Polly" on the *Nevermind* album.

Dan is like a cheerleader in the studio, and his talent was hyping the artist so they believed they were great, in order to get the best from them. He'd get overly excited about what an artist just played or sang, which could cause them to play or sing more emotionally. This technique worked with many musicians but not with Dylan, who was giving Dan a run for his money. Stone-faced, the one trick left up Dan's sleeve was his guitar playing, but with almost everything he tried, Dylan turned it down. Dan once did a great mix before Dylan arrived and then played it for him.

"Did you mix that in the daytime?" Dylan asked.

"Yes, do you like it?" Dan replied.

"No, it needs to be mixed at night."

The sessions started with just Dylan, Dan, and a Roland TR-808 drum machine, like can be heard on "Man in the Long Black Coat." For the first two weeks of recording, Dylan didn't acknowledge that I was even in the room; I was like a ghost. I would set Dylan up in a chair with his back to the kitchen counter. He wouldn't wear headphones, so I set up an Electro-Voice (EV) floor wedge monitor, like you would have at a live show. Beside Dylan's chair, I had a little Fender Champ amp and a little table and light — a place for his coffee and lyrics. I'd set up the microphone in front of him and he would move the other way, so I would move it to where he'd gone, and then he would move back. It seemed he was doing it on purpose, so finally I'd just sit at his feet and follow him whatever way he chose to sit.

I set up Dan on a chair beside Dylan to record, and I put a Vox AC30 amp in the bathroom for isolation. I also had an EV monitor set up for him to hear. Once the band came in, I put the Yamaha drum kit in the control room beside the main door; it was a tight squeeze with the drums in there.

Dylan wrote his songs on a typewriter, without a firm idea of what instrument was appropriate or which key was best, so he was always testing the water. He'd try a song on guitar and then wonder if maybe it would be best on the piano. If he went into the parlor to work it out on piano, I would move the whole setup, with drums and everything, into the parlor. When I'd get the last cable plugged in, he would get up and move back to the control room, and then I'd move it all back again. It felt like a cat and mouse game. Part of working with artists is going with the flow so they are free to create.

Dylan had a piano song called "Ring Them Bells" that had a lyric that went "the fighting was strong," but every time we listened back, it sounded like "the farting was strong." We laughed every time we heard it and Dylan would ask, "Why you always laughing?"

"Ring Them Bells" wasn't quite finished, so Dylan was always going into the parlor to work on it. We had all three pianos lined up, but Dylan always went to the Baldwin to play. Daniel was curious as to why Dylan picked that piano so he finally asked, "Why do you always play the Baldwin? Is it because of the action or the way it sounds?"

"*No*," Dylan replied. "It's because it's the only one with a stool."

Dan's face dropped. I could feel the tension in the air. There seemed to be some kind of personality clash igniting.

Daniel had an idea that a local band, Rockin' Dopsie, would be good for the song "Shooting Star." Rockin' Dopsie was a zydeco band with a scrubboard player. Dylan wasn't sure about them. After a couple of takes of "Where Teardrops Fall," Dylan, right in front of the band, asked sarcastically, "Where did you get these guys from?"

Shortly after that, things began to boil. Dan could have a bad temper, but I had only ever witnessed yelling, no violence. While recording Peter Gabriel's *So* album, in a fit of temper, he'd locked Gabriel in the barn. One night, Dylan was fumbling along, playing guitar, and when I looked over, I could see Dan breathing heavily, his eyes bulging.

Dan suddenly erupted in a rage and grabbed the metal Dobro by the neck and smashed it over Dylan's monitor, filling the air with the sound of a car wreck and denting the guitar. Dylan went white, and I stood in shock, wondering if Dan would hit him.

"I'm not fucking putting up with your bullshit anymore," Dan yelled. The room went silent. I got up and walked outside, and Malcolm Burn followed. We went into the carriage house for a drink. A short while later, we heard Dylan leave. I went back into the studio. Dan had also gone, the Dobro was lying on the floor, and I shut down for the night.

Nothing was ever said again about the Dobro smashing. The next day, I was in the courtyard working on one of the bikes when I heard someone at the gate. Dylan was standing there in his grey hoodie. Victor, his bodyguard, had dropped him off.

"Hey, Mark, do you think you could get me a Harley like one of yours?" he asked.

I told him I had a friend in Florida who sold vintage bikes like mine.

"Talk to Victor and he can set you up with the cash," he instructed.

I called my friend in Florida and he said he had a 1966 Harley-Davidson

Shovelhead for sale. I asked him to send me a couple of photos. I got them a couple of days later and showed Dylan. He loved it and asked me when we could get the bike. I promised I'd pick it up on the weekend. He was as thrilled as a kid in a candy store and kept the photo on his little side table, looking at it from time to time. Dylan started calling me by my first name and talking to me like we had known each other forever. I didn't know it at the time, but Dylan had not ridden since he'd had his motorcycle accident back in the '60s. Something had sparked his interest and he wanted to ride again.

I went to St. Petersburg, Florida, on the weekend to pick up the bike. It was electric-blue and white. The 1966 Electra-Glide was the first year of the Shovelhead motor. It had an electric start, and the paint job was amazing. The front headlight cowling was polished aluminum. I returned to the studio with it on Sunday night. I thought the bike was running a little rich, and I wanted to have my local bike mechanic tune it up. Timmy was the bike mechanic at Big Bobs Bayou Cycle. He was a big biker and knew everything about getting a Harley fine-tuned. He'd worked under Pete Hill, who was a four-time winner of the American Motorcyclist Association Drag Bike Top Fuel title riding a modified 1947 Harley-Davidson Knucklehead. I would often see Timmy at the local Maple Leaf Bar dancing to old blues music. He was covered in tattoos, with the word *white* tattooed on his right hand and *power* tattooed on his left. I once asked him how he could tattoo something racist on his skin but then go dancing to music made by the same people he was prejudiced against.

"Did they ever do anything to you?" I asked him.

"No," he replied, "but my daddy told me not to like them."

I decided it would take another generation before that stupidity went away.

Timmy had a pit bull in the shop and the poor old dog had a testicle that was the size of a watermelon — when he walked, it dragged along the floor. I asked Timmy what was wrong with his dog, and he insisted the dog was just old. Despite his character flaws, Timmy got Dylan's bike running better than my own.

Dylan showed up a little early for the session so he could see the bike and take it for a ride. I had it out in the driveway when he arrived. He jumped out of the car and couldn't believe his eyes. "It's amazing," he said.

I started it up for him and he sat on it and put it in gear and took off with no helmet. I sat there with Victor, assuming Dylan would just go around the corner but he didn't come back for over an hour. When he pulled in, he said the bike was running great, then added, "The police are so nice here — they were all waving at me."

I said, "They were waving at you because there is a helmet law here, unlike in California, and they were telling you to put one on."

It became routine for me to have the bike ready for Dylan to ride every day. I took him on a couple of rides so he would know where to escape to. We'd take Tchoupitoulas Street down past the zoo and ride onto the dirt road along the top of the levee, then down onto the river road until we crossed the Mississippi. At Highway 90, we'd follow the river road out past the big antebellum plantation homes, passing under huge oak trees that covered the road like a tunnel, Spanish moss dripping from them. It felt like time stood still out there.

One morning, I had the bike ready and Dylan went out by himself, and I heard him stall around the corner. I found him sitting on the bike in the middle of the road with people surrounding him, asking for his autograph. Dylan just sat and stared straight ahead as if he was completely alone. He never said a word to anybody. I ran up and told them to leave him alone and they left. I asked him what happened.

"It just died," he said.

I looked the bike over and saw he hadn't turned on the petcock valve for the gas, so I did it, and the bike started right up again. Then off he went on his morning ride.

Back in the studio, Dylan pulled out his song "Man in the Long Black Coat." Both the lyrics and his delivery were haunting. Malcolm Burn played the Yamaha DX7 keyboard with the special Brian Eno sounds in it, which Brian had left on a cartridge. Daniel had a white Fender Mustang, a solid-body electric guitar introduced in 1965 that attained cult status in the '90s. He played the Fender through his Korg SDD 3000 (digital delay guitar effects box) and timed his echo to the Roland TR-808 drum machine so it was in time. Then I ran the Fender into the Vox AC30 amp, which was introduced in 1958 to meet the growing demand for louder amps. Characterized by its "jangly" high-end sound, the Vox AC30 has been widely used by British musicians and others, such as Edge from U2. I set up a Roland TR-808 drum machine, only using the kick, and added an echo to it, so for every one hit we got four echoes. Malcolm then dialed up some cricket sounds. The opening line of the song is "Crickets are chirping, the water is high," so the sound really fit.

I recorded a couple of takes of the song and we listened back and picked the last one. Dylan refined the lyrics and I punched in a bunch of new lines he thought were better. Dylan put the harp on it and I added an AMS delay. The recording felt complete. I did a late-night mix, and it was done.

During another session, Daryl Johnson showed up to play some conga. I will always remember meeting Daryl for the first time because he was wearing stone-washed jeans inside out, with the pockets just hanging there.

"Your pants are inside out," I'd told him, and he responded, "*So?*" It shut me up fast.

Dylan would usually sit at the counter drinking coffee and smoking cigarettes while he worked on lyrics. We couldn't tell what he was writing because the paper had words every which way, so we couldn't read it; it just looked like a collage. Somehow, he'd pull from it. I have never seen a more dedicated writer. I always kept a big drawing tablet around in case I want to sketch something. One night Dylan asked me if he could borrow it, so I gave it to him. He turned to Dan.

"Hey, Daniel, can I draw a picture of you?"

Dylan sketched a picture, but when he turned the portrait toward us, it was an abstract drawing of Dan, who looked like an unfortunate disheveled homeless person. Dylan didn't sign it and the drawing remained in my book.

As an alternative speaker in the studio, we used a little Sony blaster. It had an aux-in on the back and I would run a line level to it, so we could listen through it as we mixed. It also had two cassette doors in the front. We would mix to a Sony DAT recorder in those days, but we had to make cassettes to listen to outside of the studio. I used a portable high-end Sony cassette recorder to make the weekly mix cassettes. Then one day, I put one of the weekly cassettes in the Sony blaster and played it to hear what it sounded like. We noticed that the blaster ran a little fast but it actually made the recording sound better — everything was so much tighter. So when it came time to master the record with Greg Calbi, we got him to make the speed of the whole record faster, to make it sound the way that cassette had.

The record was finished and Dylan had been gone for a week. Rain had rolled in on a sultry night, but fog still hung in the air and cicadas buzzed loudly in the trees. Someone came to the back gate and I found Dylan standing in the rain, his grey hoodie damp.

"I've decided to sign the drawing," he said, and then he came inside, signed it, and left without saying another word.

CHAPTER 6

THE START OF KINGSWAY STUDIO

SOMEONE IN THE GARDEN DISTRICT NEIGHBORHOOD DECIDED they didn't like having musicians as neighbors, and they went door to door to with a petition trying to kick us out. Perhaps they thought we looked suspicious — all these guys with long hair getting off motorcycles to come inside, and a big black Caddy parked in the driveway. Oddly enough, because our place had a pool, we would let all the kids in the neighborhood come and swim on Sundays, and we had a girl named Christine come over to supervise and make sure no one drowned. None of the other neighbors would sign the petition because they said that we made the neighborhood a safer place, helping all the kids stay out of trouble.

Dan hired a pair of twin boys to wash the Caddy one day, and he gave them a bucket, soap, and a couple of steel-wool pads. He came back an hour later to see if they'd finished and discovered they'd used the steel-wool pads on the paint and scratched up both sides of the car! He paid them anyway and I had the car repainted.

Wanting more bikes, Dan had me look for him, and I found a 1965 Harley-Davidson Electra-Glide and a 1947 Indian Chief. Although we were starting to look like a motorcycle club, we'd ride to the health food store every morning and get carrot juice. They called us "The Mild Ones."

After finishing the albums we'd been working on, and with our lease up, I felt ready to get out of New Orleans. Dan had done a local radio show and played some tracks off his new record. He met Barbara Hoover, a DJ, there. She looked like Elvira, Mistress of the Dark. Barbara wore all black and had long black hair, and she had one of those nasally voices, like Fran Drescher from *The Nanny*. She also had a voodoo doll business and thought of herself as some kind of voodoo princess. In New Orleans, people from that area outside the French Quarter are called "yats" because they would say in a slangy voice, "Where yo yat?"

© KAREN KUEHN

In front of Kingsway Studio with the 1936 Knucklehead (August 1990).

I was walking through the French Quarter with Barbara one day and we came across a For Sale sign on a rundown house at Esplanade Avenue and Chartres Street. I told her it would make a good studio and she told me she knew how to get in. She led me through the back gate, through a bunch of garages, and to the driveway. She called, "Teddy!" and out of an old garage, a guy emerged. He was the security guard, and he let us in the house. It was disgusting! The roof had been leaking for years and it smelled as though something had died in the place. The house was huge, however, and it had some nice tile floors and lighting fixtures, but it was simply too far gone. The upstairs bedrooms had carpet from the '60s that was rotted from the rain leaking in. It felt like the only thing the house could be used for was making a horror film.

I told Barbara we'd better leave before we got sick, but her response was "I am going to get Dan to buy this place for me."

"Good luck," I said. "This place is a dump." I had no idea that Dan was having a fling with her at the time. Before I knew it, he told me he was considering buying the house.

"Don't," I warned him. "You're out of your mind. The place is a dump and it would take years to renovate. Let's get out of New Orleans." He was always talking about going down to Mexico and I was ready to go, too.

Still, somehow Barbara Hoover convinced him to buy the house. I felt trouble brewing, but he put in an offer of $250,000, which was accepted.

The house had quite the history. It was owned by Germaine Cazenave Wells. Her family owned Arnaud's, the undisputed leading New Orleans fine-dining restaurant in the 1930s and '40s. Her father, Count Arnaud, had died and left her everything. She'd worshipped her father. Only New Orleans could produce a Germaine Cazenave Wells. She was lusty, dramatic, loud, and headstrong. Her capacities for alcohol, celebration, and men were extreme, even by the standards of the day. She was also famous for an Easter-bonnet parade that began at the house.

Dan bought the house in the spring of 1989. I hired Jimmy Mac once again to oversee the renovation, which was to be a quick fix-up in order for us to move in. In one month, Jimmy transformed the place from utterly uninhabitable to something we could live in. With a huge crew, he'd patched the roof, removed all the carpets, sanded and stained the floors, and painted the entire interior.

In the winter of 1989, before starting Dylan's *Oh Mercy* album, Dan had gotten a tip that Mediasound, a big studio in New York, was going out of business and that everything was to be auctioned off. Mediasound was a hit machine. It had opened in June 1969 in central Manhattan. The flow of artists from there included Frank Sinatra, Paul Anka, the Rolling Stones, Ben E. King, Stevie Wonder, Barry Manilow, and Pat Benatar. Dan sent me to bid on the big Neve 8078 recording console. Once I got to the auction, a lot of the smaller pieces of gear had already gone, but they were auctioning off the big Neve at 4:00 p.m.

While waiting, I looked through the studio and bumped into Dan Alexander. Alexander was a used-recording-equipment broker from San Francisco. He reminded me of a used-car salesman — balding with a comb-over, he was always talking too much and trying to say too many words too quickly and stuttering over them. I had bought some microphones and a couple of Neve microphone preamps off him in the past. His claim to fame was that he was in a band called the Psychotic Pineapple, although I had never heard of them. He asked me what I was doing there and I told him I was planning to bid on the Neve 8078 recording console. I noticed him turning red.

"I am taking that console and don't bother bidding on it," he told me.

I went outside to a pay phone and called Dan. I told him what Alexander had said and asked how much I should bid. He was silent for a second, then said, "Bid up to $90,000."

I went back into the studio; everyone was gathering in the performance room, and the console went up on the block. Bidding opened up at $25,000 and quickly rose to $50,000, at which time people began dropping out. When Alexander bid $55,000, I'm sure no one thought anyone would bid any higher. That's when I made my first bid — $65,000.

Alexander spun to look at me, growling. For some reason, the crowd of people began to cheer me on. When the bid reached $80,000, everyone was yelling "go" to me. I could hear people in the crowd asking, "Who is this little kid bidding that kind of money?" At that time, I looked like a teenager; they didn't know I had the knowledge of a fifty-year-old when it came to gear. Eventually, I bid the $90,000 that Dan had capped me at, and when I did that, Alexander blew his top, yelling out, "$120,000!" I smiled and bowed and said, "It's yours."

He could have walked out of there with the console for just $91,000 if he

LISTEN UP!

hadn't blown his cool. He sold it to someone else and I'm sure he made money on it anyway but not nearly as much as he could have.

After the auction, people came up to me and shook my hand. "Great job, kid," they said.

In the spring of 1989, I got a call from Alexander; he had found a recording console for Dan. This time it was an API and it was at the Record Plant in New York. He wanted $90,000 for it, but it had to be out of the Record Plant building in a week. Dan wanted it, so I made the arrangements. I had to fly to New York and get it out of the building before the lease was up. I had never seen an API console before and had no idea what I was getting into. The Record Plant was a legendary place. John Lennon recorded "Imagine" there. Hendrix had recorded *Electric Ladyland* there. Aerosmith, Cheap Trick, the Allman Brothers, Cyndi Lauper, and Van Halen had all recorded culturally iconic smash hits in that building. This was the famous console that a lot of those records were made with.

The night before I was to leave for New York, I woke up sick. I looked in the mirror and my face looked like I had leprosy. I had caught chicken pox from my girlfriend's kid! It was so itchy, but I had to get on a plane in a couple of hours and get the console out of the Record Plant. On the plane, I wore a baseball cap and kept a low profile. The flight attendant asked if I wanted anything to drink and I looked up at her to say no thank you. There was horror on her face when she saw the condition I was in, and she quickly moved on.

Once I got to New York and to the Record Plant, everyone saw I had chicken pox and wouldn't come close to me. I was left to dismantle the huge API recording console alone. I got boxes delivered and rolls of bubble wrap. I took pictures of the console so I knew where everything went. As I pulled apart every module, I gave each a number and then wrapped it and put it in one of boxes. Once everything was wrapped, I had to cut all the wires out of the back of the console because they ran into the floor and there was no way of retrieving them. I took a saw and cut through huge bundles of wire.

They had built the room around the API, so there was no way to carry the frame straight out the door, and there were several doors and corners to get around. I hired piano movers to get it out. I thought it was going to be impossible without taking a wall out, but they managed by building a skid plate and strapping the console to it, then tipping it on its end and wiggling it around the corners.

Jimmy Mac had flown up and rented a U-Haul to drive the console back down to New Orleans. I had asked my best friend from Canada, Ty Trepanier, to ride my 1956 Harley-Davidson Panhead down to New York to meet me so I could take my bike back down to New Orleans.

Once Jimmy got the console to New Orleans, I had planned for it to live in the main parlor. The main room had amazing terrazzo floors, and there was a beautiful pattern in the center of the parlor floor on which I centered the console. There were two marble fireplaces and two crystal chandeliers that hung in the center of the room, so it was all properly balanced. I had the console up and running within a day, and I had Mike Montero in to wire the multitrack harnesses and speaker outputs. Montero also wired the electrical panel so I had clean power.

Dan had me go to auctions to buy furniture for the house, and I also went to the local Indian rug stores. I was at Aladdin Rugs on Magazine Street haggling on a price when I said to the store owner that I had just bought a 500-year-old, twenty-five-foot-by-twenty-foot Pakistani wool rug in Montreal for $5,000. The guy laughed and said, "I am sorry, that is impossible."

I disagreed, but he informed me that Pakistan had only been a country for one hundred years.

I had to have the studio up and running in a week because Malcolm Burn was producing a record for Dan's sister's band, Crash Vegas, which would be a good test to make sure everything was running right. The console sounded fantastic.

Dan was going to be going on tour for his own album, and rehearsals for that took place at 544 Esplanade Avenue in New Orleans. Daryl Johnson was the bass player and Malcolm Burn played keys, but they were missing the right drummer. We went through a dozen players until we came across Ronald Jones. Ronald was a piano player who'd played with Little Richard but who had the best feel on the drums.

We toured the United States and Europe, and then Dan got an offer to be the music director for the Mandela concert at Wembley Stadium in London. The lineup for the first half of the show included the Neville Brothers, Patti LaBelle, and Tracy Chapman. Also on the bill were Anita Baker, Bonnie Raitt, Chrissie Hynde, Jackson Browne, Lou Reed, Natalie Cole, Neil Young, Peter Gabriel, and Simple Minds.

I was mixing the sound for the first half of the show. We held rehearsals for the Mandela concert at John Henry's studio in North London.

Patti LaBelle came in accompanied by her musical director, Bud. Bud stormed into the rehearsal saying, "I need a grand piano."

Dan told him we didn't have one, but Bud insisted they needed it for one of Patti's songs. "We can't get one, so here, play this cowbell," Dan said.

Bud just looked at him in shock.

Patti told us she wanted to do "Over the Rainbow," but Dan told her there is no way they were doing that song because it was so corny. Patti put her foot down. "Look, we are doing it, like it or not," she said.

Sure enough, they did a version of it.

Dan flew in Bill Dillon to play guitar. He told Patti that Bill was a Newfie, something people from Newfoundland are occasionally referred to as in Canada, typically in a derogatory way. Whenever Patti talked to Bill, she called him the Newfie and introduced him at the show as Newfie Bill.

Tracy Chapman showed up with Elliot Roberts, her manager. When they walked into the rehearsal, Elliot said, "Okay, everyone's got to go, clear the room out."

Dan told Elliot that if we cleared the room, there wouldn't be a band to play with, so everyone stayed.

More than 90,000 people attended the event. I did the stage setup for the first half of the show, then ran out front to the mix area through a huge crowd of people. It was hailing huge chunks of ice, but the crowd didn't flinch. Dan opened the show and then brought out the Neville Brothers. Cyril kicked into "My Blood," a track off the *Yellow Moon* record. The sound system for the show was a Clair Brothers system that really had some punch. I was warned by the house tech that the sound was too loud according to his dB meter, which measures sound decibels (dB). It was a Sunday, so I was only allowed to be at 90 dB and I was pushing 100, so I pulled the main fader down to 90 dB. As he was walking away, I turned it back up; he didn't notice.

After the first half of the show, I went back to the stage to clear it. Nelson Mandela was up next to give a speech. I was standing in the hall behind the stage, leaning against the wall, when I saw him coming down the hall with his wife, Winnie, and his security. As he got closer, I looked at him and smiled. He walked up to me. I don't know if Mandela thought I was one of the rock stars because I was dressed in leather, or if he was just being appreciative. He was a very humble and loving man.

"Thank you," he said, shaking my hand with both of his.

I said, "You are so welcome."

There was a party later that night after the show, and it was a star-studded event. I was starving, so I went to catering. Chrissie Hynde was in front of me ordering something vegetarian. The catering guys asked me what I wanted, so I asked for a hotdog.

Chrissie heard me, turned around, and said, "That's disgusting."

"It's not really meat!" I joked.

"Yes, it is, and it's disgusting you're eating an animal."

Jokingly, I countered, "Well, it's not disgusting that you're wearing leather boots!"

That was it — I'd set her off and she started yelling at me, so I turned and walked away, but I could still hear her as I ducked into the crowd.

With the Mandela concert over, we went back on tour with Dan. He thought it would be funny to play a joke on Bill Dillon: we had flowers sent to Bill at every hotel we stayed at, with a note saying, "Love, Patti." Bill thought Patti LaBelle was in love with him for the entire tour and was thinking he might marry her.

CHAPTER 7

BACK IN NEW ORLEANS

AFTER DAN'S TOUR, I WENT BACK TO New Orleans and started Chris Whitley's first record, *Living with the Law.* Dan's band was pretty tight coming off a year on the road, and they became the backup band for Chris's record. Chris was a New York bike messenger and the friend of a great New York photographer, Karen Kuehn. Karen introduced Chris to Dan, and they'd cut a little track direct to DAT called "Phone Call from Leavenworth." It was that track that got Chris a record deal with Columbia Records. Dan didn't want to produce the album, so he recommended Malcolm Burn.

I tracked the record in the wooden piano room beside the console. We were all still in the same room and I could see Chris and the band from the console. Chris was a little nervous, but maybe it was all the coffee he drank.

During the making of the album, renovations were still underway. Sometimes we'd ride to Tipitina's, a music venue, on the Harleys. Hanging around outside Tipitina's, we met a woman who told us she knew the bikers who'd turned their mansion into a recording studio, and that U2 was there recording. Obviously, she was talking about us, and we played along. Her name was Karen Brady; she was a real New Orleans gal, with that sweet, Southern soul about her. She ended up hanging out with us, and we had to let her know that the guys she'd been talking about were, in fact, us. She just laughed.

The 1956 Harley Panhead at Kingsway.

Until then, I had been overseeing the bank account, the renovations, all the studio booking, paying all the bills, doing the grocery shopping, and making records. Everything was in my name — from the car to the bikes to the bank account. Now, we got Karen to work for the studio part time, to pay bills and do the grocery shopping. This was when the studio was given the name Kingsway. Karen took on more and more work as time went on, so I could focus on overseeing the studio and making the records that came through.

Right after Chris Whitley's project, I dove into a record with Harold Budd, an American avant-garde composer and poet. Brian Eno had produced his first couple of ambient records. Harold was a piano player from L.A. with his own style, which he termed "soft pedal" — big open notes ringing out with heavy treatments on them. Harold brought in B.J. Cole on pedal steel and Bill Nelson on guitar. Bill Nelson was from a band called Be-Bop Deluxe. The album *By the Dawn's Early Light* is typical of Budd's signature minimalist style and features several short poems, each read by Budd.

In the summer of 1990, I received an invitation to go to Italy to record and mix a concert for Nusrat Fateh Ali Khan, a Pakistani musician, who was primarily a singer of Qawwali, the devotional music of the Sufis. Singer Nusrat Fateh Ali Khan and guitarist-producer Michael Brook collaborated on the album *Mustt Mustt*. Michael Brook was doing a concert with Nusrat and wanted me to come and work with them at the Time Zones Festival in Bari, Italy, in July 1991.

The first half of the show was traditional Sufis, and then Michael came up for the second half to produce *Mustt Mustt* live. It sounded just like the record. Michael was one of the first to use computers in a live show.

The festival had hired an Indian family to cook traditional food for Nusrat because, as part of his religion, he only ate traditional food. The first night we were all at a restaurant eating pizza and pasta, when I watched Nusrat wolf down a whole pizza and a big bowl of pasta — he loved Italian food. Nusrat was a big man who sat cross-legged on the floor while he sang, and when he'd get up, he would wobble from side to side, stretch a leg out, then rock the other way to get his other leg out. While in rehearsals for the show, Nusrat's manager was told not to return after he was caught sexually assaulting one of the young male assistants in the back room.

Michael told Nusrat that I'd just finished a record with the Neville Brothers, and Nusrat was so excited; he asked me to play him some of it. With a big grin on his face, he rocked back and forth as he listened, blown away by the record. He loved the Nevilles and kept telling me he couldn't get enough of them.

I also hung out with Manu Katché, who was the drummer on Peter Gabriel's *So* album. Manu was there playing with a jazz group. David Sylvian, who in the late 1970s was the lead vocalist and main songwriter in the group Japan, was also there. David told stories about not being able to leave his house at the height of his career without being mobbed by girls.

We went to an all-night disco with some of the women we met at the festival. It was interesting to watch Manu dance; he had weird, quirky moves and didn't move to the rhythm of the music, which was a bit strange because he's an amazing drummer.

• • •

Chris Whitley came back to New Orleans to finish his record in the fall. His brother-in-law, Allan, who played some bass on the record, came, too, and stayed for a bit.

Peter Gabriel showed up once Chris was finished and asked me if I could take him to see the Neville Brothers play at the Jazz Fest. I told him I would. When we got to the show, I had the manager sit us on the side of the stage. Sitting with us was actor Dennis Quaid, who was a friend of the band. Everything was great until Quaid, who'd been drinking, fell on Peter and almost knocked him to the floor. Dennis had no idea who Peter Gabriel was. Peter was a bit shaken up but laughed it off. I couldn't believe Peter Gabriel had been trampled on my night to show him a good time.

The next day in the studio, Peter was working on his follow-up record to *So*, called *Us*. He wanted the New Orleans horn sound on a track called "Washing of the Water," so I arranged to get Tim Green in on tenor saxophone, Reggie Houston on baritone saxophone, and Renard Poché on trombone. We came up with a sound that was merely blowing air through their horns and it sounded haunting.

Peter Gabriel had his own amazing studio in Bath, England, called Real World. A 200-year-old water mill, surrounded by gardens in the stunning countryside in Wiltshire, provided an inspirational setting. The magnificent main studio area, with two adjoining isolation booths, could be used alongside the Wood Room to provide a considerable number of options for recording almost anything. The seventy-two channel SSL 9000 XL G series analogue console had been custom-installed to maximize its potential in the room, and you only had to look up from the desk to be reminded of the proximity of water: the view of the millpond from the work area was intoxicating.

At Peter's studio, he'd hold recording sessions he'd call "Record Week" and would invite unique artists from around the world to collaborate with top producers. I was invited over, along with Daniel, to help out. Once we got there, we stayed at Peter's house, across the street from the studio. In those days, the electricity for the house was controlled by a pay box, so the lights and all the power would go off when your money ran out, and the hot water and the heating was automated to turn on at certain times. Because we worked a noon to midnight schedule, there would be no hot water or heat when we wanted them, and when the power would go out, we would have to sit in the dark because we didn't have any change.

Peter had a pretty cool custom Volkswagen Beetle with a high-end custom stereo that you could plug a DAT machine into, in order to listen to mixes from the studio. It was like a James Bond car with all kinds of gadgets: there was a panel of custom buttons to control the interior lighting and change the color of the dash lights, and others adjusted the height of the car. The seats were custom chocolate-brown suede with speakers in the headrests. Subwoofers were built into the bottom of the seats. It really was a whole other experience of sound.

Dan was whisked away to a little side studio they had set up in the barn in order to work. Mike Large was the studio manager and asked me if I would produce one of their African artists, Lucky Dube, and I agreed. Lucky had just flown in from South Africa with his band of fifteen people. The only studio that could accommodate us was the big room that looked out over the pond. It looked a bit like a spaceship in there, with the huge SSL wraparound console in front of a window.

I introduced myself to Lucky, but he wasn't interested in talking. Everyone was exhausted from the travel. I was trying to find a way to win him over when I mentioned to him that I had just finished a record with the Neville Brothers.

"You worked with the Neville Brothers?" he said in disbelief, his face lighting up.

I told him I'd worked on *Yellow Moon*. He quickly became my best friend. I cut two tracks with Lucky and his band, "War and Crime" and "Frankenstein." The BBC came into the studio while we were recording and asked if they could shoot a segment with Lucky and me. It was bizarre to be on BBC TV, on the news, with other producers like Phil Ramone and big stars like Van Morrison working in the little side studios, and me working in the big room with the legendary Lucky Dube, a man some people consider to be on the same level as Bob Marley, a reggae legend.

CHAPTER 8

KINGSWAY

KINGSWAY BECAME A REVOLVING DOOR FOR CANADIAN artists. Pierre Marchand was a friend of Dan's and also the keyboard player in the band for Canadian singer Luba. Dan had produced one of Luba's records and had bonded with Marchand. Pierre went on to make a couple of albums with the McGarrigle sisters, and they recommended he work with a young woman from the east coast of Canada named Sarah McLachlan. A gifted singer of emotional ballads, she was virtually unknown at the time, but Pierre took a chance on her, and by 2015 she had sold over forty million records worldwide.

Daniel let Pierre and Sarah set up a studio in one of the upstairs annexes next to the room that we called the Plant Room, which had a big skylight, to finish working on her first record. At the same time, Robbie Robertson had booked into Kingsway for a week to work on the follow-up record to his self-titled album. Gary Gersh would produce this new album, called *Storyville*. Robertson was infatuated with New Orleans and wanted the vibe on his album, and he went all out. It felt like I recorded more people that week than I had recorded in my entire life: I had Mardi Gras Indians lined up in the kitchen to come and sing. Once finished with the Dirty Dozen Brass Band, I recorded different drummers and guitar players, more singers, percussion players, then an organ player and piano players. I turned around to Gersh one day and said, "Man, I am exhausted."

He turned and replied, "Kid, this is nothing. Try doing this every day for a year."

Each room in the house had a name. Joel Ford had been working on the house and was living in the Mexican Room. Joel had done a tin ceiling in the Mexican Room and painted it to look rustic and old; the walls had treatments to make them look like the paint was peeling off. The Mermaid Room was the bedroom at the front of the house with a beautiful marble fireplace, wide plank floors, and windows that opened onto the huge front balcony. This was Daniel's room when he stayed at the house. The bathroom was amazing, with beautiful tile work and a walk-in shower with five shower heads. The floor had symbols on it of the reverse swastika, which is considered to be a sacred and auspicious symbol in Hinduism, Buddhism, and Jainism.

Across from the huge hall was the Bordello Room, also with huge windows that opened onto the balcony. Every room had a fireplace, but this one was the best — sculpted with naked women and a huge gold mirror with more sculpted women and flowers. There was a huge four-poster bed with a red velvet canopy top, with deep-purple drapes tied with red velvet rope. It really had the feeling of a bordello from the Storyville era. The bathroom had a huge claw-foot tub and the faucet was a swan's neck and head, and the water ran from the mouth. There were crystal chandeliers and a gold toilet with a black seat and a matching bidet. The walls were painted with a mural of scenes from the Sistine Chapel. This was my room when I lived at Kingsway, a far cry from the futon I had slept on in previous years.

The last of the big rooms with private bathrooms was the New Orleans Room, which had an Italian tumbled-marble floor and a beautiful claw-foot tub in the bathroom. It had an amazing Chinese bed made entirely of wood with intricate designs carved into it. I found all of the beds for the house at an estate auction on Magazine Street, but this one was special, and I later met the woman whose family had owned it when she was a child. She was the wife of Steve Nails, who owned Dockside Studio in Lafayette.

The house had a grand staircase and at the top of the stairs was a huge cross that came from Marie Laveau's grave. Born in 1794, she was an infamous Louisiana Creole practitioner of voodoo. It was said that she had put a curse on the drinking water of New Orleans: anyone who drank it would come back to New Orleans four more times before they died.

At the Kingsway Studio API console.

The third floor of the house was an apartment with a huge deck that looked out over the French Quarter. It had one massive room with a huge four-poster bed, and the bathroom was in a large center room. There was a claw-foot tub that looked into a huge saltwater fish tank built into the wall. The room beside it was a little kitchenette with a vintage fridge and a little sink and stove. If you forgot your smokes up there, it was easier to go to the store and buy more than to walk all the way back up.

The Plant Room was in the center of the rear of the house, and we opened up the ceiling to put in a skylight. In the center of the room was a mammoth pot filled with bird of paradise flowers, and the room had a bit of a jungle vibe. There was an Indian rug that I'd bought in Montreal for $5,000, something no one had wanted because it was so huge — thirty feet by twenty-five feet of red wool with a fat weave, and it was extraordinarily heavy. On each side of the Plant Room were two annexes, and those had single beds in them. They were reserved for Canadians who had drifted down, like Coyote Shivers, Tim Gibbons, and Dave Rave.

The kitchen was pretty much original, with old white subway tiles and an old gas stove and fridge, which was a huge two-door icebox style with big chrome handles. I had all new parts put in so that it ran quietly. Beside the kitchen was the Bar Room, with tile work all around it. Next to the house was a garden and a driveway leading to the garage.

Daniel wanted a pool put in, so I hired Tony Bananno, a friend who was the son of an Italian stonemason. I had a backhoe come and dig the hole for the pool, and I sent photos to Dan, who was in England at the time. The pool was being wired before they poured the cement when I got a call in the middle of the night from Dan telling me the pool was too big and I needed to make it smaller, like the size of a hot tub. I had to stop everything, buy back the dirt I had just trucked away, and fill the hole back in. Suddenly, I knew where the phrase "Dig a hole, fill it up" came from.

Dan wanted his money's worth from me, and he'd write lists in his book; he was only paying me CDN$200 per week, and it seemed I always had a list of twenty ridiculous things to do. I was busy enough running the studio, overseeing the house renovation, and keeping the bike collection running. My laundry list consisted of things like: *I want you to hang Mardi Gras beads in all the fireplaces.* He was paradoxical, wanting me to cut a bottle of apple juice with water so he'd have twice as much for the same price and then buying a $70,000 Gibson Les Paul Goldtop guitar the same day.

Tony tiled the pool with green-and-blue flagstone so it looked like a grotto. We planted banana trees and bird of paradise flowers around the sides of the pool so they would hang over it, making a lush cave.

The garage was at the back of the driveway, and I'd turned it into a motorcycle collection showroom. Between Dan and me, we had twelve bikes in there. Once he saw my Harley-Davidson Knucklehead, he had to top me, and I found him a

1947 EL Knucklehead, flat blue, and then he wanted a Harley-Davidson Hydra-Glide like mine, so I got him a turquoise 1948 Hydra-Glide, the first year of the Panhead. He had all the collectables: a 1947, the last year of the Knucklehead; a 1948, the first year of the Panhead; a 1965 Electra-Glide Panhead from the first year of electric start; a 1960 Duo Glide, second year with rear shocks; and a 1947 Indian Chief.

With my 1936 first year Knucklehead, 1956 Panhead Hydra-Glide, 1962 Duo Glide that I customized with electric start, and 1966 first year Shovelhead, it was quite the collection of old Harleys, plus one Indian. I had every bike in there on a trickle charge so the batteries wouldn't die, and I'd take a different bike out every day to keep them all running. It felt like a full-time job just managing the bikes. I'd get on the Indian that had the throttle on the left and the tank shifter on the right, then get on the 1947 Knucklehead that had the throttle on the right and the tank shift on the left and ride away, adjusting immediately.

Mason Ruffner, the guitar player who played on Dylan's *Oh Mercy*, asked me to get him a bike after seeing the collection. I found him a 1966 Shovelhead from my friend in Florida, rose and white in color, with tunable exhaust, so you could make the bike really quiet if you wanted to, and he kept the bike parked in the garage, too.

I had to shut down the house once to tent it because it had termites. It took a week to gas the house and it left a nasty smell for months, and all the books in the house smelled toxic when you opened them. After bagging the house, the roof was next on the list to replace, as the patch wasn't holding up very well in heavy rain. I designed the roof so that it had a walkway up and down each side so no one had to walk on the slate, which was fragile and could crack. I used rubber to line the roof parapet walls, so it was like a swimming pool.

At one point, I shut down the studio so Joel could do some master wood-working on the API console. Joel had built the kitchen table, which was nine feet long, and the top made out of a single piece of four-inch-thick red mahogany. He spent weeks sanding it to make it super fine, with no stain, only hand oiled, and it must have weighed 800 pounds. The API console had dark-brown fake (plastic) wood on the sides and a vinyl-padded armrest, so Joel constructed a beautiful dark-ebony wood casing around the console, with four-inch-thick sides and a four-inch-wide armrest. For the top of the console, I had him cut a sliver

LISTEN UP!

vent into the top, facing the engineer. I had an idea that when we worked late we'd need to be revived when tired, so I had a foot pedal installed that could be pressed open like a guitar-volume pedal, and two tanks would blow out oxygen. It also cooled a person down. Those old analogue consoles ran hot, and it often felt like working over a hot stove all day.

I had been using old Tannoy Gold fifteen-inch speakers in Lockwood cabinets, and I had two sets of them. One set of the Tannoy Gold speakers came from Abbey Road Studios in London, and one of them had a big gash in the side of it, rumored to be from where John Lennon had thrown a teacup at it. I had this idea to stack the speakers on top of each other, like the Grateful Dead had stacked their PA speakers, for a huge punch. I also had a pair of eighteen-inch Clair Brothers PA subwoofers, and I stacked the two Tannoys on top, making a fifteen-foot tower of speakers. I powered the subs with a Canadian amp called Bryston 4B, and the four tops I powered with four Mcintosh mono tube amps, used a two-way electronic crossover, and then tuned them with it. The speaker stacks sounded incredible; it was the best sound system I had ever heard. Because the Tannoys were Tannoy Dual Concentric speakers, it meant that all the sound came from one source, making it smoother. Other speakers have components with tweeters, and the sound comes from different areas, which makes it hard on the ears for long hours of listening. I painted them black and changed the grill cloth so it looked amazing: two black towers on each side of the console.

Once I had revamped the studio, Karen Kuehn came down from New York to shoot photos for a brochure. The studio was about to go public and open its doors to other artists — up until that time it had been private for our own projects.

CHAPTER 9

IGGY POP AND R.E.M.

IGGY POP HEARD THE CHRIS WHITLEY RECORD, and he loved the sound; he wanted Malcolm Burn and me to make his new album. I hit it off with Iggy right away. He brought in his road band to record. It was Larry Mullins on drums, Hal Cragin on bass, and Eric Schermerhorn on guitar.

I set the band up in the Piano Room, which we had just set up, with Larry's back to me. Iggy sat in front of the fireplace. I isolated Iggy's guitar and Eric's amp in other rooms. Iggy was living on the third floor and the rest of the band was on the second floor. Iggy brought his wife, Suchi Asano, and Mookie, their Siamese cat, and somehow I always got his wife's name and the cat's name mixed up. The cat pissed and shit in every plant in the house.

Iggy had a twelve-hour rule: if you finished at midnight, you couldn't start work until the next day at noon. If he saw me even close to the studio, he would ask, "Where you going?"

We got invited one night to see the Beastie Boys' show and Henry Rollins was opening. Henry was intense. After the show, we went backstage, and Iggy talked to Henry and asked him if he would sing on a track, so the next day Henry came into the studio. He was like another person, soft-spoken and very polite. Then he started singing and the wild man came out. Henry sang on a track called "Wild America," which was perfect for him.

After a week of recording, I think Malcolm got on Iggy's nerves. Iggy took little jabs at Malcolm all the time, and would say things like, "Hey, Malcolm, when are you going to start producing something?"

I had hired Trina Shoemaker to be my assistant, so part of her job was to run around the corner to see if a band was on at Café Brazil'. One night, she came back crying. She'd been mugged at gunpoint — she was shattered.

Iggy and I went to Café Brazil after we were done recording on that night. There was a jazz band and the drummer was really giving it. Iggy said, "Man, someone better pick up that kid."

I told Dan about the drummer the next day, and he asked if I'd gotten his number, but I hadn't. I had no idea who he was at all. I spent weeks trying to locate him, and it wasn't until I went to a drum clinic that I spotted him. I asked him if he'd played Café Brazil, and he had, and told me his name was Brian Blade. I asked him if he'd be interested in jamming with Dan and he agreed.

The track "Caesar" was a jam on which I had treated Iggy's vocal with some echoes, and it turned out to be one of Iggy's favorite tracks. The record American Caesar had a raw feel when it was cut, but lost some of its power with too many keyboard overdubs.

The record company said they didn't have a single, so Iggy had an idea to cut "Louie Louie." It was the only track that I didn't record because it was an afterthought, but I ended up mixing it at Kingsway.

Iggy's body is something else, cut and fit, and I asked him if he worked out. "Hell, no," he said.

I asked him how he stayed in great shape and he told me that back in the '80s when he drank he'd gotten a big belly, but he began doing a Chinese breathing technique in which he inhales and exhales, passing oxygen to all parts of his body. The only food I saw him eat was steak and potatoes. Iggy grew up in Detroit and I grew up a few hours away, so we both knew how harsh the winters in that area were. I told him that in the winter my dad wouldn't turn up the heat, and would just say, "If you're cold, put on a sweater." If we were hungry he'd say, "Eat an apple."

Iggy laughed and said it was the opposite for him. His dad would say, "Jim, are you cold? Turn up the heat!"

I guess that's the American way.

Iggy Pop in New York.

I had an amazing 1963 Jaguar XKE, silver with chrome wire wheels, black worn-leather seats, and an Alpine stereo that rocked. On the weekend, I'd take drives with Iggy along River Road to listen to the week's mixes. Iggy would tell me stories about working with Bowie. Iggy had written a song about his wife, Suchi, and when he'd played it for Bowie, Bowie asked if he could cut it for his new record. Iggy was more than happy for him to use it, and it became a huge hit. The song was "China Girl."

Iggy lived in New York's Alphabet City. His apartment had multiple colored prints on the walls; he'd had Suchi sit in different color paints, then sit on art paper. There were yellow, red, green, blue, and purple prints of Suchi's bum.

I was once sitting at Caffe Reggio in Greenwich Village waiting for Iggy to show up. He finally arrived and sat down, and a kid at the back of the café with a guitar case recognized Iggy and came over.

"Mr. Pop, would you sign my guitar?" the kid asked. He pulled out a brand-new white Stratocaster and a Sharpie.

"Sure, kid," Iggy said, and drew a big dick on the guitar. He then wrote, *Dick by Iggy*.

The kid was dumbfounded and thanked Iggy in a nervous voice. Iggy gave him his trademark sinister grin.

LISTEN UP!

The first single from the album, "Wild America," reached number twenty-five on the Billboard Rock chart. The album was not as commercially successful as its predecessor, but it did fare well in the United Kingdom and sold well throughout America in the '90s.

The Neville Brothers' *Brother's Keeper* was one of the first records to be recorded at Kingsway Studio. Bono from U2 had written something that he thought would be perfect for the Nevilles, a gospel song called "Kingdom Come." I thought it was a powerful track with Cyril singing it and Bono wailing in the background. Sadly, the track never made to the record, due to the band's collective decision.

R.E.M. came through for a week in February 1992 to start recording *Automatic for the People*. It was a writing demo period for them. They brought their producer, Scott Litt, too. I set them up and they worked on a bunch of songs, but the only thing that made it on the record was "New Orleans Instrumental No. 1."

R.E.M.'s management called me about helping the band flush out songs for their next record, which would become *Monster*. They wanted to work with just me, without Litt, so they could be free of any outside opinions. I was living up in Ojai, California, at the time, so I flew in to meet the guys at Kingsway Studio in the fall of 1993. I assumed everyone would stay at the house, but Michael Stipe wanted to be the only one who stayed there, so the other band members stayed in a hotel.

There was only one rule: there were to be no razor blades in the studio or the house — they all had to be removed. For cutting the tape, I had to bring in a razor blade and then have it taken away. I never questioned why, just did what they asked.

The first time I saw everyone in the studio with a laptop was in 1993. Everyone would sit on the couch, their faces lit by a blue glow from the screen.

I set R.E.M. up in the Piano Room, where I normally recorded, so it was easy to communicate. Sessions started around noon each day, much of the time spent trying out new gear. Mike Mills had gotten a new Mesa / Boogie amp that had tremolo. I plugged his bass into the amp and turned on the tremolo on the amp and he thought it was a cool sound. Peter Buck also had a couple of new guitar effects he was interested in, but mainly he tested out the house Vox AC30 guitar amp. He had never seen the AC30 with the top boost on it, and after trying it, he wanted one. Bill Berry came with nothing, not even sticks. We ended up using the house Yamaha Maple recording custom drum kit, just a little four-piece.

Michael Stipe would lie on the couch, singing along as the band recorded, so one day I gave him a handheld mic, a Shure SM58, so he could record his ideas. He looked at me a little puzzled and said, "I can lie here and sing?"

I told him he could, and he said, "Wow, I have never done it like this before."

Michael could hear his voice coming out of the speakers, and he was happy to work this way.

I was experimenting with filming, too, back then, and I filmed a lot of the sessions. The band made me erase the footage in which anyone was smoking pot, but I handed over the film to them, so maybe one day it might be shown. Most of the songs I recorded the ideas for ended up making it onto the record, and they used some of the tracks I recorded as well. The band went on to Miami and then to L.A. to finish up. *Monster* went to number one in quite a few countries and went four-times platinum in the USA.

R.E.M. didn't work too late so everyone could still go out at night. One night, Bill Berry drank a little too much and ended up staggering around the French Quarter, only to find himself staring down the barrel of a gun. Although the French Quarter is very tourist oriented, it still has some dark side streets, and people who go down them are easy targets for robbery. Drug addicts prey on people on the outskirts of the Quarter, keeping an eye out for drunk people heading back to their hotels. A British couple was killed after refusing to give up their wallets. Bill still had his wits about him, despite being drunk, and he handed over his wallet without any trouble. The thief ran away and Bill somehow made it back to his hotel and to his room. I'm not sure why, but for some reason, he got up in the middle of the night and left his room, maybe looking for something else to drink. He went back to his room but accidentally went to the room across the hall from his, got into bed, and woke up looking down the barrel of *another* gun!

Bill's first thought was that the thief had found him, but then he realized it was the police. They asked for his name and he told them he was Bill Berry from the group R.E.M., but they didn't believe him. After being robbed, he obviously had no wallet to prove his identity, and he was registered in the hotel under an assumed name!

The police wouldn't let him go, and he asked if he could call the band's manager to vouch for him. Jefferson Holt, the band's manager and accountant, traveled everywhere with R.E.M., so he was around at the time. Jefferson confirmed to the police that, in fact, they did have Bill Berry and that he was in New Orleans recording. The police ended up letting Bill go, but when he told them he'd been robbed and lost his wallet, they didn't bother to make a report, telling him instead that it was his own fault for being drunk. The New Orleans police were notorious for being crooked and didn't care when people were robbed — it was just more annoying paperwork for them.

New Orleans is the only place I know of where you can buy a cop to be at your event or party; you make a deal with them, pay them cash, and they will do what you need. I had a 1969 Chevrolet Chevelle SS with a 454-cubic-inch engine, royal blue, with Mickey Thompson 50 series tires on the rear. The car was a monster. It would do wheelies when you floored it — the ultimate muscle car. One day, I had parked it in front of Kingsway while I ran in to use the bathroom, but when I came out four minutes later, it was gone! If someone had hot-wired it, I would have heard it fire up because the engine was so loud. I called to see if it had been towed and they didn't have it, so I called the police to make a report. I never saw that car again. Months later, there was a sting operation, and it was discovered that some police officers were eyeing up cars they liked then having them towed to a secret tow yard and putting their names on the windows to claim them later.

CHAPTER 10

THE BIRDHOUSE

IN APRIL 1993 I JOINED THE NORTH AMERICAN and European tour for Dan's album, along with Brian Blade and Daryl Johnson. We finished in Los Angeles, California, in September 1993, and I moved into the Chateau Marmont for a couple of weeks while I regrouped and began gathering up gear in road cases that I could take to Mexico to create a studio. Once I had arranged all the gear, I set up shop in Encinitas, California — a coastal beach city and popular surf town in San Diego County — at the home of my friends Uva and Garth. Their house was an old converted train station that they named the Derby House. Uva had covered the walls inside with interesting materials, like corduroy and denim. Uva was a painter and had huge wall-sized paintings; a painting of a huge white cow hung in the living room.

I had made a deal with Amek USA to buy a console in a road case from them. I got an Amek Tac SR 3000. It was a live console that had lots of sends and a punchy equalizer. I had the Studer A80 mk2 tape recorder shipped from Kingsway Studio, and I bought a pair of Electro-Voice Century 500 speakers from Westlake Audio and a pair of Clair Brothers eighteen-inch subwoofers. I spent a month at the Derby House receiving and setting up all the gear, and I bought a Ford Explorer to get around. Once everything arrived and was wired, I packed it all back up and rented a house in Ojai, California. It was a large house on an orange grove, with a pool and two little Hansel and Gretel–like cottages. John Lennon had lived in the house once after breaking up with Yoko Ono in the '60s.

The main room had a cathedral ceiling and wooden floors, with quite an echo because of all the plaster. I got a huge green army tent and hung it in the big cathedral room and laid down that huge Indian rug I'd bought so long ago in Montreal. The room was now dense and dry-sounding and smelled like old canvas. I hung Indian tapestries on the inside to make it feel like Morocco. That was where I set up bands, and I put the control room down the hall in one of the bedrooms. The plan was to eventually find a place in Mexico and ship all the gear down there.

I flew down to Cabo San Lucas in early November 1993. My friends Uva and Garth had a house there, and Uva said she could show me a couple of places. I checked into the Palmilla Resort just outside Cabo San Jose. The resort had been built in 1956 as a fifteen-room luxury hideaway by Don Abelardo Rodriguez, the son of the president of Mexico. It could only be reached by yacht or private plane, and early guests included Hollywood celebrities like Lucille Ball, John Wayne, Bing Crosby, and former United States president Dwight D. Eisenhower. Uva and I drove around for two days, but the luxury properties she showed me were big, tasteless vacation homes, built by rich L.A. types — nothing had any charm. She wondered if her friend Ken might rent us his unique house, and the following day he invited us to see it.

Ken had built his house into the side of a mountain, like in a spy movie. From the street there was nothing to see other than a wooden door in the middle of a rock. Once you entered the concealed building, you walked down a winding stone pathway lined by tropical plants and natural rock walls. The path opened up into a big open area that was the living room and kitchen. The kitchen was built into the rock walls, and a large round table had a Lazy Susan so you could spin your food around. It had a propane fridge that didn't make a sound. There was a fireplace built into the rock wall, and a palapa roof covered the area while huge plate-glass windows opened like an accordion, revealing the Sea of Cortez. This led to a large outdoor area with palm trees and a lagoon-shaped pool. The pool went under another set of plate-glass windows into the master bedroom — you could actually roll out of bed into the pool and then swim outside. The bathroom was like a cave, with an outside shower covered with a palapa roof.

The Birdhouse in Cabo San Lucas (January 1994).

The rest of the house was open to the environment, so birds could come and go and lizards and scorpions could run wild. There were two other bedrooms in the rear with private bathrooms, both more modern. I made a deal with Ken to rent the house for six months starting in January. Down at the bottom of the Baja Peninsula, it only rained six days a year, and that was usually in September; the average temperature year-round is about 75 degrees Fahrenheit, and with its desert-like low humidity, it was total paradise.

I hired Rock-it Cargo to ship the gear from Ojai, California, to Ken's house at the tip of the peninsula. They picked up the gear on January 3, 1994. I drove down in the Ford Explorer with Brant Scott, and the gear was to arrive a week later. We did the 1,000-mile drive nonstop, ripping through Baja like it was a race. There were a couple of hundred miles of washboard roads, so we had hours of being shaken. Once we got there, we checked into the Twin Dolphins Hotel, which boasted an amazing cove to swim in.

We waited for Ken to leave his house, but he took his time. Hurricane Calvin had wiped out the whole corridor between San José del Cabo and Cabo San Lucas. There was no water because the main feed had been washed away with the storm, so all the water had to be trucked in. Ken finally moved and we took over. The house was nicknamed "the Birdhouse," because of the birds flying in all the time.

A week later, the gear had not shown up. I went into San José del Cabo to use the phone and called Rock-it to see where everything was. My agent at Rock-it said that because NAFTA had just come into play on January 1, everything was being held in California until they could clear customs. He said that it should only be another couple of days before the shipment would leave. Three days later, I called back and the agent said the gear would be going out at the end of the week. It had been two weeks by then, and the gear still hadn't left L.A. Brant and I could only do so much, so we went to the beach every day and explored every place to eat and drink. By January 15, the gear remained in L.A., at which point Rock-it informed me that they couldn't move it because the borders weren't prepared for importing this kind of equipment yet.

I had told my friend Garth about the issue, and he said his Mexican mover could get the gear in without any questions asked, but I had to fly back to L.A. to give it to him. I had a flight booked for L.A. on January 17, but when I went to the airport, I was informed that all flights to L.A. were canceled because of a huge earthquake.

Instead, I flew in the next day and took a cab to Glendale, where I had one of my motorcycles stored. I rode it to the Chateau Marmont to stay. That night I felt an aftershock that felt like another big earthquake. I slept with my clothes and shoes on, ready to jump out the window because the tremors felt so bad.

I had arranged with the Mexican shipper to meet me at the Rock-it Cargo terminal at the airport. The Mexican truck showed up, and it was an old beat-up stake truck, not even covered. The entire back was open with only wooden fence sides. Still, we loaded everything and the driver left. I didn't know if I would ever see the gear again. The next day, I flew back to the Baja California Peninsula to the Birdhouse. I was shocked when two days later the truck arrived! It seemed incredible that a big shipping company couldn't get the gear in, but an old Mexican man with a one-truck moving company could drive it there like it was nothing.

When the truck showed up, all the gear was in a transport trailer, but the driver wouldn't pull it up the huge hill to the Birdhouse. To make matters worse, when the driver jumped out of the truck, he only had one leg — a wooden peg, like a pirate's. I saw a truck coming up the hill filled with workmen who had been working on a house down by the sea. I flagged it down and offered the guys $200 cash to take the gear off the transport trailer, put it onto their truck, and move it up the hill and into the Birdhouse.

Cutting it close for time, Dan's band was showing up the next day and I had to be up and running, ready to record. Once all the gear was in, I set it up right away, pulling an all-nighter to be ready. Brant was leaving the next day and "Wayne the Brain" was flying in to be my assistant.

The sessions at the Birdhouse were mostly instrumental, and a lot of great tracks came out of there. One evening, I cut a track with Daryl and Brian called "Frozen Reggae." Dan felt the song was an afterthought, but he was out for the evening. Thirteen years later, the track resurfaced on Dan's *Black Dub* album as the song "I Believe in You."

I had brought a Dutch PA system (Axys) with me down to the Birdhouse; it was a three-box system with two eighteen-inch subs, a side, and a top, completely self-powered and packing a punch. I used the PA in the rear of venues for a surround-sound effect, and I used a joystick panner to spin guitar around the venue — quadraphonic sound at its best.

The sound in the Birdhouse was incredible because of the rock walls and the grass roof, which gave it a dense sound with no reflections. A Spanish-speaking woman named Loose was the housekeeper, and she cooked amazing meals for us and taught us how to catch scorpions. Loose kept a mason jar with alcohol in it, which was full of scorpions. She said, "If you see a scorpion on the floor, grab the kitchen tongs, and put him in the jar of alcohol." She claimed that once the scorpion was dropped in the jar, it spit its venom into the alcohol, making an antivenom.

Loose warned us to beware of the black centipedes because they were deadly if they bit you. They could be a foot long, with hornlike stingers on their heads, and the Mexicans called them "Hundred Legs." Daryl saw one of the black centipedes crawling up the wall and tried to catch it, but even though he grabbed it with the tongs, it actually bent them and got away.

One day, Brian was recording a take on the drums when he let out an "Ohhh . . ." He always made funny sounds while playing the drums so I assumed that's what was happening, but then he jumped up like a hot tea bag had been thrown down his pants and danced around the room like he was on *Soul Train*.

"I just got bit on my leg," Brian said.

He rolled up his pant leg and there was a huge, throbbing bump where a scorpion that had crawled up his pant leg had bitten him.

I ran over and grabbed Loose's jar of scorpions. I dipped a paper towel into the jar and applied it to Brian's leg. About half an hour later, the bump went down and Brian was fine.

People in Mexico lived close to death. There was always a new cross along the roadside where someone had recently died. Sunday was the Mexicans' day of rest, and often they would get really drunk. One Sunday, we were driving back from San José del Cabo and an SUV was clearly tailing us. It was a mountain coast road, with cliffs down to the ocean, so I pulled over to let the driver pass. The SUV had a family inside, and as it passed us, the kids in the back window waved. It raced by but it was a stone road, and when they went around the big bend ahead, my heart sank as we watched the car drive right off the cliff in front of us. We quickly pulled over, expecting to see the SUV destroyed, but there was a house at the bottom of the cliff with a palapa roof, and the SUV had flown down about ten stories and landed on the roof of the house, the rear of the car sticking out. We ran down the cliff and saw that, although the occupants of the car were badly shaken up with cuts, everyone was alive and walked away. Fortunately, the home owners were at the beach that day.

A group of Canadians had heard that we were recording on the Baja California Peninsula. They found our secret location through a woman named Chia Rafelson, who lived in a little artist town called Todos Santos. I had started hanging out with Chia, and she took me to the other coast to see Todos Santos, a desert oasis on the Tropic of Cancer with ancient palm and mango orchards and beautiful views of white sand beaches and the Pacific Ocean. It has a cool vibe, like in Oaxaca. Chia's mom, Paula, owned a really cool restaurant in Todos Santos called Café Santa-Fé, a great Italian restaurant. Paula and her husband, Ezio, had decided to clear out of L.A. and move to Mexico to start a restaurant. Ezio was master chef and had built the restaurant with a wood-burning oven to make the pizzas like they do in Italy.

Paula is married to Bob Rafelson's brother, but she had dated Bob during the height of his career. Bob was partners with Bert Schneider, and together they'd created a company called Raybert Productions. Bob directed the movie called *The Postman Always Rings Twice,* which starred Jack Nicholson. He also produced *Easy Rider,* which starred Dennis Hopper, Peter Fonda, and Jack Nicholson. Raybert also created a TV show in the '60s called the *Monkees.* Paula was one of the original cage dancers at the Whisky a Go Go. Hendrix hired her to be his assistant and she would go into the studio before he got there and deck it out with psychedelic tapestries, incense, and lava lamps. Paula told us crazy stories about babysitting Jack Nicholson and Dennis Hopper while they were on acid and wouldn't get out of the bathtub.

One day, we were eating with Paula at the Café Santa-Fé when I noticed that she had a huge Frida Kahlo painting on the wall. I asked her how she got it, but she said it was a reproduction painted in Mexico City by artists at the university. At that moment, Drew Barrymore and her boyfriend, Eric Erlandson, the guitar player from Hole, came in and sat with us. Chia went to school in L.A. with Drew. Drew and Eric had come down to hide out for a while. Chia had broken up with her boyfriend, Balthazar Getty, the child actor from the movie *Lord of the Flies*. Drew, Balthazar, and Chia were all part of the Brat Pack'. I told Chia that our time at the Birdhouse was up and that I needed to find another place to record.

Chia showed me an old hotel on the main road called Hotel California. It was rundown and noisy because huge trucks drove by all the time. Then she showed me an old sugarcane baron's dilapidated estate, called Casa Dracula, built in 1852 by Don Antonio Domingues. Casa Dracula is the largest and most famous historical house in Todos Santos. The name was inspired by the casa's unique gothic arched windows. There's said to be treasure buried somewhere within the walls.

The imposing brick structure had two floors and fourteen-foot ceilings, with each floor measuring approximately twenty-five-hundred square feet. There were three bedrooms, a foyer, a salon, and a bathroom upstairs, and two large principal rooms on the ground floor. In an adjoining outbuilding was a bathroom, a kitchen, and a guest bedroom. I thought it was the perfect place to record, so I spoke with the owner to arrange a deal to work there for six months. First, though, I had to leave for a month to produce a record for the Tragically Hip. They were Canada's top band at the time and were touring the world with Midnight Oil and Ziggy Marley. I was going to produce them back in New Orleans at Kingsway. I left Wayne the Brain at the Birdhouse to pack up the studio.

CHAPTER 11

THE TRAGICALLY HIP

I SPENT THE MONTH OF APRIL 1994 in New Orleans producing the Tragically Hip record *Day for Night*, which was released in September 1994. It became the band's first album to debut at number one on the Canadian Albums Chart. I had done some demos in Kingston, Ontario, Canada, at the band's warehouse / rehearsal studio. In January, it was so cold I wore a snowmobile suit and a Russian army–issue hat. I discovered the drum treatment for the song "Thugs" there.

The band decided that they wanted to make the album by playing all the songs in a live set, the idea being they would perform the song without burning it out. Two weeks into the record, I felt like I didn't have one good take under my belt, and I was getting nervous. I told Dan what was happening because he'd gone through this kind of thing with U2; he told me the best solution was to edit the best bits of all the takes to make one good one, which is what he'd done.

Each morning I would get up early and review the best parts of the songs, then begin editing them together. Once everyone showed up at noon for work, I would play the tracks I had edited, but I'd tell them that it was the last take from yesterday and everyone would agree that it was the best of all the takes and should be used.

These guys were beer drinkers like no other band I had ever seen, and they'd go through at least twenty-four beers a day and a quarter pound of weed a week.

They brought their assistant, Billy Ray, and his job was to roll joints all day. Billy got the job from a letter he'd written to the band saying he was their biggest fan and would work for free, so they took a chance on him and he was with them throughout the rest of their career. I hope he got paid eventually.

Billy took a big interest in the Harleys and would polish them. I let him ride one of my bikes and he got hooked on motorcycles from that point. I ended up selling him his first bike, my Norton Dunstall 810. They're rare and now I wish I hadn't sold it. He ended up blowing the motor and selling it to Bob Rock, another producer.

The song "So Hard Done By" had a real tight sound, but I didn't want to use a normal-sounding guitar for the solo, so I put Robbie Baker's guitar through a pocket amp the size of a cigarette pack that ran off a 9-volt battery, and I got a barking little guitar sound. Daryl Johnson came over to put congas on the track, too. The record was a bit of a stretch for the band because their other records were straight-up rock records and they'd never really experimented

Day for Night (1994).

ALBUM ART

LISTEN UP!

THE TRAGICALLY HIP   65

with sounds before. Johnny Fay, the drummer, appreciated me pushing him and was into the drum treatments I was using. We ended up becoming good friends and I still get calls from him to check in.

One night while we were recording, I noticed a guy sitting on the stairs, rocking out. After the take, I turned around and he slapped his leg, then said, "You guys rock!"

It was Brad Pitt. He was in town filming *Interview with the Vampire* and somehow Karen Brady had bumped into him and invited him over to see the house. Brad's major motion picture debut was in *Thelma & Louise.* In the scene in which he has sex with Geena Davis's character, the background music is Chris Whitley's song "Kicking the Stones," which I had recorded. Brad said he loved that track and was a big fan of Chris's, and I told him that the song had been recorded in the room we were in, which he thought was cool. Brad decided he wanted to buy the house and have Karen run it for him, but his father and his investment broker told him that it was not a good investment.

In 2017, Gord Downie, the lead singer for the Tragically Hip, passed away. He had been diagnosed with glioblastoma, an incurable brain cancer, and yet he carried on with a national tour and with recording, and he brought awareness to the issues facing the Indigenous Peoples of Canada. There is a Native American saying about two wolves of the psyche, and that the wolf you feed will be the stonger one. Gord chose not to focus on the cancer but instead to feed truth and love, which expanded as he pushed for accountability with respect to how Canada treats its Indigenous population. He generated awareness of the issues facing Indigenous Peoples and brought the horrors of the residential school system into everyday conversations, along with the deep need for reconciliation. Watching the country grieve after Gord passed reminded me of the reaction to John Lennon's death. The outpouring of emotion was on a national scale. The country shared in the sadness, and even the Prime Minister cried while addressing the press. Gord was a great man who made a lasting impact, and it was a privilege not only to have worked with him but to have known him as a person.

CHAPTER 12

CASA DRACULA

WHEN I FINISHED RECORDING THE TRAGICALLY HIP, I headed back to the Birdhouse. I arrived and found Wayne the Brain had all the gear packed up. I got an open trailer with a double set of wheels and attached it to the Ford Explorer. It took several trips to move the gear from the Birdhouse to Todos Santos's Casa Dracula, which was located just outside the town center. You could walk through the palm grove to get to the beach, and it felt like walking through a jungle in Vietnam. There were miles and miles of empty beach, which left a person feeling like they were totally alone, like in *Planet of the Apes*. Todos Santos is a beautiful oasis town near the west coast's best surfing beach, called Cerritos Beach.

I set up the studio in the main salon, a rustic room with a log beam and plaster ceiling and walls of peeling paint. All the floors were terra-cotta. French doors opened to a courtyard with a cement fountain surrounded by a mural of "birds" of paradise. The house had minimal furniture, just beds, a kitchen table, and chairs. I lived there with Wayne, and I set up Daniel on the top-floor penthouse over at the Hotel California.

Food was limited, with only three places to eat: Café Santa-Fé, Todos Santos Café, or a taco stand. The day the studio was up and running was the same day we went back to work, and we reviewed a lot of what we had done at the Birdhouse. I had spent a considerable amount of time at the Birdhouse treating

Casa Dracula (April 1994).

drum tracks by Brian Blade. I would take Brian's best grooves and loop them in an Eventide H3000, an ultra harmonizer that combines pitch, delay, modulation, and filtering. I had a system in which I'd send the drums to multiple different effects and then, using the mute buttons on the console, I would perform effects on top of the drum loops. There was one that Dan really loved and that we used for a track called "Jimmy Was." It ended up being used later in Billy Bob Thornton's film *Sling Blade*.

While working at Casa Dracula, we would drive out to an abandoned airfield in order to listen to our mixes in the car. It was the same airfield where drug planes landed from Colombia. There was a cool effect that would happen when you walked out on the tarmac: the heat vapors coming up from the pavement would make anything invisible from the ground up. If you walked along it, your body would disappear and your head would appear to be floating in the air.

One night we were out there with the doors of the car open, listening to our mixes, when out of the vapors a truck sped toward us. It was the Federales — the Mexican Federal Police. They pulled up, machine guns drawn, yelling.

I turned the stereo down. The truck was full of Federales and they surrounded us, likely assuming we were drug lords waiting for a plane full of cocaine to arrive. Wayne looked like a caveman with long hair, Dan had long hair and a headband, and I was dressed like a biker with jeans, cowboy boots, Harley shirt, chain wallet, and black Ray-Bans. We had Chia with us and she was wearing almost nothing because it was so hot. We probably fit the drug bill.

The Federales acted like they had just made an enormous bust. I tried to speak to them in English, but they acted like they didn't understand. They searched the car and they found Dan's bathroom bag, with a baggie of fennel seeds inside, which they thought were pot seeds. They kept saying, "*La marihuana!*"

Things turned ugly. The police had Wayne on the ground, face down, with a machine gun at his head. Dan was on his knees with his hands on his head. I thought they might shoot them. Chia spoke fluent Spanish and tried to explain to the head officer that we were musicians from Canada and we were there recording music. I asked Chia to tell the police that we were working with Vicente Fernández. He is a singer, actor, and film producer nicknamed El Rey de la Música Ranchera.

The Federales yelled to all the other officers about Vicente Fernández, and they all laughed for a moment, but then suddenly stopped and started yelling again. *Well, that backfired*, I thought.

Chia then said to the Federales, "I have seen you before — you eat dinner at my mother's restaurant, Café Santa-Fé."

The officer's face suddenly relaxed to a smile.

"*Sí. Paula es tu madre?*" which means, "Paula is your mother?"

"*Sí*," Chia responded.

The head officer was friends with Paula. Next thing we knew, we were all free to go. We had all been certain we were either going to die or go to prison.

The Mexican Federales are notorious for making people disappear. On the trip down from Tijuana, you pass through many spot checks and they show the drug busts on a big board, like photos of tanker trucks cut open to reveal cocaine. There are also fake Federales who pull people over and take all their money. I once got pulled over in Cabo San Lucas by the police and I paid them $50 and they let me go. You never know what can happen.

Soon after this, I left Wayne and Daniel in Todos Santos, as I had to fly to Montreal to mix the Tragically Hip's record. Wayne stayed on, packed up the studio again, and shipped the gear back to California. He drove the car back to the United States by himself. I had made arrangements to send the gear to my friend Fred Drake's house in Joshua Tree, which was the beginning of Rancho de la Luna Studio. Fred Drake and David Catching started the studio where bands like Queens of the Stone Age and Eagles of Death Metal would later record. On the long list of acts who recorded there are Dave Grohl, Iggy Pop, Daniel Lanois, Foo Fighters with Joe Walsh, and the Mutants, plus many more.

CHAPTER 13

EMMYLOU HARRIS AND BILLY BOB THORNTON

SAN FRANCISCO FELT AMAZING. CHIA RAFELSON, MY girlfriend at the time, had made the apartment feel like home. Every day I could hear the "hoot hoot" of an owl outside. I kept looking out my window trying to find it, but I couldn't.

One day, I finally met my neighbor upstairs, a young gay man. He introduced himself to me and said, "I'm sorry, I hope I'm not disturbing you every morning."

I said, "What do you mean?" I had no idea why he would worry about that.

"My lover is a little loud," he told me, and I suddenly realized it wasn't an owl I had been hearing . . .

Chia and I flew to New Orleans to get my car and bikes, which were being stored at my friend Big Al's, out in Lafayette. I had a trailer hitch put on the Jag, rented a little box trailer from U-Haul, and, after loading up, started the long drive back to San Francisco.

I had been getting calls to produce a couple of records. One of them from was a Texas guitar slinger, Ian Moore. I had flown to Austin, Texas, for a meeting, and he was now coming to San Francisco to make the record *Modern Day Folklore*.

Through Zac Allentuck at Coast Recorders studio, I met someone who had a warehouse for rent in the Mission District. It was a three-story building with a roll-up door that you pulled into, and it could fit at least six cars. The top floor was one big open span with huge skylights and wooden floors. The second floor had five rooms that I could turn into bedrooms, and I thought it was a perfect place to make Ian Moore's album.

It had been a couple of months since I'd left Joshua Tree in the middle of the night when I received a call from Dan.

"How's Frisco feeling?" he asked.

I told him how cool it was, that there was a really great motorcycle culture there, and lots of cool coffee shops with tons of bikes parked outside of them. There were amazing places to ride once you crossed the Golden Gate Bridge.

"What happened to you?" he asked me. "You just split in the middle of the night."

"I tried to talk to you about it but you wouldn't listen." I explained I'd been uncomfortable there. I had been freaked out living with Fred, who was really sick at the time. Sadly, Fred had AIDS, and it freaked me out as he had sores all over him. Daniel wanted me to stay with Fred and it scared me so much that I had to leave. I had never seen anybody that sick, and staying with him was too much for me.

"That's all you have to say?" was his reply.

"What are you going to do with all your gear there?" I asked. He said he didn't know, but that San Francisco might sound cool, so I told him that I'd found a really great warehouse with tons of space to store cars, bikes, and gear, and it had living quarters. I made him an offer: I would supply the location if he supplied the gear. He'd have six months' free rent and I'd have six months with gear to produce the records I'd be making. I would help him on his own music, too. He thought it sounded interesting but needed to think about it. An hour later he called back, said he wanted to move forward, and we found ourselves partners. This is where our relationship changed; I was no longer working for him but working *with* him.

I secured the warehouse and arranged for Wayne the Brain to help me fix up the place. He turned all five offices on the second floor into bedrooms, painted them, and got beds and lamps. The warehouse had a hydraulic elevator that didn't work. My dad was an elevator mechanic for a university in Canada, so I flew him down to see if he could fix it. He spent a couple of days working on it and said that it was so old that all the seals had disintegrated. It worked on a piston that a pump filled with water and that pushed the elevator up; the seals were made of leather and there was no way to find replacements. He made

Bella Vista: Billy Bob Thornton session.

some calls and found a place that made parts for ships. The strange coincidence was that it was located at the end of the street we were on. Natoma Street was a little street between Ninth and Tenth Streets, south of Mission Street. My father went over there and met the old man who custom-made the seals on the spot. My dad came back and fixed the elevator, and we were able to take gear up to the third floor. We flew down to Joshua Tree and packed up the studio at Fred's. I rented a twenty-four-foot U-Haul and filled it to the brim. We drove nonstop back to San Francisco and brought the gear inside in the middle of the night so no one in the seedy area would see all the expensive equipment. Someone lived in the dumpster up the street and there were a lot of homeless people on Mission.

The studio on the third floor looked amazing, with the big Indian rug laid down and Chinese globes hung for the lighting. On the walls, I had tacked up huge Indian rugs to dampen the sound. I went to thrift stores and bought a couple of amazing mohair couches and armchairs.

Ian Moore came in with the band and we began the record. Ian was a guitar snob. He had a Marshall stack with a 50-watt Plexi-head and a 100-watt head, a great amplifier used by the Who, Eric Clapton, and Jimi Hendrix; it had even been used as a guitar amp at Woodstock. Ian wasn't happy with his guitar sound and made a comment that I didn't know how to get one. He called his friend Eric Johnson and asked him what he needed. Eric told Ian to use a combination of a couple of amps, a Fender and Marshall, and to take out the batteries in his pedals, shorting them out to lower the voltage to help with tone. We tried all those things, but Ian still wasn't satisfied. I was getting frustrated, and I told him that the tone came from him, not me. We butted heads and he was insistent that the only thing wrong was the way I was recording.

Finally, I said, "Okay, let's try a test." I invited Billy Gibbons, from ZZ Top, over. Billy had been in town picking up one of his cars, which had just been painted. He pulled up in a 1934 Ford 3-Window Coupe Street Rod 302. The paint was a black purple, the color of a black light, with a silver metal flake, like on motorcycle helmets from the '60s. It sounded like a dragster. The interior was simple, leather with minimal gauges, but with a killer Mcintosh stereo. Billy climbed out. He was a small man, unhealthily thin looking, wearing a weird hat that looked like a shag rug.

"So what do you think?" he asked about his car, and I told him I'd never seen such a cool paint job before.

Billy came up to the studio and I showed him the rig we were using.

"Yeah, just use the Marshall Plexi 50-watt head and the Marshall cabinet," he instructed.

I recorded Billy playing Ian's Stratocaster through the same rig and it sounded incredible. Ian, with the same guitar and same amp, played the same thing, and I recorded it and it sounded like shit. I played them both back and Ian was baffled that Billy's sounded so good and his didn't, even though they'd used the exact same gear.

"Hey, man, it's all about the touch," Billy said and smiled.

I felt a bit smug.

Billy showed us a little black box that looked like a Nintendo game of today. "See this? You can make a whole record on here." He'd made an entire song on the plane ride there. This was at a time when everyone was working on tape, computer recording still years off in the future.

Michael Villegas was a talented drummer from Texas. I loved his sound and we really hit it off. I used Michael on a couple of other records after this one. Bukka Allen (son of revered Texas songwriter Terry Allen) contributed piano and we got a great organ sound. After the record was finished, it was sent to someone else to mix, but I never thought it sounded as good as the mixes I had done.

While making Ian's record, Dan had begun an album with Emmylou Harris in Nashville; later they moved to Kingsway. I recorded some synthesizer bass on "All My Tears" with Daryl Johnson. I had gotten a new Novation bass station module, and I found a great bass sound for "All My Tears." I mixed the song and finished off other overdubs with Dan and Emmylou Harris once they came to San Francisco. Once we were done, we rehearsed for a show in Boulder, Colorado, and then took the tour bus from San Francisco to Boulder.

Once back home, N'Dea Davenport from the Brand New Heavies came in to cut her debut solo record with me which was self titled. She was married to Brady Blade at the time, Brian Blade's older brother, and Brady also played drums. The same Novation bass station used on "When the Night Falls" by N'Dea can be heard on Emmylou Harris's "All My Tears."

The band consisted of Brady Blade, Daryl Johnson, and Glenn Patcha on keyboards. Doyle Bramhall II (who was in the Arc Angels with Charlie Sexton) was a guest. Doyle's father, Doyle Bramhall, had played drums for legendary bluesmen Lightnin' Hopkins and Freddie King and was a lifelong collaborator with childhood friends Stevie Ray Vaughan and Jimmie Vaughan.

Emmylou got invited to play Neil Young's Bridge School Benefit on October 30, 1995, at the Shoreline Amphitheatre. Included on the bill were Bruce Springsteen, Chrissie Hynde, Beck, and Steven Tyler. There was a tradition where the night before the concert Neil had a big party. He held it at his house up in Northern California's Half Moon Bay, at Broken Arrow Ranch, situated on 140 acres off Skyline Boulevard. The road wound through redwood and eucalyptus trees and rolling hills and had beautiful views. Neil Young's house was a huge log cabin that had been added onto several times. I loved the house which was built on different levels with several nine-foot Steinway pianos; the photos on the walls composed a musical history lesson from Bob Dylan to Joni Mitchell.

The next day at the Bridge Show, Emmylou Harris performed. Working with Dan, she had left behind her traditional country sound. It was a bold move for her to diverge and choose a path of personal songs that fused soul, gospel, and folk. It was the first time she'd let people hear her new sound.

On the drive back from L.A. to San Francisco, I drove through a little Mexican town an hour north of L.A. called Oxnard. I came across a building for rent called the Teatro, which had been a porn theater in the 1940s. I called the number on the sign and talked to the Asian man who owned it. He said he wanted $1,500 a month for rent. I thought the theater was in pretty rough shape but had potential. I told Dan that I was considering renting it for the studio. At the time, he was listening to recorded tracks with Gary Gersh, and they drove up the coast to see it. He called me back and said it looked cool, and that he was into me moving the studio down to Oxnard. I flew down to Burbank, rented a car, and drove up to Oxnard to see the inside. A migrant Mexican farm worker was living in the front ticket booth. Oxnard in those days was the agricultural center of strawberries and lima beans. When you pass Malibu and the Ventura County line, the land spreads out flat with miles and miles of fields. The town of Oxnard is situated there. The town center was kind of rough, full of used-car lots, but it had a little Mexican restaurant called Cielito Lindo Cafe, across the street from the Teatro. Saul's Pawn Shop was on the street, as was Gordon's Western Wear, a great place for vintage Levi's and Wrangler jeans. There weren't many white people on the street. A Mexican pool hall was where all the excitement was to be found.

The owner of the Teatro opened the front doors and led me inside. The whole concession stand was still there — with the popcorn machine half full of mouldy popcorn! The place stank. There were two padded doors with little diamond windows in them, and when we passed through, I found all the seats still intact and the screen still there. The ripped curtains on the walls were beige and stained from the roof leaking. There was a stage in front of the screen and two halls on either side, with exit doors leading to the alley. Back in the concession area, there was a men's bathroom on one side and a women's on the other. Upstairs was the projector room (but the projector was long gone), a room with a toilet, and an office. Overall, it was pretty dirty and it would take a lot to get it into shape.

I was still working on a record with N'Dea Davenport at that time, and I sent Wayne the Brain down to start the demolition at the Teatro. We drove down and I bought Wayne a pickup truck to use for the job. I had a budget of $5,000 to get the theater into shape and Wayne had a month to pull it off, and so while I was finishing up with N'Dea, Wayne was down in Oxnard ripping the place apart. He took out the ticket booth in front of the Teatro, and he said the hardest thing was kicking out Pedro, the Mexican migrant worker living in there. Pedro moved from the ticket booth to the bushes in the parking lot. The parking lot was huge and could fit ten tour buses if need be.

In November 1995 Wayne moved inside and started ripping out the seats using a sledgehammer. He left the back three rows and then cleared out the whole middle, then left five rows in front of the stage in case we wanted to do some shows in there, or to use as guitar rests. Then he built a wooden deck that covered the middle of the theater. Wayne was Canadian, and he came by his deck-building skills naturally. The capacity to build a deck is in our Canadian blood. It was fifty feet wide by seventy feet long. He hung up the curtains that had fallen down and then spray-painted the curtains black, painting the floor black, too.

I needed a place to live because I couldn't live in the theater, so I rented a big A-frame house on Malibou Lake in Agoura Hills. It was a bit of a swanky pad with a redwood deck all around and a big redwood hot tub that overlooked the same mountain that Paramount Pictures took its logo from, as well as being the area where the television series M*A*S*H was filmed in the '70s. It had four bedrooms, four bathrooms, a big living room with a stone fireplace, and a loft above the living room. The home also came with a tennis court. Anyone who recorded at the Teatro would be staying there. I bought a white 1975 Cadillac Eldorado convertible for driving clients to the studio.

Once Wayne finished renovations, he flew to San Francisco to help pack up the gear there. We filled a twenty-four-foot U-Haul with studio gear and towed a trailer behind it with bikes. We also filled a fourteen-foot U-Haul and put a trailer with the Jag on it. The Ford Explorer was also packed to the roof. I drove the twenty-four footer, Zack drove the fourteen footer, and Wayne drove the Explorer, making a

LISTEN UP!

convoy. We drove through the night to avoid traffic and arrived in the morning. We dropped off the U-Hauls at the Teatro and then went to crash at the Malibou Lake pad, deciding it would be safer to move the bikes and gear in late at night so no one would see what was going into the theater.

I had not seen what Wayne had done up to this point, and we waited until midnight to move in. Pedro was asleep in the bushes. We walked in the front door and the lobby was painted white and gleaming, a far cry from the filthy place it had once been. Black carpet had been laid down and the concession stand was gone. I opened the door into the theater and the transformation was incredible, it was all black with a huge platform in the middle of the room. Wayne had gone above and beyond the call of duty and created an incredible work space. Within two hours we had everything in, although it took another two weeks to unpack and set up the studio.

The first session in the Teatro in February 1996 was a score to a little art film called *Sling Blade*. Billy Bob Thornton was the unknown director and writer. Billy had been in a few cool movies: *Dead Man* with Johnny Depp, *Chopper Chicks in Zombietown*, and *One False Move*, which he also had cowritten. It was Billy's dream to make this movie, *Sling Blade*, about an intellectually challenged man named Karl Childers. Billy had worked hard on developing this character, especially the way he walked and talked. He got Miramax and the Shooting Gallery to fund the film and made it for a million dollars. Essentially, there was no money left for the film score, and he offered Dan $25,000 to score the film. Because there was not a lot of money in the budget, Dan brought in a couple of Canadians who worked cheap, Tim Gibbons and Russell Wilson.

We used some music recorded over the last couple of years and some new guitar recordings that I had been working on. Dan had a loop pedal called a boomerang, and he'd stack guitars into it, which I would then alter with my effect treatments — a performance on top of his performance. This is where the opening track of the movie came from, a piece called "Asylum."

In the scene where the kid and Karl are walking down the street, there is a track called "Jimmy Was," and it was one of the pieces of music that came out of the Mexico recordings. The murder scene was performed to picture. It is the piece called "Orange Kay," based on the Kay Fuzz Tone guitar pedal Dan used. I dialed up a thunderous sound on his guitar, which was disturbing and perhaps went a little against the grain of the scene, but it worked great. I had placed a lot of the music in the film myself and would show it to Dan when he came to the studio. Tim Gibbons had a really great song called "Lonely One," and I placed it in the dinner scene.

One day while Dan was out, Russ and I also wrote a piece of music called "Telephone," a little melody we built using an AMS DMX 15-80S delay harmonizer. I would trap a sound in there, and I could use the number pad and have different pitches on it, or play a melody on the pad. Dan loved it and I dropped it in the phone-call scene in which Karl calls the police to tell them he just killed someone.

Dan thought *Sling Blade* was a little art film and it would be lucky if anyone saw it, so he said he would give me a producer credit because I had done most of the work. I never got it on the film, but I did on the soundtrack. I am sure if he knew the film would win an Oscar, then he wouldn't have offered.

While recording at the Teatro, you could get Mexican food from across the street at Ciletos, or you could have Mexican from down the street. There was a little burger joint on the corner called Buddy Burgers, and Billy Bob would always ask for the French fried potatoes in his "Karl" voice.

Billy suffered from bad migraines, which made it hard for him to keep focused. He would let me try whatever I thought was right for the picture. I put echoes on Robert Duvall's voice when he was in his house talking to himself because I thought it made it just a little bit weirder, and Billy liked it.

Emmylou Harris came in and did a beautiful version of "Shenandoah" that was used in the baptism scene. I had produced a track for Bambi Lee Savage (Shannon Strong), a sweet song called "Darlin'," which I slid in and which everyone loved. The track "Blue Waltz" was a piece of music I had recorded in Stockholm at a sound check live to DAT. I'd had a crazy sound on Daniel's guitar and an octave sound on Daryl Johnson's bass, and again it fit the movie.

Sling Blade came out only in select theaters. The print of the film was dark and didn't look very good. It didn't test well with audiences and in opening week it only made $36,644.

The following year, in 1997, Billy Bob won an Oscar for Best Writing and for Best Screenplay Based on Material Previously Produced or Published, and he was nominated for Best Actor in a Leading Role. Several other awards would follow.

LISTEN UP!

Billy invited Daniel and me to the Oscar after-party at the Mondrian Skybox. Dan took Emmylou as his date and I took Kim Wayman, a beautiful singer with whom I was working at the time. We saw Billy at the party holding his Oscar. The awards presented to actors at the show are just models, and the real ones are sent at a later date, but Billy had snatched the model on his way out the door, and at the after-party he wouldn't let go of it. Billy Bob became a star overnight, and his whole career took off, with offers rolling in.

The Teatro was quickly shaping up. Dan's brother, Bob Lanois, had found a Neve console owned by a guy named David Moyles in Toronto. It was a Neve 8068, which is rare, and the kind used by the likes of Steely Dan, Nirvana, Pink Floyd, and Dire Straits. Bob never saw it working, just sitting on a skid on its side in a warehouse. Daniel bought it and had Rob Mitchell drive it down from Toronto. When the console arrived, I started to assemble it, painstakingly untangling the rat's nest of wires; it fired up but was in rough shape. I set it up in front of the other console so I could chip away at getting it going. We had shipped a Steinway piano over from Kingsway Studio in New Orleans and another Hammond B3, a classic organ that can sound like a carnival, big band, small jazz group, percussion, and so on. It was used by people like Bryan Adams and Eric Clapton. The Teatro began to look like a playground of musical instruments.

One of the last records I worked on at the Kingsway studio was Luscious Jackson's *Fever In Fever Out*. They had done the first leg of the album in New York and then came down to New Orleans. Tony Mangurian had produced their first record and came down to help out. The New Orleans sessions were more band based, with the group cutting live off the floor. They brought in DJ Alex Young to scratch. We spent about ten days there, then we all flew to Oxnard, California, to work at the Teatro to finish off overdubs and mixes. Because I had two consoles set up, we could work on two songs at once.

The band all stayed at the Malibou Lake house, but it kind of freaked them out because they were from New York and not used to being so isolated in the country. They couldn't just walk out the door to a store, which they didn't enjoy. Living on top of a mountain and surrounded by natural beauty isn't for everyone.

The Teatro was forever changing. I moved the Neve into the main position and now the Amek was the side console. I updated the speaker system to a pair of Westlake BBSM 12 monitors with the Clair Brothers eighteen-inch subs under them and made it sound super hi-fi. Daniel had used the Westlakes on U2's record *The Joshua Tree*.

I had the Brunswick pool table from Kingsway shipped out and put it in the lobby, so when you walked in the front door it felt like walking into a pool hall. I had found a box of old Mexican movie posters upstairs in the projector room and made a collage on the wall. The posters were from risqué soft-porn movies, similar to British movies like *Carry On*; they were mostly topless movies like *El macho*. I got a remote-control box from Home Depot that remotely turned lights on and off, and I used it to control six 16-mm film projectors up in the projector booth. There were different films on each one. Some had old black-and-white Russian films and others had driver-training films in color. Mostly, these were a camera strapped to the front of a car and the film of it driving through the streets of Miami in the 1960s, showing lots of cool old cars. The device also controlled a mirror ball and an oil wheel, like they had at Jefferson Airplane shows in the '60s, projecting oil dripping on the screen behind them.

I found two weather balloons at the army surplus store up the street and I blew them up to fifteen feet, then had them on round metal air-conditioning ducts, so they looked like big lollipops on each side of the stage. I had film loops of angels spinning around, and when I projected the angels onto the weather balloons from behind, they looked like holograms — the angels spinning inside.

When we listened back to recordings, I could control all the lights, turning them off, then on, so they would be superimposed over each other; faces would come out of the road of the driving movies. When the chorus of a song would hit, I'd turn the lights off and turn on the mirror ball so the room felt like it was spinning, then move on to the oil wheel, then the hologram angels — an art form unto itself.

I had moved into quadraphonic sound, too, using the Dutch PA towers in the rear, which made the sound come from everywhere. I had also hung two speaker clusters from the ceiling on the left and right. I did surround mixes using a joystick panner. I'd mix the guitar so it spun around the room to the right and then the hi-hat from the drum kit spun around going left, so it felt like the sound was always moving around. Combined with the visuals, it was a sight and sound experience like no other. Most of the people I work with have lyrics that conjure up images, and so I see movies when I hear music. I've always been experimenting with aesthetics, and I think images and music enhance each other.

LISTEN UP!

Chris Whitley asked me to produce his next record, *Terra Incognita*, and he wanted to do it at the Teatro. He brought the Lounge Lizards' drummer, Dougie Bowne. It was meant to be a three-way production between all of us. Most of the record was cut two-piece, just Chris and Dougie, except for the tracks cut to loops. Chris was the first one to use the Teatro for his record cover. Wayne had painted the walls of the projector-room bedroom upstairs an intense slaughter-house red, and Chris was photographed wearing a mariachi vest sitting against the blood-red walls.

One day we had a problem with a bad buzz from Chris's guitar. The buzz happened every time he put it on. When I would put it on, it was quiet, but he'd try it again and the buzz would occur. I thought maybe it was something in his pockets, but they were empty. He was wearing leather pants and no shirt, so we couldn't locate the source of the problem. At one point I asked if he'd had an operation and had metal in his leg, but he said he hadn't. I told him to take off his pants.

"Really?" he said in disbelief.

"Well, that's the only thing I can think of," I told him.

He took them off and sure enough the buzz was gone. There must have been something in the leather pants conducting the buzz, so he played without pants. I projected cartoons onto his chest, trying to make him play crazier.

Chris had a destructive streak in him. If anything got too pretty, he had to put a dissonant chord against it to turn your ear. The song "Weightless" could have been a beautiful single. I thought there were a number of really great tracks on the record like "Cool Wooden Crosses," "Clear Blue Sky," and "Aerial," all of which I thought broke new ground sonically and lyrically.

Mike Watt from Minutemen came in to play bass on a couple of tracks. His playing was so frantic that he fell off the chair he was sitting on; he hit the floor but kept on playing. I played Chris a drum loop I'd made of Brady Blade playing my 1970s blue Pearl kit, which had a killer sound, so we used it for the song "Aerial." I brought Wayne the Brain back in to assist me on the record; it was the last album I worked on with Wayne.

CHAPTER 14

DYLAN AT THE TEATRO

I BUMPED INTO BOB DYLAN ONE DAY in L.A. at Jerry's Famous Deli on Ventura Boulevard. I was having lunch with Brant Scott when Dylan walked in with his manager, Jeff Kramer. Dylan came right over to the table to say hello and didn't waste any time getting to the point.

"How did the *Oh Mercy* outtakes get leaked?"

I was caught off guard. Although I could have said that I didn't know, I felt Dylan had a right to the truth. While on tour with Dan in New York, Malcolm Burn had some DATs in his luggage with the outtakes on them. I'm not sure why he had them, but for whatever reason, Malcolm decided to change hotels and left his suitcase in the van. The van was broken into; the suitcase was the only thing they took.

Bob was understandably pissed and informed me that someone had just released a bootleg record with those mixes.

"Why did Dan let him have copies?" he asked.

"I don't know," I said. "He may not have known."

"Doesn't matter. It was his responsibility and this should have never happened." He paused. "Thanks, Mark, for telling me the truth." He walked off.

I felt terrible; I had basically ratted out Malcolm. But at the same time, I didn't want to be yelled at for something I had nothing to do with.

It was late summer 1996 when Dylan paid a visit to the Teatro. He was living in Point Dume and drove over in his old Chevy pickup. He had done a live recording at the House of Blues in Atlanta during the Olympics, and he asked if we would mix it for a Japanese release. I think he was perhaps testing the waters, and if it went well, he might make another record with Dan and me.

I spent about a week mixing the recording and then Dylan showed up one afternoon. It sounded great, and there were a lot of classic songs. I was on the last mix when Dylan said, "This one has a harmonica on it." It had been recorded by him just playing it into the vocal mic.

"Is there any way you can make it sound electric?" he asked.

I told him I'd worked with King Biscuit Boy, a Canadian blues legend, and I'd run his harp through an amp. I set it up and let Dylan hear it, and although it sounded better, Dylan asked, "Can't you make it a little more dirty?"

I put the harmonica through a green Ibanez tube screamer pedal, overdrove the signal, then put it through the amp, so that when he played the harp, it had the sound of the dirt heard on Little Walter records. Dylan loved it. Once his harp part was finished, his vocal came in dirty through the amp, and when he heard it, his face lit up.

"I want that sound on all the songs."

I remixed all the songs again using those vocal treatments.

Dylan drove in every day and he said he listened to the only radio station he could tune in between the Ventura line and the Oxnard township line. It was a station that played old blues, like Little Walter, and some jazz, like Charlie Parker — all from the 1940s and '50s.

"Why do those records sound so good and alive?"

I told him it had to do with limitations.

"Why can't my records sound like that?"

"They can, if you use the same approach and use old ribbon mics."

At that time, Dylan was also interested in the singer-songwriter Beck (who, ironically, was once involved in an anti-folk movement in New York) and the technology of using drum loops. Dan had told Dylan that he could provide that same thing Beck was doing in terms of a drum loop. I suggested to Dan that we should get Tony Mangurian in to try some loops and test a couple of ideas. I got Tony on the phone and flew him in from New York the very next day.

Dylan told Dan he had some songs for him to hear. He went to the piano and played part of a song and then asked, "What do you think of that one?"

Dan said, "That's great, but I would need to hear the lyrics before I know for sure." But Dylan wouldn't sing.

The next day, Bob showed up and went right to the piano and played another song, again with no vocal or lyrics and again he asked, "What do you think?"

Again Dan said, "That's great, but I really need to hear some lyrics."

The next day Dylan arrived, went straight to the piano, and was working out a song with a gospel vibe. Tony started playing a hip-hop beat on my little 1970 blue Pearl drum kit against Dylan's gospel. In a haunting growl, Dylan began to sing, "I can't wait . . ." then continued, "I can't wait, wait for you to change your mind, it's late, I'm trying to walk the line . . ."

The hair on my arms went up. I was recording everything, so I captured how it all fell together. Dylan sang a couple of verses and then stopped, maybe not wanting to give too much away. We listened back and marveled at how amazing it sounded. Dylan loved it. I copied the two verses and made a longer arrangement so we could hear what it would sound like with a full accom-

paniment. Dylan left for the night and we knew we had something amazing.

Tony said, "I think Bob really liked my playing."

Daniel jumped right in and said, "He wasn't responding to your playing; he was responding to the sound of the drums."

Tony and I just looked at each other. It was a low blow.

A natural-born storyteller, Dylan would talk for hours sometimes, sharing tales from his past. He would say things like, "You know when Bob

The Teatro studio (1995).

Dylan was playing Newport Folk Festival in 1965 when he went electric? That crowd wasn't booing him. It was a bunch of people in the back causing a scene and people were booing them."

It was weird to hear Dylan talk about himself in the third person.

He remembered talking to his mother on the phone when she said, "What's going on? All these people are saying you are the new spokesman of the '60s."

"Yeah, they're putting me up on this pedestal because they're reading into my lyrics."

He said "The Times They Are a-Changin'" was written the year before it was used as an anthem against the politics of the day and that he had not written it as a response to anything.

I asked him how he ended up with the members of the Band as his band. He said some girl in New York told him that he should check out these guys from Canada who played with Ronnie Hawkins. He said that he just took a chance and hired them for a tour.

Dylan also told the story about being signed to a record label. He was playing little coffee houses around Greenwich Village and his name was getting out there; there had been a little write-up about him in the *New York Times,* but John Hammond had already been talking to him. He said that John Hammond invited him up to his office and offered him a deal, and Dylan just signed it right away. Dylan said that he was friends with Albert Grossman. Albert wasn't his manager but was merely looking out for him at the time. Once he told Albert what happened, Albert said, "You did what?"

Dylan told him that John Hammond had offered him a deal and he'd signed it.

Albert said, "Oh no, you've got to get out of that deal. Look, I'm going to drive you over there right now and you are going to tell him it's not a legal deal because you're too young and you need a parental cosigner."

So Albert drove Dylan there and said, "I will wait here in the lobby and you go up and get out of this deal."

Bob Dylan went up and told John Hammond that he was too young and needed a parent to cosign for him and he wanted out of the contract.

John Hammond said, "Bob, that's okay, I can sign for you as your guardian."

"Really?" Dylan said, so John Hammond signed for him.

Dylan said when he went downstairs to the lobby, Albert was waiting for him and asked if he'd gotten out of the deal, and Dylan told him that John had signed as his guardian and now it was legal. Albert couldn't believe it.

Dylan said that Albert was monumental in his career because he'd gotten some huge artists of the time to cover Dylan's songs. Albert managed Peter, Paul, and Mary and got them to cover "Blowin' in the Wind," which went to number one, as well as a couple of other songs, all of which helped the sales of Dylan's records in the future.

Dylan told us that he had been excited to begin recording. His first record was mostly folk standards, plus two original compositions, "Talkin' New York" and "Song to Woody." Dylan said that he recorded "House of the Rising Sun" but used the arrangement that his roommate Dave Van Ronk had come up with. Once the album was done, he brought it home to play for Dave; he had never told him that he'd used Dave's version. When Dave heard it, he was mad and asked Dylan what he'd done that for; he'd planned to record it himself. Dylan told him that he'd been short of songs and did it last minute.

The stories went go on and on. Dan, Tony, and I would just sit and listen, and Dylan would keep talking, each story leading into the next. Dylan once admitted to copying another guy's whole shtick — an American folk singer who was largely unknown, although big in Europe. One night he was in the Village, standing onstage in front of the mic and just about to start his set, when he said he saw the guy walk through the front door of the club. It was Ramblin' Jack Elliott. Dylan said he was so nervous that Jack would discover he'd stolen Jack's whole thing that he ran off the stage and out the back door.

Dylan also talked about needing a rest from the whole New York scene. He was tired of running from the crowds; it became impossible because of people following him. He said he often couldn't go home because there would be a big crowd of people outside his house. He'd have to let someone know that Bob Dylan was uptown at a small club so the crowd would leave to look for him.

He told us about getting a call from Kris Kristofferson asking if he'd go down to Mexico to be in a film, *Pat Garrett and Billy the Kid*. It seemed like a breath of fresh air to get out of New York, and he took the whole family down there. He was also asked to score the movie. The film was shot on location in Durango, Mexico, and lasted from late 1972 to early 1973. Dylan said some recordings were done in Mexico City and then more were made in Burbank, California. That was the impetus for his moving to California. He never moved back to New York but settled in Malibu and lived in a house by the beach. He had his family there for a little while until one day a stranger just walked in and began talking to him. Dylan realized he needed something more private.

He was driving up the Pacific Coast Highway with a realtor who was showing him places, when he suddenly saw a billboard in Point Dume that read *How to become a millionaire* and listed a phone number. He called the number and a different realtor answered, one who was selling land in Point Dume. He told Dylan that he had this amazing property with no one around, so Dylan went to look at it, just a regular ranch-style home, and he bought it. After he'd moved in, the realtor called back and said, "Look, if you don't buy the piece of land beside you, someone will buy it and you will have a neighbor." So Dylan bought that, too.

Dylan had begun to renovate the house when the guy called again and said, "Look, if you don't buy the piece of land on the other side of you, someone will buy it and you will have a neighbor on that side."

Dylan purchased that land as well. The sign he'd seen was correct, only it was the realtor who became the millionaire.

Dylan loved to tell stories, but any time he did, he would stop halfway through and ask, "Did I tell you this already?"

When we'd tell him we hadn't heard it, he'd always carry on but often pause a second time.

"You sure I haven't told you this story?"

Dylan also talked about a guy who once approached him and claimed he had invented something incredible and wanted Dylan to invest in it. The guy told him to come to a theater in Brentwood. Dylan's interest was piqued, so he went. When he arrived, there was a bunch of people sitting in chairs, impatiently waiting to see this incredible thing. Some men came out with ladders and started fixing something in front of the screen, so people got up and left. Then another group of men carried in some scaffolding.

People yelled, "When is it going to start?"

It had been over an hour and no one had come to say anything about what was going on. More people got up and left; by now two hours had passed and the only thing that had happened was that stuff was moved around by some guys.

Eventually, there were only a handful of people. At last a guy came out and said, "Thank you for experiencing our new invention."

People were shocked; they hadn't seen anything other than men moving objects.

"What you just experienced wasn't real — there were no actual men working here!" the man informed them.

People yelled in disbelief.

"What you experienced was our new invention. We were able to make it look like there were real people working right in front of you, but it was all being projected."

Someone yelled, "But the lights were on!"

The guy replied, "Exactly!"

Dylan had finished the story so I asked him if he'd invested in it, but he said no, he hadn't believed it.

He talked of recording with the Traveling Wilburys in the Hollywood Hills. He understood having Jeff Lynne there because he would produce his ass off, and George Harrison: "Well, yeah, he was a Beatle; and it doesn't get any better than Roy Orbison; but Tom Petty? What the hell was he doing there?"

At the time it made sense, because Tom Petty wasn't quite a legend, but over time, Tom rose to those heights, which Dylan later acknowledged.

While making the Wilburys' album, he was also doing his own record, *Under the Red Sky*, with Don Was as producer, at Ocean Way studios. Dylan would leave the Wilburys and head over to where Don was doing the session. He said he'd arrive at the studio and Don would have the building full of musicians like Elton John, Stevie Ray Vaughan, Eric Clapton, David Crosby, and George Harrison, and Bob would say he wasn't ready because he didn't have his songs together. He claimed that once the record was done, he asked for an accordion and then said he wanted to play it on every track.

Dylan shared tales from the road, explaining that he believed he was the first to make use of planes for touring, and that the first one they had was a postal plane. It wasn't luxurious at all but quite military-like, with hard metal seats. They did a tour of the east coast of Canada in the winter, and the ferries couldn't get the gear to their stop because of an ice storm. He said the flight was rough with turbulence and that the winds actually flipped the plane upside down; although he thought that was the end, the pilot somehow righted the plane and landed safely.

When we were ready to start recording *Time Out of Mind* at the Teatro, Dylan said that he couldn't make the album that close to home. He felt there would be too many distractions with his family nearby, and that he needed to go somewhere far away; he suggested Miami. My heart sank — the Teatro had an amazing sound. We were to start in early January, so I volunteered to drive a bunch of the gear and a couple of motorcycles to Miami, although it meant giving up my Christmas holiday in order to drive from coast to coast and still have time to set up. I rented a cube van and loaded it with three Neve side consoles and the same vintage mics I used. I wanted to have the same gear in order to have a good starting point.

I arrived in New Orleans on Christmas Day and stayed at Kingsway Studio with Karen Brady, eating pizza and watching movies. I left the next day and took my friend Nicole Barrie with me for the rest of the drive. Nicole was a young, aspiring actor who ended up with an acting career, working eventually for Angelina Jolie. I promised to fly Nicole back if she came along for the drive.

We arrived in Miami two days before New Year's Eve. We stayed at the Marlin Hotel, owned by Chris Blackwell, who also owned Island Records. The hotel was an art deco masterpiece built in 1939 by Lawrence Murray Dixon, a renowned architect. It was the coolest scene in those days, with a nightclub in the lobby and a recording studio in the basement. They gave me a two-bedroom suite because the room I'd booked needed some renovations. The new room had a real island feel, with plantation shutters and painted in tropical colors of bright yellow and hot pink with Caribbean folk-art paintings on the walls.

I was excited to go to Criteria Studios, where we would be working. Lots of legendary records were made there, like Fleetwood Mac's *Rumours*, the Eagles' *Hotel California*, and *Saturday Night Fever*.

I offloaded the bikes at the hotel and headed to the studio to start my setup. The studio was on the outskirts of town, and I pulled up to a bleak, worn-out looking building. I was booked into the big studio with the classic Neve 8078 console. The live-room was white plaster, with a big soundstage. Nothing sounded good in there.

I asked if it was the same room in which all those great records were made, and they told me that those albums had been recorded in another room.

"Well, that's the room I want," I told them.

They told me I couldn't have it because it was now the tape vault. I asked to see it and they led me to a small, dingy room. It had the original orange shag rug, dated wood paneling, and a terrible musty smell. I thought it was a shame that a room that played a part in creating so much great music was left to rot.

I made the decision to set up all the gear in the control room, including the three Neve BCM 10 side consoles. I then did the band setup. Once Daniel rolled in, I shared my concerns about the room and he agreed that it was a bit of a turkey. I showed him the other room and he just shook his head.

"Well, what are our options?" he asked.

"We could rent the Masonic Temple on Lincoln Road in South Beach, and I could rent a bunch of gear and set up there."

He thought for a moment. "What about the Bee Gees? Don't they have a studio here?"

I called and asked if it would be possible to record there, but they immediately said that it was private and the Bee Gees didn't want anyone to use it.

I had ordered one hundred fourteen-inch reels of Ampex 456 two-inch tape for the session, so I could get eighteen minutes per reel running at 15 IPS. This enables you to get more tape time, yet you get more tape hiss. The reels were stacked to the ceiling.

Dylan wanted to use his live band, which consisted of Dave Kemper (who worked with the Jerry Garcia Band) on drums, Tony Garnier (who had been with Dylan for years) on electric bass and upright, and Bucky Baxter on pedal steel guitar. Bucky is a multi-instrumentalist who had played with people like Steve Earle and R.E.M.

We made the decision to see how it sounded recording with the band. I made Dylan a little "apartment" out of gobos, with windows and a table with lamps. As usual, Dylan wouldn't wear headphones, so I set up the little vocal amp that I used on the House of Blues mixes so he could hear himself sounding like a blues guy coming out of the back of his "apartment."

Once set up, we tried "Cold Irons Bound." I treated the drums with an Eventide H3000 digital audio processor, making them sound a little overdriven, and combined with the vocal amp on Dylan's vocal, it gave the track a dirty flavor.

Because we spent a couple of days getting set up, we lost a bit of time. Dave Kemper, the drummer, had an art opening back in L.A. that he had to fly back for over the weekend. Kemper did not return. Dan felt like Dylan needed someone who had feel, but Bob wanted someone on his side whom he trusted. Dan called in Brian Blade and Dylan called in Jim Keltner, a drummer known for his session work with people like Elvis Presley and John Lennon. Dylan also wanted some guitar players to add to the band, which included Nashville's Bob Britt, a real Nashville strummer who had played with the likes of John Fogerty and Leon Russell, and Cindy Cashdollar, known for her work with Asleep at the Wheel and Duke Robillard.

Augie Meyers, a Texan studio musician who played with the Texas Tornadoes, was also brought in to play organ. He brought his Vox organ, one of the best-known organs of the '60s and used by the Animals and the Dave Clark Five. You can hear it on the intro of "Love Sick Skanking."

Dylan asked me if I had heard of Jim Dickinson. He's a producer as well as a pianist and singer who fronted the Memphis-based band Mud Boy and the Neutrons. I told Dylan I'd worked with Jim a couple of years past in New Orleans. I offered to call him and see if I could get him to come down and Dylan said, "Let's do it!"

I called Jim and asked if he could get to Miami the following day to start on a record with Bob Dylan. He merely asked what time to show up and then dropped everything he was doing to jump on a plane.

There were eleven to twelve people playing at the same time, and things got a little crazy. I put Jim and Brian side by side facing Dylan. I would pan Brian to the right because he was on the right from Dylan, sitting in his chair looking at them, and Brian held most of the hi-hat feel. I used a real simple mic technique — one AKG C24 stereo mic between them, one capsule pointed at Brian, and the other at Jim. I put a Coles ribbon mic in front of each kick drum and then one RCA 44 ribbon mic close to Brian's hi-hat.

As I've mentioned, Dylan writes on a typewriter — only words, no music — so sometimes he's unsure of which key best suits his voice. He is the master of key change and he knows lots of old chords no one uses anymore. We would do three takes in a row for each song, but Dylan would change the key each time. This was easy for him, but the other musicians struggled with the changes and made clumsy mistakes.

Dan, losing his mind, flipped out on the band.

"If I hear another person strumming, I'm going to vomit! If you don't know the changes, don't play!"

He stormed out the door and slammed it so hard the glass broke.

After cutting three takes, the band would go into the control room to listen, and I would do a mix on the fly and print it to DAT for a reference because we were moving so fast. There wasn't time to listen later and put down a mix, so that was my only chance. On the song "Love Sick," I dialed up a crazy vocal sound with flange on it. When the band came in to listen, I rattled off a mix from that playback, and that's the mix that's on the record. I just pegged it right away and could never better it.

There were some songs that sounded better than others. "Not Dark Yet" was one of those songs that when everyone heard it back, they knew it was going to be a classic.

Whenever Dylan and the band came into the control room to listen, he'd sit beside me so he could smoke my American Spirit Blue cigarettes. He smoked the cheapest brand, GPC, but he liked Spirits.

One day after listening to all three takes, Dylan asked me, "Which take do you think it is?"

I told him I preferred take two, and he asked how I knew.

"I don't base it on how well it was played," I told him. "It's based on how it made me feel."

"You're right," he agreed. "That's the same one I felt, too."

This happened every time on each song, with us agreeing on the best takes, and I began to win his trust. I think he appreciated someone who told him the truth, who wasn't just a yes-man.

I had a technique when keeping notes in my workbook: I'd write the first word and last word of each line of the song, and then on every playback I would fill in the gaps; because Dylan kept most of his lyrics in his head, he would often confer with me on what I had written in my book. Often, he'd want to change words or whole lines. On "Not Dark Yet," he wanted to change the line "behind every beautiful thing there's been some kind of pain."

I told him I'd change it but that it was my favorite line in the whole song.

"Really?" He seemed surprised. "Okay, let's keep it then."

Perhaps he had a better line in his head, but he kept the one I liked.

On a playback of the track "Can't Wait," Dan was just not satisfied and told the band it sounded "junkie."

Keltner was quick to reply, "Is that East Coast junkie or West Coast junkie?"

Everyone laughed except Dan. You could see the storm brewing in his eyes, and I wondered when he'd unleash it. We had cut three different versions of the song and each take had a name. There was a "funk" take, a "rag doll" take and a "Pink Floyd" take.

After listening, Dylan said, "Let's try a couple more. I don't think we have it."

A friend of Dylan's was sitting with me in the control room, a young, pretty blonde. She flirted with me and chatted while I worked. Dan was out on the floor playing guitar with the band, and he gave me his evil eye, watching me laughing with the girl behind the glass.

The last take we had listened to was take two, the "rag doll" take. I hit the locator on the tape recorder to get to clean tape so we could record some more, but when I punched the button, I realized we were recording over the intro of take two. With analogue tape, there is no going back — once it's gone, it's gone. I stopped the band and quickly went to clean tape. They did three more takes and they felt a little better.

When the band came back in, we listened to all of the takes and everyone liked the last one. Dylan then asked to hear take two from earlier. My heart sank. I cued up and played what was there, but because I had erased the first hit off the top, you could hear it slurp in. I played the whole track and no one said anything. Dan then asked me to play the whole intro.

"Where the fuck is the rest of it?" he asked. I told him very quietly that the machine located to the top of take two and I had jumped into Record, but I'd stopped it and went to clean tape.

"WHAT THE FUCK DID YOU DO, HOWARD?" Dan's face went red and he spun like the Tasmanian Devil. He grabbed a metal stool and threw it toward me, and it hit the wall behind me, smashing all the dimmers for the lights in the control room. All the lights in the room flashed on and off like photo flashbulbs, and he lunged toward the console and kicked it as hard as he could with his big motorcycle boots, denting the bottom.

"You *fucker!*" he seethed.

Dylan was sitting beside me the entire time and leaned toward me and asked quietly, "Does this guy have a mental problem?"

I just looked at him and said, "I think so."

Dan stormed out and I asked everyone to take a break while I fixed things. Everyone left the control room. Chris, my assistant engineer, cleaned up the broken dimmers, but the stool was too bent to be of use again.

This was only one of the many insane temper tantrums that I suffered through over the years working with Dan. He was a creative person but a control freak, and his abusive outbursts haunt me to this day.

Following this episode, Dan was exiled from the studio. I edited a version of "Can't Wait" while everyone was out, taking the intro of the "Pink Floyd" take and cutting it onto the "rag doll" take. Everyone came back to listen and Dylan said, "I like it better this way."

In fact, the "rag doll" intro was not as good as the one we used, so it was a lucky accident.

The sessions started each day around four o'clock and finished around eleven. Once back at the hotel, it became a routine that Augie and Jim would come over to my room to have a late-night toke. Augie told stories about his time with two legendary bands, the Sir Douglas Quintet and the Texas Tornados. Augie had a bad leg from polio, and it would just give out on him; he'd be standing one minute and on the floor the next. A couple of times in the control room, I was busy listening back when I felt a huge bang behind me. Turning around, I'd see Augie on the floor. He was a big guy to fall so far. He told me he had an old pickup truck and when he had to shift, he had to grab his leg and push down on the clutch and then bring his leg back to disengage it.

Jim shared stories about being the only piano player in town. He had played piano on the Rolling Stones' "Wild Horses" at Muscle Shoals Sound Studio in December 1969.

The day after cutting "Can't Wait," Dan was determined to get back to the gospel version we cut in Oxnard. He flew in Tony Mangurian (a producer and drummer known for his work with Willie Nelson) to get back to that hip-hop feel. Brian or Keltner could not cop that hip-hop vibe, so into the fire Tony went.

Before Dylan arrived, Dan would work up the band by imitating Dylan. One day, Dylan came in a bit early and heard Dan imitating him doing "Can't Wait."

"What the hell are you doing?" Dylan asked.

Daniel said that he really wanted to get back to that Oxnard gospel-version vibe.

"No," Dylan yelled. "It's done!" Wearing white golf gloves, he grabbed Daniel's 1940s Martin 00-18 by the neck and, holding it like a baseball bat, swung it in slow motion through the air. Dylan went to Dan and swung the guitar again in slow motion, stopping before hitting him in the head.

Dylan dragged Tony, the bass player, over and asked, "Tony, in the whole time you have known me, have I ever done anything the same way twice?"

"No, Bob," Tony answered.

"See? It's done," Dylan said and walked away.

We tried it one more time, this time with Tony Mangurian on drums and Dylan on piano, but only got about halfway through before Dylan threw in the towel. Poor Tony didn't get a fair shake.

Dan talked about getting his brother, Bob, down to document the making of the album using film and photos. Dylan agreed. When Bob arrived, he decided he hated the light in the room, which was lit with fluorescent lights like a gymnasium, bright and stark. He got an idea to cover the whole studio with candles, and he went out and bought $1,000 worth of candles, then spent all day setting them up. The studio was lit by a soft glow.

Dylan showed up at 4:00 p.m. and walked through the back door.

"What the hell's going on?" he asked. "Is someone having a séance? Get rid of the candles and turn the lights on."

Bob was devastated and was sent home two days later.

The energy in the studio had become weird by this point. I remember sitting at the console and Dan leaning over and saying, "It's sounding great, guys," and then Dylan turning to me and asking, "Do you hear someone talking?"

I just smiled back at him and said, "No."

Because Dan was banished from the control room, he worked on mixes in another studio room by himself. It must have been uncomfortable for him because Dylan wouldn't talk to him, so he'd have to come to me and tell me what to say to Dylan.

On the console, I had two channels for Dylan's vocal: one was a clean vocal recorded with a Sony C-37A microphone and the other was an amp vocal. I would take his clean vocal and send it through a tube screamer, then into a little vintage Gibson amp. Dylan would always ask me how much amp vocal I had against the clean vocal, and I would say it's about 60-40, 60 being the clean and he would say, "Make it 50-50," and smile.

Going through all the tracks on the console, he once asked, "What's on that track?"

I told him it was Dan's guitar, and Dylan said I should get rid of it. He asked me what was on the other track and I told him it was his own guitar.

"Turn that up," he instructed.

There was a seventeen-minute song on the album called "Highlands." We recorded it twice and picked the latter version. I had done a rough sketch of the lyric on the fly, so I knew where all the verses were, as well as the first and last word of every line. Dylan decided he wanted to change some lines here and there. Because he didn't wear headphones, I had to have a pair of speakers in front of him so he could hear the track. I had to match the loudness of the band so that when I punched in to record his vocal mic, it would have the same amount of leakage in it. The crazy thing was that he didn't want to hear his vocal on the track, only out of the vocal amp. When I punched in his vocal, I had to pull the fader down, but then I couldn't hear him to punch out. To solve this, I had another mic in front of him that I fed into the control room into a little battery-powered Peavey guitar amp with a mic input.

Dylan would ask me to go to the thirteenth verse and go in for the third line, so I would cue it up, he would hear the top of the thirteenth verse, then at the third line I had to pull down the fader and punch into record, then bring up the Peavey amp so I could hear him, then punch out and bring the fader back up. He figured it out and started calling out things like, "Go to the third verse and go in for the fifth word."

Bang! I would be in and out.

"Then go to the fifteenth verse and go in for the last word."

By then he was just playing with me, seeing if he could get me to crack. Eventually, the game bored him and we were finished.

At the end of the session, I made Dylan a cassette with all the songs on it. Daniel didn't want one. There were more than one hundred reels, and I compacted them down to five reels with all the master takes. I got Rob Mitchell to drive the truck back to California and I flew back to Oxnard with the masters. I thought my arms were going to fall off carrying them through the airport.

CHAPTER 15

DYLAN'S
TIME OUT OF MIND

AFTER THE MIAMI SESSIONS ENDED, IT WAS a couple of months before I heard from Dylan again. The phone rang in the middle of the night.

"Hey, Mark, it's Bob."

"Hey, Bob, how are you doing?" I was barely awake.

"Good," he replied. "But I've been thinking about the record . . . do you think there is anything there?"

"Yes, and I think we should finish it."

He thought so, too, but wondered if Dan had abandoned it because he hadn't called.

I told Dan what Dylan said, but Dan decided he wasn't interested in making another blues record; it had been done before and was better left that way.

At that point, I figured that the album would never see the light of day if Dylan was questioning whether there was anything worthy there and Dan wasn't interested in finishing what he called a "blues record." Months went by before I got another call in the middle of the night.

"Hey, Mark, it's Bob. I wanted to tell you that I was playing the record for my friend at his apartment in Santa Monica and we got a knock on the door. It was his neighbor from downstairs who asked what we were listening to and where he could buy it. My friend said it wasn't for sale and that it was still being worked on, and the neighbor said it was amazing and that he hadn't heard anything like it." Dylan paused. "You think we should finish it?"

"Yes, come up to the Teatro and let's finish it," I told him.

Dylan came to Oxnard in the spring. He showed up every day wearing the same thing — white-and-black checkered chef pants and a velour leisure wear V-neck shirt, like Bobby Darin. He wore black boots with little bells on them that would jingle when he tapped his foot. He sat in the same mohair chair every day, rubbing his feet on the ground and his hands on the arms, wearing the mohair off.

I projected the same round oil wheel on the screen every day, the one that looked like a bright red sun with yellow dripping through it. One day Dylan said, "I like that one," as though it was the first time I had projected it.

I knew Dylan had an interest in boxing and talked to him about my father being a featherweight champ in England. Dylan said he had a boxing gym and would go there and spar with the boxers in the mornings. I set up two huge white paper panels, photo backdrop rolls, on each side of the console, fifteen feet wide and extending from the ceiling to the floor. I found some old black-and-white 16-mm film footage of a boxing match, made two film loops out of them, and scratched the film so that when I projected it, it looked like the fighters were boxing in a storm. Dylan loved it, and when we listened back to the mixes, he would ask me to project the boxers.

I had moved to Ventura and was living in a small house overlooking the ocean. They would hold motorcycle flat-track races at the speedway, and I would go and watch the races on Saturday nights. They had all ages racing, from kids to seniors. I told Dylan about the races and he liked the idea of going.

"There are really old guys racing in their fifties," I said, then realized he was over fifty, so I corrected myself. "I mean, in their seventies."

He smiled.

We reviewed each song, going through them to see if he had any lyric changes or if they needed any more support musically. We were working on a song called "A Girl from the Red River Shore" (which didn't make it onto *Time Out of Mind*) and Dylan wanted to change a couple of lines. I punched in his new lines, but it didn't match the character of the vocal that was on there; he seemed to be singing in another voice that didn't sound like Bob Dylan. It was like he was tapping into the voice he'd used on "Girl from the North Country" with Johnny Cash. I ended up replacing the whole vocal with this new sound. The next day, Dylan came in and I played it for him, but he didn't like it so we went back to the old vocal.

On some tracks, like "Love Sick," I was never able to better the rough mix that I did in Miami, so that was the mix that went on the record. Other tracks like "Can't Wait" went through multiple mixes and changes. The song "Dirt Road Blues" was created from a cassette tape Dylan had from a sound check. He asked me if we could use it, and so I made a loop of the best eight bars and the band played on top of it. Because it was a sound-check recording, Daniel didn't like it — he said the steel part sounded like the *Bugs Bunny / Road Runner Hour*. That's why Winston Watson played drums on the album.

"Standing in the Doorway" was a classic right from the start, and very little was done to what was cut in Miami, other than the good mix we did at the Teatro. "Million Miles" was also built on a loop that Dan and Tony Mangurian had played on top of a Little Walter loop. Little Walter never made it in the mix, just the percussion they played. Dylan added some new guitar to "Tryin'

Inside the Teatro (1996).

to Get to Heaven." "'Til I Fell in Love with You" had another working title — "Doing Alright" — and it received a rearrangement and some edits. "Not Dark Yet" was another classic right out of Miami and would only be remixed at the Teatro. "Cold Irons Bound" was the only song Dave Kemper drummed on. I used a crazy overdrive treatment on his drums to make it more exciting. "Make You Feel My Love" was the track that Daniel hated and didn't want on the record. He thought it was corny and offered it to Billy Joel thinking it would suit him. "Can't Wait" went through many levels of reconstruction, and then a final mix came through that everyone loved. "Highlands" was another song built on a loop of Tony and Daniel, and there were two versions cut in Miami. Although they were both were great, the second one had a different set of lyrics that were better, so that was the one we used. The band performed on top of the loop, and at seventeen minutes it was the longest song I had ever recorded. I bettered the mix at the Teatro.

Not all the players made the cut at the end; only what best fit the song was kept. Once all the mixes were final, I gave Dylan a cassette made on a Maxell XLII-S, and we sat on it for a few weeks before mastering. It was during that time that Dylan got sick. The news reported he was in hospital suffering from a heart condition that he'd contracted from inhaling chicken shit. I worried he might have gotten it from the Teatro because there were pigeons that lived under the marquee and dust was floating around. All I could think was *Oh man, we may have killed Bob Dylan.*

Once out of the hospital, Dylan was on heavy medication. When he called, he sounded like he was running at half speed, with long gaps between words. He came up with a sequence of songs and wanted me to try it. Dan had left everything in my hands, not wanting anything to do with the mastering.

I mastered with Joe Gastwirt at his place, Oceanview Mastering in L.A. Mastering is usually a one-day event, and when we were finished, the album sounded great. Joe made me a reference CD to give to Dylan, and on my way home, I dropped it off in Point Dume. Dylan's place looks like a big open lot with old junky cars and old satellite dishes, a couple of shipping containers, and a guard tower. When I pulled in, huge bullmastiff-type dogs approached the car. They sniffed me and followed me to the guardhouse. There were different guys who worked in the guardhouse, but I had met this particular guy before and he recognized me. I told him I was dropping off a CD for Bob and he nodded. Then I noticed that there was wire in his mouth; his jaw was wired shut as the result of a fight he'd gotten into at a local bar. Dylan once told us that he decided to test his security guys one day and jumped over the fence and fell and broke his arm. His security guys never showed up, so he replaced them all.

After the guardhouse there are two roads, but one is a dummy road that goes nowhere, so it's a 50-50 chance if you storm the gate that you will pick the right road.

The next day, I got a call from Dylan. He'd listened to the CD on his blaster and said it didn't sound good when he played it at seven, but if he turned it to twelve it sounded better. Then he said that when he listened to the cassette I gave him, it sounded twice as good. I told him that I would go back to mastering and see what I could do. The next day, Joe and I concluded that Dylan liked the sound of the tape, so we bounced the record to a half-inch mastering tape recorder then ran it through a couple of tube compressors to keep the warmth of it. Joe made me a CD and I dropped it off at Dylan's house again.

The next morning, I got a call from Dylan and he said the new CD sounded different when he played it at six on the blaster but not as good at eleven. He said the cassette I'd given him still sounded better. I told him that I'd bounced it to tape, but he felt it still wasn't good enough.

The next day I went back to Joe's and said, "I don't know what else to do."

Joe suggested we try to run it though the record lathe that they cut the vinyl lacquer on, which would give the sound of a vinyl record, so we went through the process and I dropped off the CD. I didn't hear from Dylan the next day and I tried calling him, but no one answered, so I thought, *Maybe that's it! He must like it!*

Then he called in the middle of the night once again.

"Hey, Mark, it's Bob . . . I've been listening to the song 'Doing Alright.' Can you take the first verse and put it where the last verse is and then take the last verse and put it where the first verse was?"

I told him I'd do it in the morning and drop it off. This song would become "'Til I Fell in Love with You."

"The mastering still doesn't sound as good as your cassette," he added.

I was at my wit's end. I realized there was one more thing I could try. I dropped off the edit of "Doing Alright" at Dylan's house in the morning and then went back to the Teatro. He called me back at noon and said the edit was good so I could drop it in the mastering that day.

I packed up the Tascam 122mkIII cassette machine that I had made his cassette on, along with a couple of new Maxell XLII-S ninety-minute cassettes, and drove down to see Joe. When I got there, I carried in the Tascam cassette machine and plunked it down on his mastering desk.

"What's this?" Joe asked.

"This is it!" I told him. "It's going to save us! We're going to run the whole record through this and that's going to be it."

All of Joe's great work would still be intact, but we would be running it through the Tascam with the Maxell cassette in record mode and print that. We added the new edit of "Doing Alright" and made a new CD. I dropped it off at Dylan's gate and headed back to the Teatro. By the time I got back there, Dylan was calling. I picked up the phone.

"That's it! Sounds great," he said.

I didn't even get the chance to tell him how I did it; all that mattered was that he liked it.

"Can you do one more edit for me and cut out the last verse on 'Doing Alright'?" he asked.

The next day I walked into Joe's place, and from the look of disappointment on his face, I could tell he thought it hadn't worked.

"I need to do one more edit on 'Doing Alright,'" and then very quietly I added, "He liked the mastering."

"I didn't catch that last bit you said."

I let Joe relax. "He *loved* the mastering," I told him.

I have never seen a bigger smile on anyone — it stretched wide like the Joker's on the animated Batman television series.

"No shit," he said in his Brooklyn accent.

We had spent over a week going back and forth, and we were both exhausted.

"Dude," he said, "we are celebrating." He lit up a big joint.

We did the edit and made the CD. I dropped it off at Dylan's gate and that was it — we were finally done.

I didn't see Bob again until the night of the Grammys when he won Album of the Year, Best Contemporary Folk Album, and Best Male Rock Vocal

Performance for "Cold Irons Bound." I'd been asked to come and mix Dylan's on-air portion of the show. When he accepted the award for Album of the Year, he thanked me and said, "It's not every day that you get a sound like this." It made me feel good.

Later that night, I attended the Sony Grammy after-party along with my pregnant wife, Elisa, and Dylan invited us over to his table. When I introduced him to Elisa, he put his hand on her stomach and said, "Congratulations. Is this your first?"

We told him it was.

"Did you hear I said your name on TV?" he asked.

I told him I had and thanked him.

"Well, we know you're the one who did all the work," he said.

I smiled and said, "Thanks."

Dylan really took care of us and put us up at the famous Waldorf Astoria hotel.

CHAPTER 16

IGGY POP

IT WAS AT THE GRAMMY AWARDS IN New York on February 25, 1998, that I bumped into Iggy Pop and Don Was. Iggy asked if I would be interested in recording his album; it was being produced by Don Was in New York that spring. I told him I would. Don said that he wanted to make it on an 8-track and that it was going to be stripped down. I told him that I had a Tascam 8-track recorder that I'd been using and could bring it, and he thought it would be cool.

I went to New York in the spring of 1998 and stayed in Soho at the Mercer in the penthouse loft. It was tiny but had a cool vibe with a bookcase wall.

We weren't working in a normal studio. They decided to make the record at the bass player Hal Cragin's rehearsal room over on Mott Street, three stories underground, in a tiny dungeon of a room. I tried to do what I could to make it a little more inspiring by hanging a couple of Indian tapestries, but it was so damp and dirty that there really was no helping it.

Iggy wanted to work from 10 a.m. to 4 p.m. so that he could be home to watch CNN news. I set up a little rig in the dungeon with a little Tascam mixer and the Tascam DA-88 digital 8-track recorder. I brought some outboard effects with me and a couple of cool old microphones. I also brought a rack of API pre-amps. We didn't have any speakers, so I bought a pair of Canadian speakers that I liked called Paradigm minis, which were available at a local high-end stereo store, over on Broadway. At the stereo shop, the guy tried to sell me a pair of B&W speakers, so I tested the Paradigms against them.

He put on a CD and said, "This record has the highest fidelity of any record out right now . . . check it out."

It was Willie Nelson's *Teatro* record. The salesman wouldn't shut up about the speakers, so we tested the two sets and even the guy couldn't deny the Paradigms sounded better. For $200 they were the cheapest and yet sounded the best. I never told the guy I made that Willie Nelson record because he probably would have kept talking and I needed to get out of there.

Back at the studio, it was pretty cramped by the time Larry Mullins set up his drum kit. It was just Iggy, Hal, Larry, and me in the room. Don spent a lot of time up on the street because his phone didn't have reception that far underground. While recording, I would dial up treatments and have a different headphone mix from the band, and it could get really crazy on some tracks. For the song "Corruption," I put a filter flange on Larry's kit.

Once we had a take, I played it back for them and Iggy said, "Wow, that sounds cool."

Don had come down to listen and didn't know what to think. "Can I hear it dry without all the effects?" he asked.

I played it back without all the effects, but it sounded boring.

Iggy yelled, "Stop! Put them back on." He thought it was much more exciting with the effects.

I put down a mix at that time, which would become the mix that went on the record, and it also became the only song with a video. Iggy was in the process of a divorce and going through a rough time. His wife, Suchi, had hired a New York lawyer and was trying to get his publishing as far back as the Stooges. She ended up with his New York apartment. Iggy said he was thinking of moving to Miami — that he'd seen a house there that he liked, including the furniture inside. He wanted to buy it just like that, so he didn't have to buy anything else. He also explained that he had been married before but only for a few hours. When they'd gotten home, she'd put doilies on his Marshall amp and he realized she had to go.

I told Iggy I was getting married in France in the summer and he said, "No, run, don't do it; you will regret it."

Iggy had written some really great songs for the record, including one called "Nazi Girlfriend." It was about a girl he had once dated in the neighborhood, who was controlling. She wouldn't take off her high heels in bed. One day in a restaurant, he said, "Oh no, there she is walking up the street."

Iggy hid behind the menu so she wouldn't see him.

"Miss Argentina" was a song about the woman he was dating at the time. He played her the song, but she got mad at him, saying what he wrote wasn't true. Larry had been studying the tabla, an East Indian drum, up in San Francisco at the Ali Akbar College of Music, so I got him to play on the song. He asked if I could use two mics so they could have control of the low tabla.

"That would be cool, but I was instructed by Nusrat Fateh Ali Khan's brother, who was his tabla player, that the tabla is a single sound and must be only recorded by one mic," I told him.

"Well, okay, if you say so," he said.

Iggy had a reputation for flashing himself while onstage, and I thought that was just part of the show. But Iggy showed up one day wearing plastic see-through pants with no underwear. We went out for lunch and everyone could see everything. It was New York, so people didn't react, not even the waiters at the restaurant. Hal said, "That's nothing. Iggy sometimes wears a plastic bag over his dick on the bus."

Iggy walked with a limp because he'd hit a rail while crowd-surfing in Rio. He went to jump into the crowd but everyone cleared out, so he hit the guardrail and messed up his hip.

Once we had everything tracked, Iggy asked Whitey, his road guitar player, to come in to put some big guitars on a couple of tracks. Whitey had been the guitar tech and got the job when the guitar player quit. Iggy had told him, "You're in, kid."

Larry had a similar story; he'd followed Iggy on tour with his drums in a station wagon. He kept sending notes to Iggy saying, "Your drummer is weak. Let me audition in the parking lot and I'll show you. I know all your songs."

About halfway through the tour, Iggy fired the drummer and said, "Get that kid in the parking lot who keeps sending those notes."

Iggy had had a terrible experience when a record he'd worked on hadn't been safety copied and got erased. There had been no backup. At the end of

LISTEN UP!

our recording, he panicked and we had to go to another studio and make safety copies so that wouldn't happen again.

Don felt he didn't have enough solid material to finish the record so he got John Medeski, Billy Martin, and Chris Wood — Medeski, Martin, and Wood are an American band who were known for their unconventional funk and hip-hop — to cut a track with Iggy. Then I invited Iggy and Don to come to the Teatro to finish the record there. I spent a week mixing and redoing a couple of overdubs, like Johnny Depp's on "Hollywood Affair."

After Iggy's record was finished, I got married in France and honeymooned in Marrakech, Morocco. We arrived at the La Mamounia hotel. A modern palace, our room was beautiful and overlooked the pool. We were warned not to walk the streets without a guide; naturally we didn't listen and ventured into the heart of the souks, Jemaa el-Fna, Marrakech's ancient central square, which was full of snake charmers, medicine men, and food vendors. We ate on the street and the square in the souk was full of everything, from piles of different colored spices to exotic colored dies.

A man in a royal-blue robe invited us to look at his treasures: a clutch of ostrich eggs, a pair of dried chameleons, a jaguar's skull, an assortment of vials, jars, powders, homemade lotions, dried damask roses, a half-gallon pot of lizard oil, and a shoe box half filled with human teeth. His stock in trade was sulphur and antimony.

Some of the things we saw were shocking, like an old man sitting on a pile of black coal. Everything was for sale. Haggling is the way of life there, and the vendors get offended if you don't haggle with them.

There was a stand selling Moroccan tea sets with eight colored glasses, a silver tray, and a silver teapot. I asked how much for the set and then crossed the lane to another stand selling the same thing. I asked the vendor how much he wanted for his set and once he gave a price, I told him the guy across the way was offering me two sets for that price. He said he would match it if I bought from him instead. I told him I would be right back, and I went back to the other vendor and told him that the other guy had offered me three sets for the price he wanted for one. The first vendor then said he would also give me three sets for the same price, so I ended up with three tea sets for the price of one.

I noticed large pillows to sit on in the lobby of the hotel, all different sizes

ALBUM ART

Avenue B (1999).

and made of exotic materials. I asked where I could buy some and was told that I couldn't buy them because they were custom-made. So we went to the fabric district and picked out beautiful fabrics with dingle balls (furry little balls of wool) and exotic trimmings. It cost me $5 per pillow to have them made, including the labor and material, so I ordered a dozen. The honeymoon ended up being an exotic shopping trip to furnish our house back in L.A.

After a couple of days, we had seen and bought everything we could, so we took a trip out to the desert on camels to camp overnight. It was like something out of *Lawrence of Arabia*; we stayed in a huge tent full of rugs and sheepskins. The staff cooked our meal in a tagine pot outside — a fire-tender lamb that melted in your mouth, with carrots and potatoes drenched in tangine spice, which we ate while lying outside on big exotic pillows. We were served wine in metal goblets by veiled women.

Once we finished, a small group of musicians played clay drums, darbuka, and djembe, and other stringed instruments made from goat gut. There were also metal castanets and violins that they played from their waists. It was an incredible sound. After the band played for a while, belly dancers came out, wearing bells on their ankles and veils over their faces, and it was incredible to watch how fast their hips moved.

We watched them while we smoked hookahs, huge pipes with multiple hoses, and the hash was flavored with exotic, sweet fruit. Then we were served hot Moroccan tea with mint leaves and cubes of sugar in a glass. It was an overload for the senses. We slept in a bed covered in the finest Egyptian cotton sheets and woke to the smell of breakfast — eggs baked over the fire in metal jaffle holders, served with sausage, carrots, handmade breads, and the traditional mint tea.

LISTEN UP!

With five days left in Morocco, we decided to fly to the city of Fez. It was beautiful where we were staying in Marrakech, but it was modern. I was in Morocco because I love mosaics and wanted to stay somewhere with a true Moroccan feel. We were told if we wanted that, we would have to go to Fez and stay at Palais Jamaï hotel. So we flew to Fez on Royal Air Maroc. Once we got out of the airport, we caught a cab and found ourselves on a guided tour we didn't ask for. The taxi driver took us to a pottery warehouse out in the country. We took a tour and then told him we had to go.

By the time we got to the hotel, it was getting dark and we had wasted most of our day. We checked in and went up to the room, which was disappointing, as it was nothing but English Colonial furniture and no mosaics. I began to think it had been a mistake to go to Fez. I didn't even put down my bag but went back to the front desk. I told them I wanted a room with mosaics and a Moroccan vibe. They told me they didn't have any rooms like that, so I showed them something I'd ripped out of the Royal Air Moroc magazine, a picture of their hotel with a room that was all mosaic.

They told me that was the Presidential Suite, so I asked to see it. They informed me it was $5,000 a night, but I insisted they show it to me.

We waited until a man clad in a white robe with a red fez showed us to the room. It was located on the other side of the hotel in a private wing. We walked down a long tiled corridor until we came to a set of two doors that were at least fifteen feet tall. Once he opened the door, we stepped into a mosaic palace. The ceilings were at least twenty feet high and the walls were covered with royal-blue mosaic. The suite was a masterpiece and the attention to detail was staggering. Huge doors entered into a step-down living area, and a mammoth archway led to the bedrooms, one on each side of the main salon. In the bedrooms, steps led up to a four-poster bed. Four magnificent chandeliers hung in the center of the main salon. The bathrooms had steps down into the tubs and huge French doors opened onto a private courtyard full of exotic plants. It was beyond words.

We went back to the front desk and I asked to speak to the manager. They told me he was busy but if we waited in the lobby, he would come see us when he was done.

"I don't have time to wait. It's late and I want to talk to him right now," I said.

They made a call and the manager emerged from the back room, and he invited us to sit with him on the couches in the front lobby. He had one of the employees light the big hookah pipe on the table. I thought he was smoking hash, but it was a flavored tobacco. He offered us a tube and we all smoked from the hookah. I introduced myself as Howard — Mark Howard — and said that this was a very special time for us because we were just married and we wanted a memory to last us a lifetime.

I asked him when he'd last rented the room and he proudly told me Tom Hanks had stayed there last year.

"So you haven't rented it in a year?" I asked him.

"No, I haven't. It is $5,000 a night U.S. if you'd like to stay there."

I told him I did want to stay there, but that $5,000 was a little bit over my budget.

"Look, I can do it for you for $3,000 for the night," the manager offered.

"You are so kind," I told him. "I'll tell you what — it's late and we are leaving early tomorrow. Would you take $500 cash and this would give us an amazing gift for life?"

"No, I can't do that . . ." He paused. "$1,000 cash."

I thanked him and told him it was an amazing offer, but that I only had $600 cash.

The manager shook his head and then suddenly said, "Okay. Deal."

I gave him the cash right then and thanked him. He walked us up to the room and gave us a key. He introduced us to a young man named Omar.

"He will be your servant and at your disposal while you're here," he told us. We couldn't believe we had just scored the Presidential Suite. We threw our bags down and walked around the room in disbelief, wandering out the French doors into the garden, where we discovered our own private pool. It was a hot and sticky night, the air heavy with the scent of blooming jasmine, and we went for a midnight swim.

When we went back into the room, we found that the manager had sent fruit and sugar-covered pastries, piled high in pyramids on trays set out on the coffee table. Despite our deep discount, they went all the way and treated us like royalty.

We woke early in the morning. The room was so beautiful and palatial I didn't want to leave. I had Omar bring breakfast.

Omar told us if we wanted to go down into the old medina, a maze-like section of city with very narrow brick lanes and tight doorways lining them, we'd need a guide because we could get lost or could easily be pulled into one of the doorways and go missing. We needed to be out by noon, so we had to hurry. We walked out the front door and entered the medina, and Omar had been right — it was a labyrinth. I found myself a little nervous, so I bought a bag of peanuts and dropped them as we went along so I had a trail to follow back out.

We found two little kids to show us around and I told them I wanted to buy some carpets, so they took us to a large emporium. Carpets hung on the walls and layered on the floor were huge pillows and tin tables with hookah pipes, which served as a place to sit while salesmen pulled out rugs to show us. I'd point to a rug, which they'd pull down and roll out, and then I'd ask to see another. We smoked the hookah and it had hash in it. Tourism has cleaned up these things so now hash is only sold to tourists secretly. We continued looking at rugs and I found a beautiful red rug, nine feet by twelve feet, and two long orange kilim-style runners, twelve feet long, and a little purple rug just four feet by five feet.

I asked the salesman how much he wanted for everything, and he told me it would be $3,000. I offered $600 but he laughed and said I was insulting his mother.

I asked him what his mother had to do with it.

We kept haggling until we came up with a price we both agreed on. I asked how I'd get them back to L.A., and he said he would ship them. I told him it was too risky, that I had no way of knowing if he would actually do it. We rose and prepared to walk away until he said that he would pay for shipping. I decided it was worth the risk because I wouldn't be out too much money. I had bought single Chinese rugs in L.A. for way more! I gave him my address and phone number and put the charge on a credit card so there would be a trail if he ripped me off. We carried the two kilims with us because they were small and we could deal with them. The kid-guides took us to a leather shop but it smelled terrible because they were dyeing the leather right there in big clay vats and laying it out to dry. We ended up buying a leather bag and a leather ottoman.

Running out of time, we headed back to the hotel and arrived at noon. I asked the front desk if they could check on our flight. We went back to the room and the front desk called and said that the flight had been delayed until the next day. I told them we were out of money and couldn't afford to spend another night. The manager was away, they told me, but we could stay the night as a gift for our wedding. We were thrilled.

We flew back to Marrakech the next day and relaxed by the pool. It had been an adventure, and it felt as though we needed a vacation to recover from the one we were on.

CHAPTER 17

WILLIE NELSON

BEFORE STARTING TO RECORD WILLIE NELSON'S *Teatro*, Dan was interested in another Neve console that had become available in Atlanta. I flew there to see the Neve that John Lennon had worked on in 1980 at A & R while recording in New York. The console had been bought by Triclops Sound Studios in Atlanta and was modified by Fred Hill, a Neve console restorer. He'd added on another console that had been owned by the Good Brothers, a Canadian group that'd won Juno Awards for eight consecutive years, so the console now had forty-eight channels. I bought it, packed it up, and had it shipped to the Teatro. It arrived three days before we began the Willie Nelson sessions.

I worked day and night setting the console up and tore the whole studio apart to install it. Adam Samuels was my assistant at the time, and he helped me move the console into place. I put the Neve console we already had beside it so there was just one huge console, an eighty-channel Neve 8068 with flying faders. It really looked impressive. I'd built a platform behind the console to hold a Mexican wedding wrap-around couch and rearranged the Westlake twin twelve-inch monitor speakers so they were on their ends. I worked hard on getting everything just right. I hadn't told Dan the console had arrived and was really hoping to impress him with the new setup.

Dan came to the Teatro the day before the session, along with Emmylou Harris, who would be singing with Willie. They came in the front door and we hung out and talked for a while in the pool room, until he walked through the padded doors into the studio and fell silent.

"What the *fuck* did you do?" he screamed. "How could you risk putting in a new console without testing it?"

Furious, he stormed back into the pool room and I could hear him going off. I followed him and told him that the console was in amazing shape — no buzzes — and sounded great. I assured him it would be fine, that the other Neve was almost unusable at that point, cracking and cutting in and out with every knob turned. He calmed down, but being the nervous type, he was still on edge, something that often made people uncomfortable.

What most people don't know is that there are two versions of Willie Nelson's *Teatro* album. Willie came to the Teatro to cut three songs in the spring of 1999. Emmylou Harris came to sing with Willie, and together they sang in a way I'd never heard before, Emmylou shadowing Willie's singing for a unique sound. Dan played guitar as a part of the band. I set them up in a big circle with Willie in the middle, Emmylou to his left, Dan to his right, and then the two drummers, Tony and Victor, to his right as well. Brian, the guitar player, and Bobbie, who was Willie's baby sister, on a Wurlitzer, continued the circle toward Emmylou. Mickey was on harp right next to Emmylou, completing the circle so that everyone had a visual line to Willie.

This was a collection of musicians we'd been working with over the years — Tony Mangurian was a left-handed drummer, while Victor Indrizzo was right handed. I set up the two kits beside each other, so the kick drums were side by side. Victor used a big twenty-four-inch CC bass drum, tight and punchy. Tony used my 1970s blue Pearl twenty-inch double-headed bass drum with a big, floppy sound. They shared an ashtray between them. There is no bass guitar on the record except for the song "The Maker." Mickey Raphael played bass harmonica — the same bass harp sound heard on the theme for the *Sanford and Son* TV show. Bobbie played the keyboard, Wurlitzer, electric piano, and organ. Brad Mehldau, a jazz pianist and composer, came in to play piano and vibes, and Brian Griffiths was brought in from Canada as the token Canadian guitar player.

Willie Nelson during the making of *Teatro*.

Recording began at noon. Willie would come up with a song, the band would quickly learn it, and we'd put a version down. Once I'd recorded it, I'd play it back right away, usually just one or two takes. As we listened back, I would lay down a mix as a reference so we would have something to listen to at the end of the day. Things moved really fast. One song led into the next; by the end of the night, we'd recorded ten songs.

Tom was Willie's guitar tech. In the bus parked outside, Tom rolled up a huge blunt, like a Jamaican spliff. Willie said, "Light it up so I can have a smoke with my coffee."

I told them, "I've got a lot to do to set up, so I'll smoke with you guys tonight."

I left the bus and headed into the studio to get set up for the day. Tom came in about twenty minutes later with Willie's guitar, called Trigger. Trigger is a stereo guitar with two cables that go into a stereo amp. Tom got Trigger out of its case and just stood there in front of Willie's amp.

"Tom, did you lose something?" I asked.

"Yeah, have you seen Willie's guitar cables?"

I told him he was staring right at them on top of the amp. I was happy at that moment that I hadn't smoked anything.

Willie came in, sat in his chair, and started to play, as if smoking hadn't affected him at all. We were working on a song called "I Never Cared for You."

I told Willie that I really liked the song and asked if he'd just written it. He told me he'd written it back in the '40s. I thought it was amazing he could just pull it out after all those years and remember it.

As we went through the songs, I noticed a problem with Brian Griffith's channel. I wasn't getting any signal from his guitar, so I checked all my patches, but they looked good. I walked over to Brian to see if something was broken on his end. I could only see his head from where I was sitting because he was behind a little isolation wall. When I walked over to him, I saw that he wasn't even playing, just sitting there staring off into space. I assumed he was a victim of the Willie batshit weed he'd smoked on the break. I waved at him to play, but he just gave me a glazed look and continued to stare off into the distance. There wasn't much I could do.

Willie would occasionally tell me stuff from his past. He once drove his 1969 Corvette Stingray with Kris Kristofferson riding shotgun, racing Waylon Jennings in his 1970 Corvette Stingray out on the country road outside Willie's Texas ranch. They were neck and neck when Willie reached over and turned off the air conditioning and pulled out in front to win the race. Waylon asked him how he'd sped up, and Willie laughed and said he was just better than Waylon and wouldn't tell him what he'd done.

Willie had had some problems with the IRS, and they found him liable for taxes back as far as 1972. The court ordered him to pay $6 million. Willie asked the IRS to wait for payment until settlement of a $45 million lawsuit he had filed against his former accounting firm, Price Waterhouse, for allegedly leading him astray. The agency refused and seized most of what Willie owned. They put it all up for auction, but Willie fans bought up his personal things and just gave them back to him as gifts. While we were making the record, Willie said that he'd just made his last payment to the IRS and it was finally over.

By the end of the next day, I had recorded another eleven tracks. I made a CD for Willie and we all went onto his bus to listen. Willie had a new Bose system and everything sounded amazing. That was it — the record was done, and

LISTEN UP!

we picked the best fourteen tracks out of the bunch to make the album. It was mixed on the spot.

As a joke, I asked my wife to make a copy of a photo I had of the front of the Teatro. On the marquee, I wrote *Willie Nelson* in magic marker. He loved it so much that it became the cover of the record. The record never won any awards, but it became a sonic reference for many audiophiles.

Daniel never acknowledged that everything went off without a hitch.

I ended up mixing a couple of live shows with the same band from the record. We did a show in Boulder, Colorado, at the Fox Theatre, for an annual radio conference, as well as Farm Aid and the *Late Show with David Letterman*. It was a whole different vibe being on the road with Willie. After the show, his bus was a crazy party, so full of smoke it was hard to see, with girls lifting their shirts and asking Willie to sign their breasts, which he did with a black magic marker.

Wim Wenders, the famed German filmmaker, walked into the Teatro and was fascinated by the lighting. It was lit like a theatrical stage; there were pin spotlights on the piano and one just on the drums, but everything else was dark. You couldn't really tell the size of the room, and every detail was lit like in an art gallery. Wim had come to see about doing a film on the making of the *Teatro* record. When he walked in, the first words out of his mouth were "This is perfect. I don't want to change a thing. The lighting is brilliant."

It was late July by the time we started the filming at the Teatro. Transport trailers showed up with an army of gear, and crews of workers stormed around the space. It felt like an invasion. They gridded the ceiling with pipes to hang lighting trusses from, and by the time they were finished, I had never seen it so bright. What happened to "the lighting is perfect," I wondered.

I did a similar setup as I'd done for the record, but I put Willie, Emmylou, and Daniel on a little riser. I was behind them in the center of the room, with the huge Neve console. We treated the recordings like a show and invited guests to come and watch. I had gotten a couple of diner booths from Cielito Lindo, the Mexican restaurant across the street. Some celebrities came out, like Woody Harrelson, Harry Dean Stanton, Robbie Robertson, and Marianne Faithfull.

The Pussycat Doll dancers, a singing group that had previously been a burlesque troupe, danced behind the big movie screen and only appeared as silhouettes. Harry Dean Stanton also did a dance sequence with one of the Pussycat Dolls to one of the songs.

I had made friends with the Oxnard police department when I'd donated money to buy kayaks and bicycles for their Police Activities League, which helped underprivileged kids stay out of trouble. Normally, you would have to pull permits to stop traffic for filming and for police security, but because I had a good relationship with the force, they did some favors. For instance, while we were filming the street scenes, they stopped traffic, and they also put a man outside Willie's bus to protect him from anyone trying to follow him. The police were so helpful and so kind. At one point, I was a little worried that they might do something, because when Willie opened the door of the bus, a big cloud of pot smoke rolled out. The police were just cool about it and turned a blind eye, content that their town was getting attention from one of the biggest country stars in the world.

I recorded a whole new version of the record for the filming at the Teatro, and it was just as good. The film versions are the actual takes of the new recordings without overdubs. I mixed these versions to picture so that when the camera panned to the harmonica, I'd make it louder so it matched the footage. I was just about to start producing a record for Marianne Faithfull, and she came in early because she and Wim were friends. Wim wanted to get her in the film, so there is a scene in which Marianne is sitting in an armchair smoking while Willie and the band are playing.

About a week after filming, Wim invited us to his house in the Hollywood Hills to show us a rough cut. Wim had shot it on Super 16-mm black-and-white film, so it had a gritty texture. I had been so disappointed when they had come and flooded the Teatro with all those lights, but because the 16-mm film was so dark, it needed a lot of light. When Wim showed us the footage, there was my lighting; he had managed to capture the lamps and spotlight look that I'd created. He had maintained that moody, smoky feel.

CHAPTER 18

MARIANNE FAITHFULL

MARIANNE FAITHFULL CALLED FROM FRANCE TO ASK me about making her next record. She said that Elton John had written a song for her called "For Wanting You." She played me a demo over the phone. It was definitely dramatic and would fit her perfectly.

She'd been having tea with Roger Waters, of Pink Floyd, and had asked if he would write a song for her. He said he had written a song in the '60s about Syd Barrett that had never been recorded and he thought it might be perfect for her. She said that she also had a couple of songs that she had written. It sounded like we had enough ideas to proceed. I suggested she come to the Teatro in California, as I would have access to some great players and the Teatro already had a full arsenal of musical instruments. She flew to L.A. a couple of days early to get adjusted. In the 1960s Marianne Faithfull was one of the most beautiful women in the world, a pop star alongside the Rolling Stones. She'd had a number of hits and was in movies like *Girl on a Motorcycle*. She struggled with drug abuse in the 1970s and '80s, although she still managed to produce brilliant work at various times, including her album *Broken English*.

I rented Marianne a beautiful shabby-chic house right on the beach. The shag carpet and all of the furnishings were white. She stayed there with her manager, François Ravard. The moment Marianne arrived in L.A., she sent François to the hospital's emergency department to get her some pills to help her sleep. She had been down this road many times before and knew she would need something strong to make her sleep and get through her jet lag. François waited for about four hours before he saw a doctor. He claimed he hadn't slept in days and needed something to knock him out. He was given a prescription for temazepam.

Marianne reminded me of a queen, always speaking very properly and always polite. When she arrived at the Teatro, I was walking her in when out of the blue she said to me, "You know it's not true."

"What's not true?"

"The Mars bar."

"Of course not," I replied. "Silly rumors."

It had been said that when British police raided a party at Keith Richards's home in 1967, they found Mick Jagger eating a Mars bar out of Marianne Faithfull's vagina. It seemed an odd thing to tell me right off the bat.

Marianne asked Barry Reynolds to play guitar on the record. He'd cowritten with Marianne in the past, including the song "Broken English," which got her signed to Island Records. I used the rhythm section of Brian Blade and Chris Thomas. I brought in Glenn Patscha, a great New York keyboard player. These guys would eventually tour with Marianne once the record was out.

Marianne wanted to cover Leonard Cohen's "Tower of Song," which would be the album's only cover. Marianne had five songs of her own and the rest were given to her. One of my favorites was one she had written with Barry called "File It Under Fun from the Past." She said it was a song she had written about Mick Jagger.

We would work from noon until about six or seven o'clock — not a stressful schedule. All the songs came together. It was a nice mixture between the songs she'd written and those written by legendary songwriters. Most of the takes were her live vocal, right off the floor. I used the same mic on her as I had on Dylan and Willie — the Sony C-37A. She said that Bob Dylan once showed up at her house and knocked on the door, there to apologize for something that had happened years before. She said it was Dylan who led her to me. He warned her to be careful of who produced her, because, like him, she had a unique voice.

Marianne told stories of her days with the Stones and other crazy adventures. She'd signed a bad deal with a manager that lasted twenty years, and he got all of her songwriting publishing royalties, so when she wrote the song "Sister Morphine," Jagger and Richards took the credit for it so her manager wouldn't steal that money. They put the money that song made into an account for her. It seemed a pretty cool thing for them to do. While we were making the record, the bad contract was coming to an end, and she now receives the song-writing credit for "Sister Morphine."

With Marianne Faithfull (1999).

Marianne said that she suffered from a heroin addiction while she dated Mick Jagger. On one occasion, Marianne was flying to L.A. to meet Mick, but when she arrived, the Stones' manager kidnapped her and took her out to Joshua Tree to get clean. Once she'd gone through withdrawal, he drove her back to L.A., placed a big red bow on her, put her in front of Mick's door, and rang the bell. This was his present: a new, sober Marianne.

Marianne told the story of living with a girlfriend in London while she was dating Mick. She went home one night and when she reached the flat upstairs, she found her friend, nodded off, in an overflowing bathtub. Marianne tried to get her out but fell in the tub, too, because she was also loaded on junk, at which point she passed out. While they were both in the overflowing tub, it fell through the floor into the flat below. Somehow they were both fine. They gave quite a shock to the poor guy downstairs, who could never have imagined two beautiful girls falling through his ceiling in a bathtub and landing in front of the television he was watching.

Anita Pallenberg, an Italian actress and fashion designer, was dating Brian Jones, and Marianne explained that she, Anita, Brian, Mick, and Keith were all driving in a car one evening. Brian said he felt unwell and asked that he be dropped at home. It was that night that Anita took up with Keith Richards.

Marianne eventually went off the rails with heroin and hit rock bottom, living on the street. She was forced out of England and went to live in Dublin. The band U2 looked after her and gave her a little cottage to live in. She cleaned up her drug addiction while in Dublin, but because it was Ireland, she found it impossible to stop drinking.

While we were making her album, Marianne would pop over to the Mexican place across the street for a drink. She was incredibly proper before leaving, saying things like, "Oh, look it's cocktail time. Just going across for a little drink."

After a few cocktails, she'd return and burst into the studio hollering, "Mark, you fucking cunt! Why are you making us work *so fucking hard*."

I would simply smile and say, "Oh Marianne . . . it's not that hard."

I cut ten songs for the record at the Teatro but didn't mix them until a few weeks later in London. At the time we made the album, my wife was pregnant and already past her due date; I worried she'd give birth while we were still working. On the last night of recording *Vagabond Ways,* we had a little celebration. I hadn't smoked during the whole recording period, but on the last night I thought I would have one hit off a joint. Because it had been so long since I'd smoked, man, did I get stoned. We said our good-byes and I went home. It was around midnight and I'd just gotten into bed and drifted off when my wife said, "It's time!"

We'd had everything ready for days, so I just threw on my clothes and we headed to Ventura Hospital. My daughter, Thea Nina Howard, was born that morning, on August 1, 1998. It seemed pretty amazing she'd waited until I'd finished Marianne Faithfull's album to come into this world.

CHAPTER 19

THE RED HOT CHILI PEPPERS

THE RED HOT CHILI PEPPERS CAME TO the Teatro in September 1998 to demo their *Californication* album with me. It was pretty low key — just me and the band and their road manager, Louie Mathieu.

It would be the return of John Frusciante. He had left the band due to a heroin addiction that had dominated his life, but he was newly clean. The drug had taken a heavy toll on his body and speech. Both his arms looked like they had third-degree burns, scars from years of open sores that came from shooting up. This may have been the first time the band had played with him since he'd gotten clean.

There were no guitar or drum techs, and the Chili Peppers set up their own gear. John was having a rough time getting it together so I offered a hand. He was plugged into the amp but he couldn't get sound out of it.

"My amp don't work," he sort of stuttered.

I looked at the amp.

"It's only the standby switch," I told him and flicked the switch to fire it up. I was concerned that maybe the years of heroin had taken its toll on his abilities. He couldn't go into a store and buy a bottle of water or pay his bills, and the fact that he slurred his words and couldn't turn on an amp made me think this was all too much. But once his amp fired up, it was like he was reborn. The band kicked

JAM 2

in with him. I have worked with a lot of amazing guitar players, but this was the first time I was truly in awe. He had that same funk thing as Leo Nocentelli (an American musician and songwriter) but John was at a different level. The band played like they had never been apart. It was an amazing thing to see: they were fresh and tight, excited to be playing together again.

Chad Smith, the drummer, known for his bombastic beats, showed up with just a pair of sticks. I set him up with the Teatro house kit. It was a 1960 Gretsch four-piece, with white frosted heads tuned up high, like jazz drums should be. The kick pedal was a Speed King, so it had a lot of bounce. Chad is one of those drummers who buries the kick pedal into the head, so he wasn't used to this floating action, but I think because of that he played more like Mitch Mitchell from Hendrix's band.

Flea, the bassist, had a routine before playing in which he would do yoga stretches on the floor and meditate. He brought in his road rig and I took a direct right off his bass.

I handed Anthony a Shure Beta 58A mic to use and he asked for some headphones. I told him try it without them; he didn't know that we were in quadraphonic sound. I had the rear PA disguised with some Indian tapestries, so it looked like cloth towers. The band was playing and when Anthony sang, his voice came out of the speakers, sounding like a live concert but crystal clear. The effects I had on his vocal made him sound great and he was excited to sing.

There was only one run-through for each of the songs and some small arrangement changes, but the band didn't labor over anything. After a couple of days, they had put down versions of all the songs on the record. Anthony was still working on finishing up some of the lyrics, and he spent an extra day with me to try a couple of the songs again. I made everyone a CD to listen to, and as reference for Rick Rubin, their producer. They ended up going to Cello Studios in Hollywood to make the record, but they had a rough time getting back to the sound they'd achieved at the Teatro. While listening to the new music they'd cut, Rick kept referring back to the recordings I'd done with them. He went through a couple of engineers trying to improve the sound. One day, Rick was walking by one of the other studios at Cello and saw my friend Jim Scott working. Rick asked Jim if he could help because they were having a hard time bettering the demos, then Jim made the record with them. This is something that affects a lot of people: it's called "demo-itis." Something happens on a demo — it feels fresher. The Teatro recordings ended up being used as B sides for some of the Japanese singles. They also used some of the jams for "Around the World" as a B side on a single and called it "Teatro Jam."

Californication became the Chili Peppers' most commercially successful album and sold fifteen million copies worldwide.

No one knows how, but some of the Teatro outtakes ended up leaked on the internet, many of them very different from the versions that appeared on the final album.

CHAPTER 20

U2

I WORKED WITH U2 ON THE *All That You Can't Leave Behind* album. Working with U2 is a little like working in a factory: everyone doing their part to make a cohesive whole. They begin their records with nothing and go into the studio to hash it out. Edge might have some seeds to a song, and maybe Bono has put down a melody on his idea catcher. In the early days working with them, they used Sony Walkmans to save their ideas on cassettes. They begin with no lyrics, just scats that Bono puts down to write lyrics to. The process is long and grueling.

Bono and Edge made three visits to the Teatro over the course of a year. The beginning was a seed session to find songs, the second was a halfway point, and they cut the record with drum machines and sequencers — very hip-hop. Bono was infatuated with the hip-hop world and really wanted to be a part of it. They had just come back from playing the record for Jimmy Iovine, president at Interscope Records. "This is fucking great," he said enthusiastically in his New York accent. "I can't believe it. But where the fuck is U2?"

It was all machines, no Larry or Adam. "This is great if you're Puff Daddy," he told them. "But you're not. *Hello,* where the fuck has U2 gone?!"

Bono tried to reason with him, but Jimmy didn't buy it. He told them to go back and put U2 on there, and they might have a record. Bono had gotten so caught up in his hip-hop, he'd forgotten they were a band, that it was the U2 sound that their fans wanted.

While I was working with Edge, he brought in his wife, Morleigh Steinberg, whom he'd met on one of their tours; she'd been one of their belly dancers for "Mysterious Ways." She was studying Japanese face dancing at the time and asked me if I could put her video on my TV screens so she could study. I had four forty-two-inch tube TVs on racks with wheels, a wall of screens. I put it on for her while recording guitars with Edge. It's a strange art form, so fascinating that I found myself distracted. Sometimes it was funny and then just bizarre, and at times there was no sound at all, just face dancing.

With Edge, I would pump his guitar through the rear PA and it would sound huge, like he was at a show, and with the track playing, it really pushed him to play more recklessly. That's something you don't get in normal studios. Normally, the guitarist is out in the studio space wearing headphones and doesn't get to feel the sound pressure.

The last leg of recording was for both the album and the film *The Million Dollar Hotel*. Wim Wenders was directing. It was an American drama based on a concept story by Bono, starring Mel Gibson and Milla Jovovich.

U2 has their mixes done by a who's who of music's stars. They will give their singles to a guy in New York, to a guy in London, and to a guy in L.A. Once everyone is finished, the band listens for who has the best mix. Oddly enough, it's not always one guy who nails it. Perhaps the guy from London had a good verse, but the guy from New York had a great chorus, and the guy in L.A. mixed the best ending. The band takes all the best parts and cuts them together to make one great mix.

With U2 it's not over until it's over. When you have money and power, you get your way. I remember mixing the song "Stateless"; I was just finishing the mix when Bono said that he wanted to change the second verse. The song had to be in L.A. within an hour for mastering. Down to the wire, I handed Bono a mic and punched him in for the second verse. I remixed the song and out the door it went. Bono has a million ideas and he wants to try them all; he might have three different chorus ideas. To him they may all be great, but I usually found one was obviously better than the others and he'd normally accept my opinion.

Usually, the end process of mastering was left to Edge, and he decided on the

The Edge listening to a playback.

sequence. He said that on *The Unforgettable Fire* they chose a 7.5 IPS tape recorder to master off because it had better bottom and sounded better. Most records were done at 30 IPS so there was less of a hiss.

I had just finished Iggy Pop's record before U2 came in. He was a hero to Bono and Edge, and they asked me if they could hear some of Iggy's album. I played them the track "Corruption," and they were floored. It had the energy they were always striving for and the sounds were cutting edge. Then I played them "Nazi Girlfriend" and "Miss Argentina." Bono couldn't get over how big the vocal sound was. Edge really liked "Nazi Girlfriend" and kept asking me to play it again and again. They were like excited little kids.

Bono can be a great guy to hang out with and share stories with, but when you're working with him, he doesn't have a lot of patience. I was mixing a track using a Studer 24-track tape recorder locked to an iZ Radar 24-track digital tape recorder synced to thirty-two tracks of Pro Tool. It was fanned out across the console so that all eighty channels were being used. Bono changed his mind and wanted me to use an old vocal for one line, but the old vocal was at the other end of the desk, ten feet away. I tried it — I had to pull down the vocal on one side of the desk, then run to the other end for the one line, then back to the other vocal to put it back. I missed the breath of the one vocal coming back. I was doing this on the fly and he could see that I was running back and forth like a rabbit. He came up to me and put his hand on my shoulder and said, "Look, man, you're going to have to do it a bit quicker than that." He may have been joking, but it kind of pissed me off. He expects perfection every time. One really challenging aspect of being an engineer is that musicians can make a hundred mistakes, but the engineer is always expected to get things perfect. Flood, a guy who worked on a lot of U2's records, quit the business for a while and moved to Russia to open his own restaurant because the stress level was so high.

U2's tours are on a whole other level. At one of their shows, I ventured underneath the stage and it was like nothing I had ever seen before. There were walls of computers, offices, kitchens, dressing rooms, and an army of people down there. They'd also have three rigs of the same show moving at all times. One show would be in L.A., and there would already be a show setting up in San Francisco, with another heading to Vancouver, each one moving along and coordinated like an army. The band stays in a hub in Miami, and they fly on a private plane after each show back to Miami to sleep in the same bed each night. Bono was given an oxygen mask so he had clean air and didn't get sick.

Bono said that B.B. King had opened a bunch of shows for them at one time, and he had asked B.B. what the secret was to keeping his voice healthy all the time, wondering if perhaps it was honey and hot water. He assumed B.B. would know because he'd been performing for so many years.

"Now look, son," B.B. said to him. "There is only one thing that's going to keep your voice healthy — you got to eat pussy every day."

Bono wasn't sure if he was serious or not, and they both just laughed.

For a small guy, Bono is a barrel-chested singer; he has one of those voices that cuts through anything and propels like a trumpet. He blows up most mics and I didn't dare put a tube mic in front of him because it would just break up. I was once recording vocals with him using a Shure Beta 58. He was behind me singing to the monitor speakers turned up loud, and it was crystal clear coming out of the speakers. I turned around to look at him and he wasn't even singing into the mic, only holding it down by his chest.

I've sometimes wondered why I wasn't invited to work on the other U2 records with Daniel. Making *All That You Can't Leave Behind* was the first time I got to see their dynamics. Bono was running the show and Dan was a cheerleader. In the early days, it was Brian Eno and Dan who would go into the studio to cook something up for U2 to work with.

Bono often bounced ideas off Dan. On *The Joshua Tree* album, the intro to "Where the Streets Have No Name" was actually Dan's guitar. He told Bono that the lyric "Where the streets have no name" was weak and that he could come up with something better, but that song became one of U2's biggest hits, so it's a good thing Bono didn't listen to him.

On *All That You Can't Leave Behind* Brian Eno and Dan asked Bono for songwriting credits because they came up with a lot of the music. Bono said, "No. We hire you guys because of what you bring to the table. We pay you a million to produce it and you get half a point. We could hire anyone, but we like what you do."

On the last U2 record Brian and Dan produced, *No Line on the Horizon*, they were finally offered songwriting credits, but the record failed to have a big single and sold just over a million copies. *The Joshua Tree* continues to be one of the biggest selling albums of all time, with twenty-five million copies sold.

CHAPTER 21

ALL THE PRETTY HORSES

THE SESSIONS FOR THE SOUNDTRACK TO BILLY Bob Thornton's movie *All the Pretty Horses* started at the Teatro in the spring of 1999 and carried on into the summer. Much of the music was previously recorded, and some musical themes were added for different scenes. It was more orchestral than *Sling Blade* had been.

I made an assembly using a bell tree with bowls, added metal, and glass. The whole thing hung from ropes. Each bowl had its own note and was played with a mallet. The idea behind having most of the music done before they started shooting was so that Billy Bob could play the music on set during filming. We were invited to come on location in San Antonio, Texas. When they shot the dance-hall scene, they wanted some of the musicians from the soundtrack to play in the dance-hall band. There was a big wooden barn with a stage that was from a real dance hall from back in the day, still intact. Matt Damon, Henry Thomas, and Penélope Cruz were all on set. There were more than one hundred extras, all in costumes, dancing around Matt and Penélope.

On film sets, there is a lot of down time. Emmylou Harris was visiting the set, too. Dan decided he wanted to perform a song with Emmylou for all the extras in the dance hall.

"I want you to record it," he said to me.

The only way I could do that was to use a sound guy's recorder and boom mic, the microphone they use for recording dialogue. The boom mic is on a long stick. Because I had only one mic, I used a technique I call "painting with the microphone." I stood in front of them, and when Emmylou sang, I'd move the mic toward her, and when she paused, I'd point it toward the guitar. I had to be fast but smooth, a tai-chi type of movement, in order to create a useable recording. The extras lined the walls of the dance hall to watch the performance. Once it was finished, everyone applauded. A lot of the people went up to Emmylou to tell her how beautiful she sounded and then came to thank me and comment on my beautiful dance. They hadn't realized I'd been recording and thought I was doing a performance to the song with a stick with fur on it. I didn't know how to respond, so I just said thank you and smiled.

Because *All the Pretty Horses* took place in 1949, all the props had to match the period. The stage gear they rented had to look like it came from that time. They had an old 1950s Gibson guitar amp on the stage as a prop, and Dan asked me to plug it in to see if it worked. I plugged it into the set power on the stage and the amp turned on, but when I plugged the guitar into the input, it was very quiet, even at full volume. Then I plugged the guitar amp into the microphone input and the amp burst into life. Dan couldn't believe the sound he was getting; the guitar was sustaining itself in a Hendrix-type feedback. He'd never sounded so good.

"Record me, record me *now*!" he barked.

I ran over to the sound guy but he had already packed up his gear. I asked if I could use the gear again to record the guitar sound and he told me I could and opened up his case at a leisurely pace. Film people tend to move slowly. I finally had it all together and set to record when they shut down the set power.

Dan wanted them to turn the power back on, but because the set was unionized, they had to turn it off. I found a plug on the wall of the barn and tried that, and although the amp worked, it just didn't have the firepower it had had using the set power, which was pumping out a hotter voltage. That made the tubes in the amp run hotter, making it much louder and giving the great feedback. Daniel was mad that I didn't get to record him with that amazing sound, and he wanted the amp. I went to see the prop guy, but he told me it was a rental. I explained to Dan that the prop department couldn't sell the amp, but he said he didn't "fucking care — I want that amp!"

I went back to the prop guy. "How much for the amp?" I asked.

He said he couldn't sell it so I asked him how much it was worth. He told me the replacement value was $2,500. I told him I'd give him the $2,500 plus $1,000 for his troubles.

"No, it doesn't work like that," he explained. He had a reputation to maintain.

"Look man, my friend *really wants* that amp and he has sent me to buy it. What about if I give you $5,000 for it?"

"Okay, we got a deal," he said.

I walked out with the amp and Dan was happy. Unfortunately, the amp never sounded like that ever again and just became a dust collector in his closet.

Penélope Cruz was very interested in hearing the music for the film, and Billy Bob asked me if I could take a CD over to Penélope's room that night. I knocked on the door and she invited me in. She was a sweet little woman and I loved her accent. She told me she didn't know how to make the CD player work and asked me to try. It was a Bose system but the speakers weren't connected, so I plugged them in and put on the CD. She asked me to stay and listen to it with her. I had been hanging out with her on the set, so we knew each other, and it wasn't at all uncomfortable. She offered me some wine and we sat on the couch and ended up talking for hours; she had just had a breakup and she cried as she told me about his cheating and lying. I found it funny that someone had found a way to mess up a relationship with a beautiful woman with a beautiful soul.

The movie was over three hours long at this point. I would go into Hollywood to watch the film as they dubbed the music in, and it sounded amazing in the big theater. They did a couple of test runs with audiences and it failed. Harvey Weinstein told Billy Bob the movie was too long and needed to be cut. Billy disagreed. He said that was how the film was shot and that it needed to stay that way in order to tell the story. Harvey told Billy he was pulling him from the film and he would have no say. They cut the movie down to an hour and half and then flushed the score we did down the toilet, even though they'd paid Dan a million dollars to do the music.

They rescored the movie with an orchestra and then retried the film with an audience. It still didn't test well. They then took the orchestral score and flushed that down the toilet, cut the film even shorter, and had Marty Stuart, the country singer, score the movie for very little money. In the end, the film was one hour and sixteen minutes long, and they used bits of all the scores. When the movie was released, it was a flop, making only $18 million. It cost $57 million to make.

We had spent five years at the Teatro, and I found it the most musical and creative installation to date. It spawned a lot of great records. Brian Blade's first jazz record, *Brian Blade Fellowship*, was recorded there when he got his first deal with Blue Note Records. I spent a week recording it and then we had a party on the last day and invited an audience to watch Brian perform the album live. It was interesting that most of the record came from that last night's performance.

Brian had also come through to overdub a couple of things for his second record, *Perceptual*. He asked Joni Mitchell to come in to record a vocal on a song called "Steadfast." I also mixed a song with Canadian crooner k.d. lang for the movie *Anywhere but Here*. The movie featured Natalie Portman and Susan Sarandon. k.d. was there with me when I mixed the song.

The bathroom at the Teatro was unusual, with a mosaic floor with a beautiful pattern on it that my wife had done, and the walls were a collage of women I had pulled out of fashion magazines. There was a claw-foot bathtub and camera set up that you could take bathroom portraits with. k.d. returned from the bathroom and said, "That was quite interesting. A little pretentious don't you think, the fashion wall, eh?"

"I see you like it," I replied.

Later that night, k.d.'s girlfriend, actress Leisha Hailey, came to hang out. Leisha went to the bathroom, and I quickly turned around to k.d. and said, "A little pretentious, don't you think?" We both laughed.

I had a few friends come and stay at the Teatro to work as janitors. Tim Gibbons, a friend from Canada, stayed with us and became one of the first janitors. Tim would be alone all night long. I had put a set of metal scissor gates across the front of the studio to stop the homeless from sleeping in the entrance and to stop people from knocking on the door and disturbing the sessions. But before I installed the gates, Tim was playing pool one night when a Mexican guy smashed the diamond window in the front door, put his arm through, and tried to open the door. Tim whacked the guy's arm with the pool cue, and the guy screamed and ran away.

On another night, I got a phone call from Tim telling me to get over there right away. He'd been in the bathroom sitting on the toilet when he'd heard a huge explosion. Thinking it was an earthquake, he flung open the bathroom door to run out and found a car parked in the pool room. A couple of drunk guys had driven off the boulevard, through the gates and the front doors, and landed in the pool room. Tim couldn't believe his eyes — the guys were bleeding, but when they spotted Tim, they put the car in reverse, backed out, and somehow got away.

When I got there, the front doors were down, the gate was mangled, and it looked like a bomb had gone off. Miraculously, the pool table was fine and just pushed into the wall. I called a board-up company and they put plywood on the front doors.

My friend Vudi, the guitar player from the band American Music Club, also did some time as the janitor, and so did Philip Brouchard.

My deal with Dan was that we each had a six-month working period. He had six months to work on his projects and so did I. That's how I could afford to pay the bills. The last year at the Teatro, Dan had taken up most of the year, with Willie Nelson, U2, and the *All the Pretty Horses* film score. The electric bill for a studio wasn't cheap, and I asked Daniel if he could help me out by paying the rent and some of the bills I couldn't afford. He refused.

I was stunned.

"How am I going to pay the rent?" I asked.

"I am sure you will figure it out," he said. "Sell one of your bikes. Maybe being a studio manager isn't for you. You don't have to do this anymore. You can just go work in normal studios, like the others."

"Well then, I'm out. I can't pay the rent, so we are done at the end of the month."

A couple of grand would have kept the studio going, and he had millions in the bank, so I pulled the plug. Although it was a bit scary at the time, I felt it was time to stand up for myself and move on. I didn't work with him again for a decade.

CHAPTER 22

THE PARAMOUR STUDIO

WHEN THE TEATRO CLOSED, I BOUGHT A house in Silver Lake near the city reservoir, in the central region of Los Angeles. Silver Lake is well known for its restaurants and clubs, and many notable people have made their homes there. I was riding around my neighborhood one day on my brand-new Harley-Davidson, going up to a high point at the top of Silver Lake, when I came upon a huge set of gates at 1923 Micheltorena Street. It was the Paramour Estate.

In the spring of 2000, I actually rode through those gates and had a meeting with Dana Hollister, the owner, to see the property. The very next day I worked out a deal to start a studio there. The vibe and feeling of the property was right. The mansion was twenty-two thousand square feet, Mediterranean revival–style architecture, and sitting on four and a half acres, with a 360-degree view of Los Angeles. I could see the Hollywood sign and the Griffith Observatory and even the ocean on a clear day. It had well-manicured gardens and a marble, Olympic-sized pool. The mansion was U-shaped, a wing on each side of the pool and the main ballroom in the center. The ballroom had gleaming wooden floors and a three-story-high ceiling, and it had been acoustically designed for opera singers. During the 1920s, well-to-do people had opera singers come to their mansions to sing for them, and the Paramour was no exception. The ceiling had ornate cloth over cantilevered wood in between the wooden beams to trap the sound and stop echoes. Two huge chandeliers hung from the ceiling, a large marble fireplace graced the wall, and a huge window overlooked the back lawn.

There was a library off the main room that had its own set of carved wooden doors and wood-paneled walls within. The main dining room held a fifteen-foot table with two chandeliers above it. The room also had a marble fireplace and a wall-sized oil painting of winged angels crying blood as they flew over people burning in pools of hot lava in hell. The main entrance off the oval driveway had a long marble hallway that ended at a large angel statue, which I found to be a bit creepy, and I waited for the day that it would cry blood like the angels in the oil painting.

Off the dining room was the breakfast room, one of my favorite rooms in the house because it felt like a little tree house with its view of the pine trees. The main kitchen was industrial, with a huge Wolf stove and three large refrigerators. My favorite room was the pool room at the end of the mansion. French doors opened to the huge outdoor pool and a spectacular view of downtown Los Angeles.

There were four bedrooms in each wing of the house, each decorated with ornate oriental furnishings. On one side of the mansion, upstairs, were the two main bedrooms with a hallway between them leading to a single bedroom. It was intended that the woman of the house would have her own room, the man his own room, and that they would meet in the room between each of theirs for lovemaking. There were a couple of other little cottages on the property as well as a horse stable that had been converted into an apartment.

Once settled, it felt like a dream that I could have a studio in a magnificent mansion overlooking L.A. I set up the studio, and the first record made was with a band from Texas called Deadman, an old-school southern rock band melded with some country. Eventually, I turned the entire mansion into one big music scene, with three albums going on at the same time.

I invited my friend Pierre Marchand to move into the pool-room suite to produce Sarah McLachlan's new record. Fiona Apple was put in the other wing working with producer Jon Brion. I was in the main ballroom producing Lucinda Williams. It was like girls' camp. The amazing thing was that it was still private for everyone, as we all worked different hours. Sarah and Pierre would only work mornings until noon, and I would work from noon until midnight. Fiona would wake up at midnight and work through the night until seven in the morning.

My studio installation at the Paramour Estate was in the grand ballroom and was opulent compared to the Teatro. I created the feeling of a lush Bohemian palace. I had huge Indian rugs covering the wooden floors, mohair chairs and couches, and a large Moroccan tin-tray coffee table in the center, all placed behind a state-of-the-art Amek Neve Media 5.1 sixty-four input surround-sound console. Huge sheepskins and pillows were piled in front of the fireplace. I hung long Moroccan kilim runners on the walls on each side of the fireplace. The rich colors of the rugs and exotic pillows balanced the cold feeling of all the recording gear. It can be intimidating for a lot of artists to walk into a studio and see all the gear, and I think it's an art to place the gear in such a way that it doesn't intimidate or distract people, and that decadent, comfortable surroundings feed creativity.

The speaker system was the biggest system I had ever used in studio. The system had stereo twenty-four-inch Hartley subwoofers that could practically shake the house, beside an eighteen-inch sub and the Westlake BBSM twin 12s.

Inside the Paramour studio (2002).

The wall of sound had a punchy bottom end. The twenty-four-inch subs would deliver a subsonic sound that could make your teeth rattle and the eighteen-inch subs were the punch. The Westlakes provided a sweet high frequency and crystal-clear vocal range.

I had a Neve BCM 10 side console with 1066 modules in it, and on the other side I had racks of effects from Eventide H3000s to Lexicon PCM 70s (the same as Pink Floyd had used to store the circular delay on songs like "Shine On You Crazy Diamond") and racks of Teletronix LA-2A tube compressors. I recorded onto a Studer A80 mk2 24-track tape recorder, also with an iZ Radar 24-track digital recorder. I set this up in the shape of a horseshoe so I could easily plug stuff in behind the gear.

I normally set the band up behind the gear and couches. I had two different drum sets up at all times, and I could pick which sound I thought worked best for each song. I had a beautiful Gretsch Broadkaster five-piece kit, an iconic American drum set, with a twenty-four-inch kick drum that had a tight punch to it. Then I had my 1970s blue Pearl kit with double heads, and it had a big open sound like John Bonham's from Led Zeppelin.

As I had in the past, I set up the band in a circle so everyone could see each other. I work differently than many people and choose to isolate the players' amps and not the players themselves because you get drastically different performances out of musicians when they're in the same room. There is nothing more uncomfortable than being sequestered in a cold, glass box — and it never sounds very good.

The cool thing about working this way is the room you record in is the same room you listen back in, and it always sounds either the same or better. The sound's impressive when you have a speaker system like I was using. The biggest problem I've had working in traditional studios with control rooms is that everything sounds great on the studio floor, but in the control room it's completely different and often doesn't sound as good. I think spending hundreds of thousands of dollars to build a room that has no reflections and is flat sounding is a bit of a joke. I've spent my life recording in almost every imaginable space and always get the best results when I put the recording equipment *in* the studio. Any time I do record in a traditional studio, I end up with the band in the control room, even the drums.

Each musician had their own headphone station on a table with a cool vintage lamp. I was using old Pioneer and Marantz solid-state receivers from the '60s. The musicians' headphone amps sounded incredible and so hi-fi. It blows my mind that big studios spend millions of dollars on all that gear and then they give the musician the worst-sounding headphone boxes. I always thought it important to pay attention to those details.

CHAPTER 23

LUCINDA WILLIAMS

I WAS CONNECTED TO LUCINDA WILLIAMS, THE Grammy-winning country singer, through Gary Briggs, her manager at the time. Gary thought of me as a producer because Lucinda loved Bob Dylan's *Time Out of Mind* album.

Lucinda and Gary came to visit me at the Paramour in the summer of 2002, and Lucinda played me some new songs that had been recorded during sound checks. She'd written some great songs and was looking forward to using her road band to make the album. The drummer, Jim Christie, and the bass player, Taras Prodaniuk, had once been in Dwight Yoakam's band, but she'd stolen them. Her new guitar player was Doug Pettibone, who had just left Jewel's band. Lucinda's rule for making the album was that only her band would play on it, and no one else, in order to keep it raw.

We began recording in early September. Lucinda was living in Burbank at the Safari Inn, and she liked that someone came in to clean her room every day. The feeling of being on the road was comfortable for her. Lucinda wanted to start at 4:00 p.m. each day because she wanted to maintain her normal schedule of sleeping late and going to the gym. This was wishful thinking, and she never got to the studio at that time.

Initially, Lucinda was a little freaked out about recording at the Paramour because she felt like there was witchcraft or voodoo going on. Granted, the place felt like a haunted house, but it was what she saw upstairs in glass cases that frightened her. Dana, the homeowner, collected bizarre things and displayed them in the upstairs hall. A child's antique prosthetic limbs, old dolls with cracked clay faces and real hair, stuffed two-headed turtles, a human skull next to a rat skull, jars with organs, and vintage medical vaginal speculums were all lovingly displayed. I called Lucinda to reassure her that there wasn't anything weird going on, that the objects were left over from a photo shoot and I would have them removed for her, which I did. She felt much better.

I hired a caterer, and they came in at 2:00 p.m. to set up for a light lunch, and then came back at 6:00 p.m. for dinner at 7:00 p.m. Lucinda wanted only healthy, clean food, nothing too rich.

I asked the band to come in around one o'clock each day so I could work on the arrangement of the songs as well as the sounds. Doug came at noon so he could swim some laps in the pool before starting. Jim lived in Ventura and would sometimes ride his motorcycle down. Taras ran a vintage shop in Burbank, so he was the closest and yet was always late. I would work with Doug on his guitar sound and turned him onto some smaller amps for better tones. I had a 1950s Fender Tweed deluxe and a 1960 Supro amp just like the one Jimmy Page used on *Led Zeppelin I*. Doug had a good selection of pedals. Once I felt like we had a good starting spot, I'd work out a great intro, then tweak the arrangement, and by the time Lucinda walked in we could focus on getting a great vocal take out of her.

Lucinda never made it to the studio at the time agreed upon, and it was typically six or six thirty by the time she'd roll in. She was usually frazzled when she arrived, and the first thing she'd need when she came through the door was a hot coffee, which she would drink on the side couch. A couple of glasses of Grand Marnier cognac would follow before I could lead her to the chair where she would sit and record. It always seemed she'd try to find any excuse not to start, and often by the time I'd finally get her going, the caterer was ready for us to eat. We'd record three takes of a song, then we'd go have dinner.

Meals were served in the dining room around the huge table, and it was always a beautiful spread. During dinner, the wine glasses overflowed. Lucinda, or Lu as we called her, only liked a wine called BV Cabernet Sauvignon. Dinners were always a lot of fun with great stories and lots of laughs, as Lu would pass the BV, and by the time dinner was over, everyone would be smashed. We would

Lucinda Williams session. © ELIZA BADALAMENTI

head into the studio and listen to the three takes recorded before dinner. They were always really great, but inevitably it would be the first or second take that had captured the magic. Lucinda's vocals were outstanding. I would say, "Great, everyone! We got a take." Lu would hate it and say that it would be much better if she could redo it.

On the Friday after our first week of recording, I said that it would be nice if everyone invited friends over and we could have a little playback party of the week's work. Lu invited a bunch of her friends and we had ten to fifteen people there. It was nice to see other people's reactions. Her friends would tell her how great she sounded, that they'd never heard her sound so good, but Lu would merely say, "Well, they're not even the finished vocals." Her friends would argue that the vocals were too good to change.

It was a bit of a blessing that Lucinda was dating Mike Stinson, who was a great drummer and was becoming a good singer-songwriter. Once we were done at night, Lu would run out to go have a drink with Mike. Some days, Lu would show up crying and upset, and she would sit on the couch and say, "I feel fat and ugly." I'd assure her she was beautiful and that she wasn't fat.

"Look at Dougie's stomach!" I'd joke. "That's fat!"

Lucinda would laugh at those jokes. Breaking her out of her funk was a challenge every day. One day, she drove through the main gates in her brand-new Ford pickup. She stopped to look in her purse and the gates began to close. When she noticed, she floored it, but the gates left a scratch the entire length of her new truck. She came into the house bawling. It took two glasses of cognac before she could say what had happened. I calmed her down and told her that they were only scratches and we'd get it fixed.

"Really?" she asked, surprised.

"Yes, it's going to be fine," I told her.

I got Lu into her chair to record and that was the day we cut "Righteously." As it turned out, she was so upset she had the right attitude for that vocal take and she killed it. I was initially worried about the song "Righteously" because it was all verses and no chorus. I thought the song really needed something, and when we worked on it, I pushed Doug to come up with a sound. He had one pedal, a custom hand-painted pedal called Fuzz Factory that he'd bought but had never used; I was really familiar with it, as I'd been using it on another record. It had a real demented overdrive sound that I thought would be perfect for the instrumental parts between the verses, and while we were rehearsing, I recorded it. Doug played a riff one time on a rehearsal take and once I heard it, I knew that was the hook we would use. I played it back for Doug. He learned it, and that became the riff of the song.

The record had some really beautiful songs like "Fruits of My Labor" and "Ventura." The songs "Those Three Days" and "Minneapolis" were about an affair that she'd had with Ryan Adams. It hadn't ended well when Ryan locked himself in the bathroom and jumped out the window to escape. Lu was left at the bathroom door crying, "Let me in! I know you're in there."

Every Friday the parties grew bigger, and it turned into a cool little scene. Everyone was so quiet during the playback of the week's work that it reminded me of being a kid sitting around with your friends listening to a whole record. It really was great, and everyone would clap after every song. Slowly, Lu's confidence in her vocals grew as people assured her that the album was amazing. This was all new for Lu, and she was notorious for firing every producer and for being very difficult in the studio. I was just lucky to find a pattern that worked for her.

Toward the end of the record, Lu said to me, "Maybe we need some keyboards on a couple of songs."

One afternoon, I invited over Aaron Embry, a local keyboard player, to try out what the songs would sound like with piano. As I was finishing, Taras walked in and saw Aaron playing on one of the tracks. Taras had been pushing to produce this record, but they had hired me. I caught wind that he had called Lu and ratted me out, telling her that "Howard had a guy in to play keyboards."

When Lu showed up that day, I could see she was mad, so I said, "Oh, Lu . . . I had a guy in today to try some piano on the record like you said, but you know what? It just doesn't work and we really need to keep this as just the band and not have anyone else play on it."

With a big grin, she said, "I am so happy to hear that. I was so upset that you had someone in."

"If we really want keyboards on anything, Jim can play it because he's really great."

I could see Taras squinting at me because his plan to drive a wedge between me and Lucinda hadn't worked. I just gave him an evil smile.

All of the vocals on the record were live off the floor. The album was cut in fourteen days, and then I mixed it. Some of my earlier playback mixes were spot on, so I used them and others just needed some touch-ups.

At the final party, I played all thirteen songs from the album, and you could hear a pin drop, it was so silent. The house was finally being used for what it was built for — beautiful parties and amazing music. Word had gotten out that it was a cool thing to be invited to. Dwight Yoakam showed up and loved the song "People Talkin'" so much that he later covered it.

Once we were completely finished, we met at Lu's hotel to listen to the record. Everyone loved it except Taras. He said his bass wasn't loud enough and that it all needed to be remixed. Lu said, "Shut up, Taras. It's fine. Everyone loves it and it's done."

I mastered the record with Joe Gastwirt. Joe and I were good buddies after all the time we'd spent on the Dylan record. Joe knew that Lucinda was difficult, so I asked him to make two masters — one done his way and one that was quieter. It needed to be Lucinda's decision, so with the two masters she had a choice. I knew she would pick the one Joe did, but if I only gave her that one, she'd pick it apart. If she heard Joe's version alongside another version, she'd see it was better and it would be easy to get her approval.

I later read in an interview that she still did not know how I pulled it off.

The Paramour hosted a lot of parties and benefits while I was there. *Vanity Fair* had their annual Oscar party there, and the Hollywood Sunset Free Clinic benefit was held on the grounds, on the back lawn. Elton John played a solo piano set and the Red Hot Chili Peppers played, too, along with a host of other artists. I also held a couple of my own parties there to make people aware that the studio was available to the public, hoping to keep it booked all of the time and make it a full-time operation. Robbie Robertson, Sheryl Crow, and Brad Pitt were all guests, and Fiona Apple played a live set. Fiona Apple moved into my studio one Christmas while I was away in France with my family. She was working on her third studio album, *Extraordinary Machine*, with Jon Brion. Once she was done with recording in my studio, they flew to London to Abbey Road Studios to record with the London orchestra. It was cheaper to fly to London and work at Abbey Road than it would have been to record it in L.A. with an orchestra. Fiona didn't like the outcome and abandoned most of the record.

In late April 2002 I produced a record for a Canadian Juno winner, Colin James. He came down from Vancouver and stayed at the Paramour. Back when Colin was just starting out, he had been picked up by Stevie Ray Vaughn to open his shows on the American leg of Stevie's tour. Although Colin was a good writer, he was desperate for a hit single but didn't have that hit machine in him, so I suggested he write with Jeff Trott. Jeff cowrote a bunch of hits for Sheryl Crow. Colin ended up writing two songs with Jeff.

Colin was still shy two songs for the record, so I recommended he cover a couple of songs. While grocery shopping in Hollywood, I heard "I'm Losing You" by John Lennon over the store PA, and I called Colin from the store and told him I thought he should record it. He wasn't sure about it and thought it might be out of his league. We ended up cutting it using double drummers. Amazingly enough, it turned out to be his big summer hit single, and you could hear it playing on Q107 in Toronto every hour on the hour. We also covered Hendrix's "Rainy Day, Dream Away" and Nick Drake's "Black Eyed Dog." Colin had never heard of Nick Drake before and laughed at the idea of covering one of his songs but quickly changed his mind once we cut it because it was undeniably a haunting version.

I brought in Daryl Johnson to play bass for Colin's album. Daryl and I had a long history dating back to the Neville Brothers' *Yellow Moon* album. Daryl has a five-octave vocal range and could play his ass off on any instrument. On tour Daryl would play bass pedals with his feet while playing a hand drum between his knees and singing a high falsetto harmony. He could play any song you could name on the piano and was the entertainer at every hotel we stayed at that had a piano. Colin was a perfectionist and would argue over hearing things out of tune. He wanted to tune Daryl's background vocals on one song. I said, "They are perfect and, if anything, it's your vocal that's a little pitchy."

Colin swore up and down that Daryl was flat. I told him that Daryl didn't sing flat.

"Okay, I am going to lie down on the couch and smoke some hash while you tune his vocals," I said.

It took him three hours to tune them and he told me to fly them into the track. I played the track back for him and he said, "See how much better it is?"

Then I noticed that I had played the wrong background vocals. I had played him the untuned ones. "You're right," I said. "Great job tuning them. They're perfect."

I left it at that and used the untuned background vocals, because I realized it was just in Colin's head. Once the record was done, we had a listening party at the Paramour on the final night. Colin was friends with the guys from a well-known Canadian sketch comedy show called *The Kids in the Hall*. Two of the comedians, Dave Foley and Kevin McDonald, came over. I realized they were even funnier in person, like so many comedians are.

My wife was pregnant with our second child during the making of this record, and it was on the day after we wrapped up, May 10, 2002, that my daughter Fiana was born. Both my kids had waited until I finished my records to be born.

CHAPTER 24

SHERYL CROW, EDDIE VEDDER, AND THE WAIFS AT THE PARAMOUR

JEFF TROTT, THE SONGWRITER WHO COLLABORATED WITH Sheryl Crow on "If It Makes You Happy," received a call from her asking if he'd produce a couple of tracks for her new record. He wanted to bring Sheryl to the Paramour and called to see if I would record the sessions. Sheryl had made her second record, *Sheryl Crow*, at Kingsway Studio, so she would feel at home at the Paramour. An all-star cast of musicians were enlisted: Abe Laboriel Jr., who had worked with Paul McCartney and Sting, on drums; Mike Elizondo, who'd worked with Eminem and Jay-Z, on bass; and Larry Campbell, who had worked with Bob Dylan and Paul Simon, on guitar. Jeff Trott also played guitar.

Sheryl was like one of the guys, telling everyone stories. She said Dylan had once called her off her bus to talk to her at a festival. She said it was raining and he was wearing a hoodie. They walked around in the rain and he told her that he really liked her songs, and maybe they could record a track together one day.

Sheryl was dating cyclist Lance Armstrong at the time, and although we were only recording for one day in total, she would stop the session in order to talk to him on the phone. Everything really sounded great, and I was a little surprised that none of the tracks made the record. I noticed that the tracks that Jeff produced were not used and he was only credited for coproducing two other tracks.

Shortly afterward, I was asked to produce a track for Eddie Vedder, the powerful singer best known for his band Pearl Jam. A new film called *I Am Sam*, starring Sean Penn and Michelle Pfeiffer, was being made, and Eddie was to do a song. At one of my parties at the Paramour, I had met world champion surfer Kelly Slater. He was good friends with Eddie, surf buddies I think, and told me he wanted to hook me up with Eddie one day. He thought Eddie would love the Paramour. Shortly afterward, we began recording a cover of the Beatles' song "You've Got to Hide Your Love Away."

Eddie was to be at the studio at noon to begin recording. He was surfing that morning at the break just south of the airport and was over an hour late when I got a call from him saying he was at the hospital and that he had cut off his big toe on the sharp rocks. I told him not to worry, that we could do the song some other time.

"No, man, I'm coming in as soon as they sew it back on," he said.

Sure enough, a few hours later Eddie, his toe in a big bandage, hobbled through the doors with Kelly Slater. I couldn't believe what a trooper he was.

"Well," he said, "the show must go on."

Eddie told Kelly to come back and pick him up once we were finished.

I knew that Eddie had worked with Nusrat Fateh Ali Khan on *Dead Man Walking*, a film starring Sean Penn and Susan Sarandon. With an amazing vocal ability he could sustain for hours, Nusrat was thought to be one of the greatest voices ever recorded. I told Eddie that I had also worked with Nusrat, and I considered myself lucky to have worked with such a master. Eddie completely agreed and said that working with Nusrat had changed his life and that he'd never had an experience like it.

The recording went pretty quickly. Eddie laid down the guitar and vocal, then I overdubbed him playing a tambourine and then a little brushes part on a snare drum. He had brought a harmonica with him, and I got him to put it on the end of the track. I mixed it and we were finished.

"What do you think about cutting a record here with your band?" I asked.

He shook his head. "It's too nice here. We need something dark and gloomy, something slightly uncomfortable, to get it out of us. We would all be too distracted here at the pool, with surfing, and too close to the city . . . People would go missing."

"Yes, I've seen that before," I said.

As we were sitting around waiting for Kelly to come back, Eddie asked if I wanted to hear a couple of tracks he had cut in Hawaii. He told me he was doing a ukulele record. *Oh, man — ukulele, is it going to be like Don Ho?* I wondered. I wasn't that hip to the ukulele at that point. Eddie played me the tracks, and I was really floored. He had a killer sound going on, and there was nothing remotely Hawaiian about it. It was pretty raw — just Eddie singing and playing the ukulele, and it had a cool vibe.

Kelly showed up and I took them both down to the best fish taco place in Silver Lake, on Sunset Boulevard in L.A. The place itself was just a little shack with seven picnic tables outside; it wasn't the best looking, but I loved the food. Because they were surfers, I thought they might think my restaurant in the city was crap, but they both were really impressed and said they hadn't thought they could get a good taco in Silver Lake.

I made a number of records with bands passing through L.A. One was a band called the Waifs, which was comprised of two skinny sisters, Vikki and Donna, from Albany, Western Australia. They got their name from their grandmother, who always referred to them as "the waifs." They showed up at the Paramour for a four-day session to record their album *Up All Night*. They were on tour, crossing America in a little VW bus with the three boys in the band.

It felt like a drug deal with them because they paid me out of a sock full of money, counting it out on the floor. Vikki and Donna split the songwriting duties, each one writing their own songs. They had worked out the songs on the road and were ready to put them down once they reached the studio. There really was no production on the songs — just a straight-up record where they picked the best take. My experience has been that some Australians can be indecisive, overthinking everything and not able to make up their minds. For me, these decisions are pretty cut and dried. The best take is obvious, so we choose it and move on. I could tell the band had been on tour for a while because everyone was a little grumpy and short tempered with each other.

Donna was the younger sister, yet taller. Vikki was the older sister and ran the show. Both had a carefree streak. Vikki swam nude every day and would walk back into the studio nude, like it was totally natural — she was that comfortable in her own skin. It wasn't shocking to me because as a child my parents took us to a nude swimming hole called Clearwater Abbey, in Ontario, Canada. The place was run by a hippie called Wally Tucker, who ran the Church of the Universe. It was an old lime quarry that had crystal-clear emerald-green water. Because of this exposure, nudism didn't bother me in the slightest.

I spent four days recording with the Waifs, then they left to go back out on tour. I never thought much about it at the time — it was just a sweet little record. The record went on to be nominated in Australia for four APRA awards, Australia's version of the Grammys. It ended up winning two awards, including Best Engineered Record.

After that, I was contacted by Peter Jesperson, the A&R guy at New West Records, who had loved the Lucinda Williams record. He'd been looking after an artist named Vic Chesnutt for many years, and he was looking for someone to make Vic's next record. Injuries sustained in a 1983 car accident had left Vic partially paralyzed; he used a wheelchair and had limited use of his hands. I knew of him from seeing him in the movie *Sling Blade*. Vic was quirky but one of the great American singer-songwriters. He could write from points of view most people never considered, like how lonely a single grain of salt must feel sitting on a table.

Peter asked me to produce the record. I had never met Vic until the day he showed up at the Paramour. He was joined by his wife, and they stayed in the downstairs pool suite. Peter said that Vic hadn't wanted to come to L.A. and almost backed out the day before starting out. Once he arrived, we really hit it off, and we laughed like we had known each other our whole lives.

I assembled a great band for him that included Daryl Johnson on bass, Doug Pettibone on guitar, and Mike Stinson on drums. Being surrounded by great players made Vic really shine. Doug was an outstanding guitar player, and I think that made Vic push the limits of his own abilities, and he took some of the solos on songs.

Vic had thousands of stories from the road, and he'd have everyone cracking up. He said that one time at a gig he needed to take a shit but his wheelchair wouldn't fit in the stall so he just backed up to a urinal. Some guy walked in and just stopped and stared at him. He told Vic he'd enjoyed the show and was a big fan.

Vic said to the guy, "Come on, can't you give a guy a break? Leave me alone."

As funny as Vic was, there was a deeper, emotional side to him as well. Vic had tried to commit suicide a couple of times. He was once on tour by himself in New York and decided on the freeway he couldn't go on. He pulled the van over and opened the side door, planning to hang himself on it. He fell and got caught hanging outside the door, dangling like a puppet, with his wheelchair out of reach. The police finally found him and took him to a homeless shelter, and he said he spent a week there trying to get out.

Sadly, on December 25, 2009, at the age of forty-five, Chesnutt died from an overdose of muscle relaxants, which had already left him in a coma in an Athens, Georgia, hospital. I was shattered to hear of his death. It's a privilege to be able to help artists create a legacy of music before they leave this world.

CHAPTER 25

TOM WAITS

IN JANUARY 2002, ANDY KAULKIN, THE HEAD of Anti- records, called me. He was a big fan of the Lucinda Williams album, and he'd pitched my name to Tom Waits for his next record. I was thrilled: I was a big fan of Tom's *Bone Machine* album.

Andy wasn't sure when Tom wanted to start but said that Tom would call me. A year passed and I assumed they must have recorded with someone else. Then in February 2003, Tom finally called.

"Hey, Mark," he said in his low, gravelly voice. "I was wondering if you would be available to make my next record."

I agreed right away.

"I understand that you produce a lot of records," he continued. "I have the producing part covered by my wife, Kathleen, and me. Would it be possible for you to separate the production and the engineering part, then record and mix my record?"

I told him I actually did that a lot. I also told him where I was working — at the Paramour — and that we could record there if he liked. Tom said that although it sounded great, he liked to work close to home so he was with family. The studio that was closest to his home was more than two hours away, and it would be a battle going back and forth every day. I suggested I do a studio installation somewhere nearer.

"Hmm . . . now that could be interesting," he said.

He told me about an old schoolhouse that people rented for events. I flew to Oakland, rented a car, and drove up to a little town called Valley Ford, just north of San Francisco. It was about a twenty-minute drive past Petaluma, a short drive past Bodega Bay, where Alfred Hitchcock had filmed his 1963 horror film *The Birds*. What a creepy little fishing village Bodega Bay was: driving in I felt a chill in the air; it was windy and disturbing because the birds really do swarm there.

Tom was to meet me there at 2:00 p.m. There was just a little general store with a wooden porch, and I imagined Tom showing up in a rusted-out '50s pickup. Cars came and went, but not Tom. I was sitting on the wooden bench in front of the general store when a woman driving a black Audi with tinted windows pulled up. The car sat there for a good fifteen minutes before the woman got out and walked over to the store. Just as she entered the building, she looked over at me and asked, "You're not Mark, are you?"

I told her I was, but she continued into the store, which I thought strange. When she came back out, she said, "Tom said he wanted to talk to you."

I explained that I had been waiting for him for an hour but he hadn't shown up. She told me to come over to the car, so I walked over with her. She opened the back door and there he was. I hadn't been able to see him because of the blackened windows.

Tom Waits climbed out, dressed entirely in denim — what we in Canada call "the Canadian tuxedo."

"Hey, Mark, it's me, Tom. Sorry I'm late, I was working on a 'preparation.'"

I didn't know what that meant but told him it was fine.

We drove around the corner to the schoolhouse, a long wooden building with steps that led up to a set of double doors. There was a big old barn beside it, and a big dirt parking lot in front. We walked in and the schoolhouse was still intact, complete with chalkboards and alphabet cards hanging above them. It was just one big classroom, with girls' and boys' bathrooms. With the wooden flooring and fluorescent lighting, it was all a bit stark, although it did have windows along the front and the possibility of good natural light.

I'd brought a few pieces of test gear like always: a voltage meter and a little cassette blaster that I hooked up to an acoustic guitar pickup to check the magnetic field. The voltage was 220 and the magnetic field was near perfect. Tom asked if I thought it would work, and I said I did. It was exactly the same size as the grand ballroom at the Paramour. He said he'd talk to the custodian and see if he could rent it for a couple of months.

Tom wanted to play me some songs he'd been working on but had no way to play them because they were on a Tascam 4-track cassette machine. I suggested he come to L.A. for a day so we could listen to the songs, and I told him that I would be able to mix them down so he could listen to them on a CD in his car.

He was enthusiastic. "Wow! That's what I need."

Tom and his wife, Kathleen Brennan, came to L.A. to work with me at the Paramour in March 2003. I walked them around the property and they couldn't believe how beautiful it was. Tom pulled out his 4-track cassette recorder and I plugged it in. The songs were recordings that he had done in the bathroom of his house, late at night while everyone was sleeping. They sounded so animalistic — he had grunted into the mic and although it was distorted, the recording featured a nice overdrive. He had done beats with his mouth and then overdubbed pots and pans on top of them, *boom chic clang*. It was so bizarre, but it was also great.

"When we make the record, we will re-record it to get a bigger sound," I said.

I mixed it all down so he had a reference, but they were mainly ideas for rhythm tracks, with no lyrics.

Tom had worked out a deal to work at the schoolhouse and we planned to start in April. He only wanted to work weekdays. I packed up all the studio gear and all the rugs and couches and loaded them into a twenty-four-foot U-Haul. I also took a Harley with me — a little 883 Sportster — so I would have a way to get around. The truck was packed to the gills, with the Sportster stuffed in the back, so the door just closed. I left the Paramour at 5:00 am to beat traffic. It took a lot longer to get to Valley Ford because the truck would only go 55 miles per hour and because going through the Grapevine, a forty-mile stretch of the Golden State Freeway, was incredibly slow. There is a gradual climb to the road and it's famous for causing cars to overheat or blow head gaskets. I arrived in the early evening, and Tom and his kids were there to help me unload the truck. I backed it up to the front entrance of the schoolhouse and pulled out the ramp. It only took an hour to unload everything. Tom said that we could start bringing over some of his instruments the next day.

Tom and Kathleen had booked me into a bed and breakfast just up the street, a musty old Victorian house. My room felt like it belonged in a dollhouse, with lots of frilly curtains and old wooden wardrobes. There was no TV or internet, and the bathroom was up the hall. Being totally exhausted from the drive, I crashed right away, but I woke up at four o'clock in the morning and, being wide awake with nothing to do, headed over to the schoolhouse to start the installation.

I had brought a Moroccan tent with me, which I set up over the control-room area and hung the walls of the tent over the front windows so no one could see inside. It was purple silk, and combined with the rugs, it felt like being in a Moroccan palace. I had everything all set up by nine that morning, so I went back to the bed and breakfast to eat.

Tom arrived at the schoolhouse at noon. "Wow! I would have never imagined it to be this cool," he exclaimed from the doorway. He called Kathleen and told her she needed to come over so he could show her.

Later on, Tom said we needed to go to his house and pick up his gear while we had the big truck. There were green rolling hills where he lived, and it felt a little like being in Ireland. We arrived at a little treed area and then carried on down a winding road that led to a set of gates. They were like a metal sculpture with gardening tools welded to them — old shovels, garden scissors, and a pitchfork. Once the gates opened, we drove down the lane to the house, which looked like a modern barn that had been converted into a house. There was a swimming pool that looked like a lagoon and a trampoline with cargo netting around it. The outside area was like an army training camp, with ropes hanging from the trees, more cargo netting for climbing, and old tire tubes stacked to climb through — it was definitely a kid's paradise.

We went into Tom's storage locker, which was bigger than a garage and looked like a half-finished studio. It was packed to the ceiling with all kinds of exotic instruments: old pianos, a steam calliope, a wooden marimba, kalimbas, and a double-key Chamberlin. I was floored by the incredible things he had, and on the walls were black-and-white photos of him and Keith Richards. Tom said that Keith and James Brown were his heroes. We loaded the truck with all kinds of musical toys and went back to the schoolhouse to unload.

Tom had assembled musicians to come in and record with him, including Bryan Mantia, the drummer from Primus, whose real name had been misspelled at some point in his career, so he was now known as Brain. He brought in an Akai MPC sampler that he'd had someone do a custom paint job on. It was on the same level as the paint jobs on the Chicano lowrider cars that bounce up and down.

Larry Taylor was the bass player, and he played upright bass. He'd done other records with Tom and they had a good relationship. Marc Ribot had been working with Tom as far back as 1985's *Rain Dogs*, Tom's eighth album. Ribot was also the guitar player from the Lounge Lizards and had recorded countless records. His eclectic sound suited Tom's music, but this would be the very first time they tracked a record together. Every other time they'd worked together, Ribot was brought in after the initial recoding and overdubbed.

Les Claypool, the bass player from Primus, would come in later and put down tracks once Larry left. Tom's son Casey would play drums on a couple of songs and do some DJ record scratching. Tom asked Casey to go into San Francisco to pick up some vinyl and gave him 200 dollars. Casey came back from San Francisco with the vinyl and Tom heard him pull in, so he opened the door.

I heard Tom yell, "Oh no!"

I ran to see what had happened. Casey had put the vinyl in the back window of the car and it had warped in the sun; it was all ruined.

"I guess that's something we take for granted," Tom said. "We know about these things but they don't get passed on down, so he wouldn't have known. We grew up with vinyl and it was common knowledge not to leave them in the sun."

Tom had just finished the movie *Coffee and Cigarettes* with Iggy Pop. It was directed by Jim Jarmusch. Jim had apparently gone to Tom and told him that Iggy didn't like Tom's drummers, and then gone to Iggy and said that Tom really didn't like his music, hoping to fire up some controversy and create dramatic tension on the set of the film.

Once we started recording, I got overexcited and suggested a lot of sounds. After the second day, Tom called me at my hotel. I had moved from the bed and breakfast to a larger hotel in a little hippie town called Sebastopol. Tom told me he was feeling like a patient and I was the doctor, that I was trying to prescribe him Zyprexa but he wanted clonazepam.

"Maybe you're right that I need Zyprexa, but let me do the clonazepam for now."

Tracking *Real Gone*: Tom Waits, Marc Ribot, and Les Claypool on bass.

I told him I understood and would cool it — basically keep my mouth shut and let him find his own way.

Tom never spoke in a normal fashion about anything. He had bizarre descriptions for everything. For instance, he couldn't just tell me to turn the vocal up; instead he would say, "Put a little more hair on it."

If we recorded something and got it on the first take, Tom would say, "That one came out of the ground like a potato — done!"

If a song wasn't working, he would say, "It's like a fat kid with a bad haircut."

I recorded a lot of things using a Sony blaster with two speakers in the front. I kept it in the boys' bathroom because that was the most live-sounding room. On the day we recorded the song "Shake It," I set Brain up in the bathroom. He was taping up his snare drum with gaffer tape while I was in the classroom getting the sound up when Tom asked, "What was that?"

LISTEN UP!

I listened and realized he was hearing Brain ripping the gaffer tape.

"That's the sound I want!" Tom said.

"What? The ripping of the tape?"

He nodded. "Yes, it's perfect."

So I went into the bathroom to see Brain, and I told him that he was going to play the gaffer tape.

"How will I do that?" he asked, incredulous.

"Just by ripping it."

Brain used a whole roll of gaffer tape on the song. Once Brain had put down the gaffer tape, he went into the stall to take a piss, but the mic was still on. When he finished, we heard the stall door slam.

"What was that?" Tom asked.

This time I told him it was the stall door slamming.

"I want him to play the door," Tom strangely suggested.

I went back into the bathroom and told Brain that now he had to play the stall door.

I told him to also hit the wall with a two-by-four piece of wood. "So slam the door then hit the wall with the wood as the rhythm."

At the end of the song, the stall door broke off and fell on the floor from being slammed. It was perfect timing.

Tom would show up every day with a cup of coffee, instructing us to not tell Kathleen. She had Tom on a special diet and he wasn't allowed coffee. She also had him going to Pilates. He asked me if I had ever done yoga, and I told him I hadn't.

"I think you should try it and go to a class while you're here."

I did, and I have been practicing yoga on and off ever since.

I tracked three different versions of the song "Circus": one on piano, another using a Portishead loop, and the one that made the record, done on a Chamberlin keyboard. Tom said he'd bought the Chamberlin from two surfers in L.A. He saw it in their garage and bought it right on the spot. The Chamberlin is a keyboard that uses taped samples of real instruments. Tom's had a double keyboard, with orchestral sounds on one side and percussion sounds on the other. I played bell sounds, then slowed them down to make them sound like church bells in the distance. I recorded bacon frying and made it sound like crackles on a record. The song eventually began to sound like something from Rod Serling's *Twilight Zone*.

On weekends, Tom would call me up and say that he wanted to record interesting things, like bees buzzing in a bottle, or ask if we could record crickets and then slow them down so they would sound like an orchestra.

Tom also coached his son's baseball team, and on one occasion he invited me to watch. I showed up at the game to find Tom hammering his fist on the fence yelling, "Go, Sullivan!"

Tom said, "Come next week, I'm running the snack shack."

I went back the next week and sure enough, there was Tom working in the snack shack. I went up and said, "Hey, Tom, get me a hotdog."

He looked flustered. "Hotdog, eh? Hmm . . . I don't know how to do that." He smiled. "Kathleen!" he yelled. "One hotdog!"

One day, Tom shared with me that he and Kathleen had thought they should buy a house when their first child was born, so Tom went to the bank only to find out that he had no money. Tom had signed a bad deal with Island Records and discovered that they owned all of his publishing rights. Tom Waits, a prolific writer whom some call a genius, didn't even own his own songs.

Kathleen really helped Tom turn his life around. At one point, she had had enough of Tom's drinking and, in the middle of the night, threw their kids in the car and left; they didn't even have their shoes because she left so fast. She took the family back to their house in L.A. Tom was in shambles and also went to L.A. He called Kathleen when he arrived. She asked him where he was staying, and he told her down at "the sands."

"The Sands Hotel?" she'd asked.

"No," he admitted, "on the sands down at the beach."

Tom went to a bookstore looking for a book on how to help his marriage and found a book called *How to Leave Your Wife*. He picked it up and took it to the counter. The woman looked at him and said, "This is the book you want? *How to Weave Your Life?*"

He had read the title very differently, thinking it was a book about divorce. He told me he bought the book anyway and that it had a lot of good things in it.

Since Tom was having marriage problems, he went to see a marriage therapist. The therapist suggested that Tom and Kathleen try a thing called mystery dating. Once a week, they were to take each other out on a date but not tell the other person where they were going. Kathleen said that it didn't work because

Tom took her to the hardware store for the mystery date he'd planned. Tom thought it was great because the store had tons of cool stuff, like a thousand different types of nails.

Tom had a great fear of performing. One time while doing a sold-out show in New York, he determined he couldn't go on without a drum that was at Kathleen's mom's house in Brooklyn. It was a marching drum with a painting on the front of the Alps and a lake. Kathleen told him he didn't need it to do the show but Tom insisted. Kathleen didn't know what to do, so she drove all the way to her mother's house, got the drum, and brought it back. The audience waited over an hour and half for Tom to go on. Kathleen returned with the drum and Tom went on, although he didn't even play the drum. It just sat there on the stage, like a security blanket.

When a song needed something, Tom would go around the room trying different instruments. Sometimes nothing satisfied him and he'd return to a huge pea-pod shaker. It was his secret weapon and always worked on any song he decided to use it on. Working in an installation studio with everything in one room was ideal for Waits, because working in a normal studio meant he'd have to run out to the studio floor, try the instrument, record it, then run back into the control room and listen, then keep doing that until something stuck. He said that was exhausting. This time he was as happy as a kid in a candy shop, experimenting with everything within reach.

Initially, I thought the mouth rhythms Tom had done on his 4-track cassette would sound better once we started the record and redid them, but I just couldn't beat the sound he'd achieved, even with all the expensive gear I had. Overloading the preamp in the Tascam gave it a thump like a kick drum, and the low-fi quality was all part of the sound. I ended up using the original recordings and bounced them to the iZ Radar to loop them so we could layer on top. All of the album was recorded on two-inch tape, but once we had the main takes, I bounced them to the iZ Radar to mix.

Tom was always concerned that his voice didn't sound good. I tried several microphones, the Sony C-37A mic amongst others, but it wasn't until I went out and bought a vintage RCA 44 that he liked the sound of his voice. I got the best vocal sound I'd ever had on the song "Green Grass," recorded with the RCA 44. It was big and warm with a huge print. Tom always thought his voice was too low, which made it unclear. He would cup his hands around his mouth, like a megaphone, thinking that if he took all the low off his voice that it would be clearer. I remember playing the track back and I was so proud of what we'd done, but he said it was too clean, that it sounded like a Murray McLauchlan record. Murray was a Canadian singer-songwriter known for making squeaky-clean records. To me, that was a low blow. I had pushed the envelope my entire life trying to stay as far away as possible from anything remotely clean. Tom made me roll off some of the low, but I still managed to keep the velvet sound of his voice.

Tom really pushed me sonically. He made a comment one day that he thought the drums sound a little beige.

"I hate beige!" I said, and I cranked the drums up and made them over-the-top exciting. "Still beige?" I asked.

Toward the end of recording, I took some control, telling Tom that he needed to step back and look at the big picture of the record. Often artists are too close to the project and can't see the obvious.

I mixed everything right there at the schoolhouse, and once finished, I packed up and headed back to L.A. I mastered the record with Gavin Lurssen at the Mastering Lab on Sunset.

The record *Real Gone* was rated four out of five stars by *Rolling Stone* and went to number one on the Billboard Independent Albums chart. Tom was nominated for Best Rock Vocal Solo Performance at the Grammys for the song "Metropolitan Glide."

After pulling out of the Paramour to make Tom's record, I never returned. Instead, I set out on my around-the-world studio installation record productions. I really thought that the Paramour was going to be a huge success, but after four years there and with the music industry slowly crashing, it only really worked for my own productions. Tom Waits's album initiated the change: I was ready to move on.

CHAPTER 26

SAM ROBERTS IN AUSTRALIA

OCCASIONALLY, MY TRACK RECORD OF SUCCESSFUL ALBUMS isn't enough to land me a gig. Sometimes a new artist doesn't know what I've done, isn't familiar with the artists I've worked with, or I've been pitched by a manager or record company to them. That's when it comes down to a meeting with the artist; that's when I've got to sell myself. Meetings backstage after shows are usually the places where I have done these deals.

Sam Roberts is a Canadian singer-songwriter who had some success with his first record. His 2002 debut release, *The Inhuman Condition,* became one of the best-selling independent releases in Canadian music history. Sam was opening for the Tragically Hip when he came through L.A. The first time I met him, it was backstage. The head of Universal Music Canada told him that I was coming to meet him. The show was at the Avalon, a concert venue right in Hollywood. I introduced myself and Sam thanked me for coming out. He felt he hadn't sounded very good on stage but I assured him he had.

I asked him if he had enough songs to make a record and he told me that he just had a couple; he was still in the process of writing. He told me he was planning to start recording in February. I was the fifth person he'd met with about producing his next album. A lot of the producers hadn't really had the same vision that Sam did for this record; they told him that they would learn all his songs so they could understand them and play with him on them.

"I don't want them to play with me," Sam informed me. He explained that he wanted to record someplace where he could surf and be warm. That was my cue. I told him that was exactly how I made records — that I traveled around the world finding cool environments in which to record. I asked him if he had ever been to Australia.

"No, but I've always wanted to surf there," he said.

"Well, that's one of few places on the planet where you can surf in February where they speak English." I got him excited about the possibility.

We talked for a while and he kept coming back to Australia.

"You really think we could find a cool place?" he asked.

I told him I'd talk to Kelly Slater and ask him to suggest a place. Sam was floored that I knew Kelly, a world surfing champion and Sam's hero, so I told him that Kelly was the person who'd gotten me a gig with Eddie Vedder.

"Would you come up to Montreal and we can try a couple songs together?" he asked, and I told him I would be happy to.

I arrived in Montreal in January 2004 and met Sam at his apartment. As we smoked hash, he played me all of his ideas and songs he'd written. I was a bit concerned. There wasn't much there as far as material was concerned. I picked out what I thought were the best songs and we booked a studio. Sam had just received bad news — his drummer had just quit, but there was a guy he wanted to try out. There was a huge snowstorm on the day we were set to begin recording, and it was nearly impossible to get to the studio. I plowed through the drifts of snow that covered the roads, nearly getting stuck every time. Somehow, everyone managed to get to the studio.

I set the band up and we tracked the songs I had picked out. I mentioned to Sam that, unfortunately, the drummer he had picked wasn't quite cutting it, and he agreed. I told him that I had heard back from Kelly, and he had suggested a place called Byron Bay, at the most eastern point of Australia, and had said that it had the best surf breaks. There were seven great surf breaks there, giving lots of options and variety. I brought pictures of a church that I had found there and of a bed and breakfast located just outside of town.

LISTEN UP!

"Wow, this looks awesome," Sam said. "That's it, I'm sold. Let's do it!"

He was going to South Africa a couple of weeks later, and he said he would meet me in Byron Bay. "I will write the rest of the songs for the record while I'm in South Africa," he said.

I sent the songs we'd just recorded to the A&R guy at Universal, and he got back to me complaining that there were only three songs, but I assured him that Sam was writing more. I explained the plan to go to Australia, and that by the time we met, Sam would have written the rest of the songs.

"There is no way we are going to do that," the A&R guy said. "First of all, we need to hear all the songs before you even start a record."

I was disappointed. By February, I was back in L.A., living in Santa Monica in a little beach house, but I decided we had to proceed. I had made all of the arrangements with the church, and Kylie, the woman who owned it, was cool with us renting it for a couple of months. A short while later, the A&R guy from Toronto called. He'd been talking to Sam, who'd convinced him that he needed to record in Australia. The A&R guy had gotten approval from the president, so they were giving us a green light. He warned me that he didn't want us going to Australia to smoke pot and surf for two months, and that if we didn't return with a hit record, he'd get into trouble for funding the most expensive surf holiday ever. I assured him that we'd take things seriously, that Sam would write some fantastic songs in South Africa, and that the album would be great.

I had one week to pull everything together before leaving for Australia. Fortunately, most of the groundwork was already done; I just needed to line everything up for my arrival. I took the heart of my studio — the iZ Radar recorder, my Dynaudio speakers, and my mics. I got Jim Moginie, the guitarist for Midnight Oil, to supply the rest of the gear. I'd become friends with him when Midnight Oil played the Tragically Hip's cross-Canada Another Roadside Attraction tour. I was mixing the front-of-house sound for Dan at the time. During the tour, all of the bands got together for a song to protest the logging of trees in Western Canada. We went into a studio at the end of the tour and cut a track, and each band contributed a verse. The Oils (as we came to call Midnight Oil) really loved how it sounded, and I ended up mixing a bunch of the songs for one of their records.

The Oils had broken up by the time I was set to record Sam Roberts;

Peter Garrett had gotten involved in Australian politics, and the other members went their different ways. Jim started a company that rented all kinds of vintage musical gear, from old drum sets to recording equipment, so I'd made arrangements with Jim to get any additional gear that I needed instead of lugging it overseas.

I flew out of L.A. and documented all my gear with U.S. customs so that when I came back, customs would know I'd left the country with the equipment and wouldn't try to make me pay duty upon return. I arrived in Brisbane County, New South Wales, Australia; collected my gear; and was going through customs when they pulled me to the side.

"What's in all the boxes?" they asked.

I explained it was my personal recording gear and that I was there to do some recording by myself for a couple of months. I showed them my customs declaration, and they informed me that I wasn't allowed to bring in more than $10,000 worth of gear. My customs paperwork clearly showed my gear added up to a lot more than that! I tried to explain that the value on the paperwork was the cost to purchase new, and that the gear wasn't worth much now because it was used. The customs officials didn't buy it, and they confiscated all my gear. They wouldn't release it until I posted a bond — which I needed to hire a shipping company to do — to ensure that I didn't sell the gear while I was there. I found a broker to post the bond, but it was going to cost AU$5,000!

The record company had arranged a rental car for me, so I drove down to Byron Bay and met Kylie at an old wooden Protestant church that had arched windows with wooden crosses embossed in the trim. The main room had a huge dining-room table, two couches, and coffee tables. There was a mezzanine that overlooked the main room. There were three bedrooms in the main church, and attached to the back of the church was another building that had four more bedrooms, each holding two beds. There was a modern kitchen at the back of the main building that opened onto the garden. After seeing the ins and outs, I thought the church was really cool and perfect for the record.

I emailed the record label and told them all of my gear had been confiscated and asked them to pay for the bond, explaining that they would get their money back once I left the country with the gear. They agreed to front the money, and I would have my gear in a couple of days.

LISTEN UP!

Sam Roberts recording in the old church, Byron Bay, Australia (2005).

In the meantime, I rearranged the church and put the dining-room table in the kitchen. Jim showed up with the rented gear, helped set it up, and stayed the night. I drove back to Brisbane the next day to get my own gear.

While waiting for my gear to arrive, I explored all the beaches and hung out in town, meeting some locals. At the local music store they recommended I talk to a guy named Simon, who could help me out with anything I needed. Byron Bay was a cool little town with a lot of wooden buildings with balcony bars and restaurants. The main drag ended at a beach called The Wreck, which was one of the surf breaks and the main beach where all the girls sunbathed.

I met a woman working in an Indonesian boutique where I was buying some tapestries and learned she was a yoga teacher, so I ended up taking private lessons from her. While at her place for my yoga lesson, I spotted a Yamaha XS650 motorcycle. It was her boyfriend's bike, and I asked about renting it.

I also met a woman who was the champion boogie boarder in Australia.

When I told her that I'd been doing a lot of boogie boarding, she invited me to go with her, so I met her at the beach. I was carrying my boogie board from Woolworths, decorated with a picture of dolphins.

"You've got to be kidding!" She laughed when she saw it.

"It goes fast because of the dolphins," I told her, and she couldn't stop laughing.

She was awesome on the board and showed me some tricks, like how to board sitting on my knees and how to spin it around. In the one week it took me to set up the studio, I'd met most of the coolest people in the town, and everyone was so friendly, they knew me by name. What a contrast to L.A., where I'd lived in my beach house in Santa Monica for two months and still hadn't met my neighbors.

Sam arrived at Coolangatta, a small airport, with his girlfriend, and I went to meet them. He was so excited to be there. Our plan was to spend a week going through all of the songs he'd written in South Africa, and he'd have time to get some surfing in before we started. The day after he arrived, we sat down to go through the songs.

"How many songs did you write while you were in South Africa?" I asked him.

"Well . . . there was a little bit of a problem," he said.

"You lost them or left them there?"

"Well, I didn't write any."

I gasped. "You have nothing?"

"Nope."

I decided we just had to roll up our sleeves and start putting stuff together. We made a schedule starting at noon every day so that Sam could surf every morning. We got started with all of his ideas — which we called seeds — and made a big chart to monitor the progress of turning seeds into songs. We recorded versions of them using percussion instruments we'd made, like boxes with stones in them.

Sam's friend, Matt Mays, another musician from the east coast of Canada, was in Australia surfing and planned to stop in for a week or so. Matt was a good musical ally to encourage Sam. Sam could play every instrument and had played everything on his first record, but this time he really wanted to use his band. It sounded great with just the three of us. The band showed up a week later and we already had a really good road map. They hired a drummer they'd never played with before, a powerhouse hard-hitter named Billy.

LISTEN UP!

The rest of Sam's band was composed of his friends from high school. They were a little freaked out because of all the insects. One day, I heard a scream from the bunkhouse, and it turned out one of the guys had seen a huntsman spider for the first time. They are huge and hairy, and this one was extra big — about the size of my hand. I told him they were harmless, and I went and got a bowl to catch it in. The whole band was in the room watching me. The spider was high up on the wall, and as I went to put the bowl on top of it, it *jumped* onto the floor, making all the men scream. I finally captured it and took it outside.

The bathroom downstairs was so scary that no one would use it. Frogs lived in the toilet, hiding under the bowl, and when you sat down, their little feet would reach up and touch your butt. Oddly enough, that wasn't the scariest thing about that bathroom — that was the funnel-web spider that lived above the toilet. It's one of the deadliest spiders on the planet.

The church was located in a little area called Newrybar, where coffee is grown. Huge fields were netted so that no bugs would eat the coffee while it grew, and it allowed the farmers to not use chemical pesticides on the plants. The coffee in Australia is smooth, not edgy like American coffee.

There weren't any kangaroos there, but there were wallabies, smaller than kangaroos, which the Australians call joeys. There was one little joey that would come to the back door, open it, and come inside. He'd go to the fridge and help himself to the food in there. It was incredible that he had no fear. He wouldn't let anyone touch him, but if ignored, he'd hop right past. There were mango trees at the side of the house, and at night fruit bats could be heard eating the mangos. One night, I was outside and could hear them in the trees, so I went over and shone a light on them. I couldn't believe what I was seeing — they were the size of fat cats. They ignored me and kept eating.

I was driving down one of the country roads at night when I felt a little bump.

"Did you see that?" Sam asked. He told me I'd driven over a huge snake. We turned the car around, stopped, and there it was — a massive python crossing the road and slithering off into the bush.

Sam and the guys went surfing every morning at a beach I showed them called Broken Head. The sand on the beach was white and clean, and it was entirely empty, like there was no one left on Earth. I had tried surfing with them, but the waves were six metres tall and I got slammed. After the first week, the front page of the local paper said seven great white sharks had been spotted at the beach the same day we were there.

After the first week of tracking, I felt I wasn't getting the results I'd hoped for. Billy, the drummer, could only play one beat and could only play loud, not the feels I was wanting. The other guys were not cutting it either, and I felt like I was going backward. I had asked Eric, the keyboard player, to work on some new sounds and he hadn't done anything. I tried talking to Sam about it, but he said, "Give them a chance." I was accustomed to having the best players available to me, and by this point I was pretty frustrated.

By the end of the second week, I had tracked twelve songs and although the record was taking shape, I didn't have a single that I thought the record company would like. It seemed more of a concept album. Each song was based on a "chemical city," a thematic through-line for all of Sam's writing at the time.

I became concerned with Sam's voice — I thought it was sounding distorted, and although I tried different mics on him, the distortion was coming out of his throat. Surfing in salt water was drying out his throat and affecting his voice. He was freaked out, thinking he couldn't sing well enough to record. By the end, I determined that the sound for the record *was* his distorted vocals.

The A&R guy flew in to hear the record. We played him the whole thing and he hated it. Sam spent the rest of the night trying to explain that it was a concept record like the ones Pink Floyd made, but the A&R guy couldn't see it. I spoke to the A&R guy in the morning and shared my concerns, everything from the drummer to not having any songs to not having strong players. He said that he couldn't play the album to his boss in the shape it was in. Sam stood by his album and said it was finished. It was over at that point, and everyone left.

Chemical City was released as a studio album in 2006 and nominated for Rock Album of the Year at the Canadian Juno awards.

I'd loved working in Australia, and although my visa was set to expire, I decided to go to Fiji to renew it. I wanted to stay on.

CHAPTER 27

RECORDING AROUND THE WORLD

IT WAS JUNE 2004 WHEN I CHECKED into Sing Sing Recording Studios in Melbourne. I had been asked to mix a record for an Australian indie / pop / rock band called Augie March. They were a really cool band and had great songs, and to date they've had two nominations for ARIA awards (Australian Record Industry Association) and have won an Australian Music Prize.

I convinced the band that if I wore tinfoil on my ears their mixes would be more dynamic. I'd heard a story that Brian Eno had done this during some of his mixes. Eno was always trying to push the envelope, whether turning the tape backward looking for new melodies or recording things at a fast tape speed and playing them back normal speed.

The guys in the band turned me on to eating kangaroo meat and told me I should take a drive down Great Ocean Road to see the Twelve Apostles, the enormous limestone rock formations that rise out of the ocean. I rented a car and took that long drive. The rental car had an icon that flashed on the dash every so often, a picture of a coffee cup with steam coming off it. For the life of me I couldn't figure out what it was. Perhaps it was picking up a signal that there was a coffee shop coming up. It turned out that people drove for hours and got tired, so the auto industry came up with a coffee-cup icon to let drivers know it was time to pull over.

When I finally reached the Twelve Apostles, I stopped to take some pictures. I noticed there were black-and-white birds on the beach. They were penguins, and I was ecstatic. When I felt like I'd had my experience, I headed back to Melbourne.

The record did well and was nominated for an ARIA award. After mixing Augie March, I spent a couple of days in Sydney at Bondi Beach before heading back to L.A.

When I landed in L.A., Sam Roberts's record company called wanting me to go to Montreal to rework some of the songs we'd recorded. I stayed in L.A. about a week before heading there. It was late June in Montreal, and it felt great. The streets were full of people, the air was warm, and there were street festivals every night. In the studio, I reworked a couple of the songs, re-recording a bunch of the drums and replacing some guitars, and Sam redid a lot of the vocals. The record company wanted someone else to try some mixes on the record, so I left it in their hands to finish. The record was a mild hit for Sam but never won any awards.

From Montreal I headed back to L.A. to begin a new adventure. I bought a new Airstream trailer to use as my private apartment whenever I made records on location. Inside, the Airstream was like a modern New York City apartment. It had a polished aluminum interior with halogen inset lighting and was super modern, with solar panels on the roof. The Airstream was totally self-sustaining. Right off, I made a couple of records in California, one at Joshua Tree for Tim Easton, and then one in Malibu for a wealthy family, the Nortons. The father was a real-estate tycoon who'd sold one of the Enron buildings and developed resorts.

The Nortons had a son who had a serious immune deficiency disease, the sort that has caused some children to essentially live in "bubbles," and he wasn't allowed to leave the house because he could pick up germs and die. His last wish was to make a record, and he wanted me to produce it. I brought the studio to their house and parked my Airstream on their property. They had just moved into a huge modern house with a lap pool. The main living room had huge glass windows that overlooked the ocean, and that was where I set up the studio and recorded the album.

The son, Nathaniel, was a big fan of Dylan's *Time Out of Mind*. I got Jim Keltner, a drummer who'd played on the album and had previously worked with some of the Beatles, and Tony Mangurian, who'd worked with Dylan playing

LISTEN UP!

drums and percussion, on the record. Daryl Johnson, who'd worked with the Neville Brothers, played bass, and Michael Chavez played guitar.

I cut the record in a week and then mixed it right away. The whole family was there during recording. The Nortons had two beautiful daughters; one was a yoga teacher and the other was a dancer. The mother was a singer, and she had the same disease as her son, so we all had to wear special shoes once we entered their house. After completing Nathaniel's album, they published on their own label and Nathaniel recovered from his sickness 100 percent. My next stop was Mexico.

Once Dan caught wind of my mobile setup, he wanted to fund another recording venture in Todos Santos, near the tip of Baja California, Mexico. The next thing I knew, I was driving south of the border in my new Chevrolet Avalanche truck, with a new BMW HP2 mega dirt bike in the back of the truck, and pulling the Airstream behind it. I had had the studio assembled on the inside of the Airstream, and it turned out to have better sound than many huge studios.

I arrived in Todos Santos in April 2005. I had made arrangements with Paula, the woman who owned the Café Santa-Fe in Todos Santos, to park the Airstream in her empty lot. However, once I got there, I discovered her lot had been damaged in a storm, and there was no electricity to plug into in order to run the studio. She told me that I could park the trailer at her friend's house instead, as her friend had an empty lot with power next to her house. I went over to meet Susanna Acevedo, a lovely lady in her sixties, who lived alone and really enjoyed my company. She said that her ex-husband was a musician and she was used to having music around. It wasn't until much later that she revealed who her ex-husband was: Neil Young. Susanna was Neil's first wife and he had written the song "Oh Susanna" about her. That same month, I got a call from Emily O'Halloran, a woman I'd met at Sing Sing studios in Australia. She was a friend of the assistant who worked there. Although unknown, I thought Emily was a great writer and had the most incredible low voice, like Marianne Faithfull's or Nico's. I had mentioned to her if she was ever in L.A. she should look me up, and I would cut a tape. I was happy to hear from her, and she said that she was stopping in L.A. on her way to New York and wondered if I would still be up to cut a track. I told her it was good timing for me as I was between projects. I picked Emily up at the airport and told her she could stay with me for a couple

Recording Kaizers Orchestra, East Berlin (2005).

of days because I had an extra room. We didn't waste any time, and although she was a little jet lagged, we started recording the following day. One song turned into several. Emily had never made a record before or even played with a band. It started out as just me and her; I played the drums on a couple of tracks and she played guitar.

Before I knew what happened, we were going everywhere together, from cutting tracks in Jamaica to flying to London to using some of the biggest studios in L.A. It had turned into a full on rock 'n' roll romance. The record took longer to make than expected due to the other records I was working on throughout.

We would leave for Berlin for a month, then come back and do a little more. I finished mixing the record at Sonora Recorders in Los Feliz in L.A.

Emily ended up putting the record out on Tear Stain Records, and it received rave reviews from media sources like *Mojo* and *Uncut*, many giving her five stars, saying what a great writer she was, and comparing her to the Cowboy Junkies, Nico, and Marianne Faithfull.

It was during this time that I got an invitation to produce one of Norway's biggest rock bands, Kaizers Orchestra. They wanted to make their album in Berlin. Actually, the place where they wanted to record was in the former East Berlin, at the DDR radio building. This building was built by Hitler for radio broadcasts, and it housed over more than 20,000 workers during Word War Two. There were many different rooms for recording, but the most impressive were the two orchestra rooms: each was the size of a New York City block. Between the two rooms was a control room bridge where the radio broadcast was done, so that while one orchestra played live to radio, the other waited, ready to start as the other finished. This way the musicians got breaks between performances.

The rooms were huge, with five-story ceilings and ornate wood carvings along the walls. The floors were in the shape of a horseshoe, with different levels where the orchestra players performed. At the back of the rooms were theater-style seating, where Hitler and his generals sat during performances.

Kaizers Orchestra was a unique setup, from the accordion to drums made from oil barrels. The drummer would play these huge oil barrels with crowbars — it was very industrial. I would take it to the next level by attaching guitar pickups to the oil barrels and then run them through distortion pedals and into Marshall stacks.

One of the rooms we worked in was a Foley room. Foley is when sound is made for films. For example, if someone in a film is punched in the face, the Foley artist records a fish being slapped on a table, and that sound is dubbed into the movie. There was a set of stairs in the room to record marching, and other rooms had sandboxes. It was like a typical studio with a glass window to look through. I tracked the band in there.

One day, the band was in the performance room when the assistant brought me a cup of tea. I went to set it on the console, but it slipped and spilled all over my shirt, so I took off my shirt and hung it over the lamp to dry.

The band was in the middle of a take when I looked behind me and found my shirt was on fire. I ran to grab it, but what the band saw through the glass was me running through the studio on fire. I put the flames out but the shirt was burned pretty badly, so I had to go shirtless for the rest of the session.

Schnitzel became a running joke for us — in Germany everyone loves it. Everything we ordered to eat came with a schnitzel on it. If we ordered a pizza, it came with a schnitzel; if we ordered Thai food, it came with a schnitzel; so the band bought me a shirt that read *Schnitzel*.

Kaizers Orchestra's album did really well and they had a number one hit in Norway.

CHAPTER 28

MUMFORD & SONS

THE HOTEL CAFE IS A CLUB IN L.A. where a lot of new bands get to showcase. I got a call from my manager, Sandy Robertson, to go to check out a new band from the United Kingdom called Mumford & Sons. They were on tour across America with two other acts, Laura Marling and Johnny Flynn, all traveling in the same van, backing up each other so the band stayed the same but the singers changed.

Mumford had a pretty driving sound with a lot of strumming, and Marcus playing the kick drum while playing guitar and singing gave the band a unique sound. After their show, I met with them in the back alley. We hit it off and chatted a bit about making a record, although they seemed more interested in hearing stories about working with Dylan.

They asked if I'd be interested in trying a couple of songs with them one day, and I said that I would. I didn't hear from them for a couple of months, and then just before Christmas 2006 I got a call asking if I could come to London to work on two songs. The band didn't have a record deal yet, but they had a spec deal to pay to record the songs. They could cover my expenses, like flight and food, but they had no money to pay me. They said that if they got a deal, they would use me to produce the record. They were a great band so I agreed, but asked they fly me over on Virgin Atlantic because I had points and could upgrade my seat.

My girlfriend, Emily, and I flew to London two weeks before Christmas. One of the band members picked us up at the airport at 7:00 a.m. He was driving a little car, and our bags only just fit. They'd booked us into a hotel by the studio. The lobby was just big enough to stand in, and the check-in desk took up most of the space.

"Mr. Howard, we have been expecting you," the clerk said. I was traveling with my equipment, so I had a couple of big pieces of luggage and asked for help taking them up, but they informed me I wouldn't be able to take the luggage to the room and would have to leave it downstairs.

"That is outrageous!" I told them. "You mean I have to come down to change my clothes?"

I asked to see the room, was given a key, and told to take the lift up. Leaving everything in the lobby, we went up to our room. It was ridiculous. The lift itself was the size of a phone booth and there was no way a fat couple would have fit, so it's no wonder they thought my luggage was an issue. On our floor, we headed down the hall to a set of stairs and then around a corner to our door. We opened it and the door slammed against the bed — a single. Emily and I were exhausted: we were jet lagged and hadn't slept on the flight. There was no way we could both sleep in a single — the room was so small that there wasn't even room to stand beside the bed.

We went back down and told the women at the desk that the room wasn't sufficient and that we wouldn't be staying. We ordered a taxi, loaded everything in, and found another hotel up the street — a proper one with a proper room — and checked in. We crashed as soon as we got settled and woke up at eight o'clock in the evening, a bad idea because then we wouldn't sleep at night and I started work the next day. We were starving and headed out to eat. It was raining, which we weren't prepared for, so we got drenched. The only thing open was an Indian restaurant, so we ate there. I was up all night because of the long nap but couldn't sleep in because I had to be at the studio at 11:00 a.m. to set up. I left Emily in the room and went to work. I called the people who were funding the recording and told them about the hotel room situation and that they needed to deal with it.

"If I'm not getting paid, then you could at least give me a proper room," I explained.

They booked us a room at the Garden Suites, just across the road from the studio, and admitted they'd been trying to save money by putting us in a hole in the wall.

Mumford & Sons were at Metropolis Studios, where I had mixed Marianne Faithfull's record, and I really liked that studio because it was ultramodern, and I was in a better mood just being there. We were working on the ground floor in studio one. It had a big SSL recording console and although it had a small performance room, it would do.

The first day went great and we cut three songs. I recorded them live off the floor so I could get a true performance out of the band. I used an 808 kick drum sample as I had to replace the kick that Marcus normally played. The band hummed and hawed over the tempos, but we finally got it to work.

I called Emily and had her move to the new hotel. I worked until 11:00 p.m. and dragged myself back to our new room. Unfortunately, I was so tired I fell asleep again, only to wake at 3:00 a.m. and find myself up until morning. I crawled into the studio the next day. It's a horrible feeling having to work when you haven't slept properly in several nights, and I felt like I was firing on three cylinders instead of six. It was our last day at the studio, and then we would move to Olympic Studios to mix. We cut three more songs and finished up a couple that had been recorded the day before.

The band members tended to bicker, each wanting their ideas to be heard. I kept to my guns and plowed through, keeping focused. I may have been a little short with the boys, as my patience was wearing thin because of utter exhaustion. We made it through the day and everyone was happy to be finished.

The next day we went to Olympic Studios to mix. This was the studio where the Rolling Stones had cut a lot of their records. I was informed once I arrived that this would be the last day that the studio would ever be open, that they were closing their doors for good, forced to do so because of real-estate prices. Olympic was owned by Abbey Road Studios, and they just couldn't afford to keep both studios open.

We mixed downstairs while U2 was working upstairs. It was a rough day with still no sleep for me, and the band wanted to change all kinds of things. I had to mix six songs in one day and redo lots of parts as well. I took a break around midnight and went upstairs to see the U2 boys. They were all huddled in one of the mix rooms finishing up. I saw Dallas Schoo, Edge's guitar tech, and he showed me around the big studio. They were just tearing down and everyone looked pretty worn out. Dallas said he would pop his head into the studio to see if I could say hello. A few minutes later, he waved me in. The band was done for the night.

"Mark, how goes it, man?" Bono greeted me at the door.

I told him I was just mixing downstairs with a new band, Mumford & Sons.

"Sounds like a funeral home," he replied.

Brian Eno was there waiting for his CD, and he asked me if I'd heard from Daniel.

"No, not for a bit," I said. "But I heard he was hiding out in Jamaica."

"Good place for him." Bono laughed.

I could see how tired Bono looked.

"You all look a bit shattered," I commented.

"A bit? Ha! It's been over a year and a half of this, so we passed shattered months ago."

Eno got ready to leave. "That's it. I'm out, boy. Nice seeing you, Mark, and good luck mixing."

It was 3:00 a.m. and I only had five out of the six songs mixed. I went back into the studio with Mumford.

"That's it, guys. Honestly, I'm spent. I'll mix this one another time."

"No, we really need it mixed for our EP."

EP! Nobody had said anything about an EP to me. They told me they were going to sell it on the road. I felt a little used at that point, but I agreed to finish it. I mixed the last song and finished around 4:30 a.m., and I guess they got a free EP out of me.

They might say that U2 was the last band at Olympic, but they left at midnight and I worked until 4:30 a.m., so really it was me and Mumford & Sons who closed the doors.

I talked to my manager once I returned home and asked him to see if he could get me some money for the work I'd done. The deal had been to do a couple of songs as a test, not an EP. The company replied that there was no money, so I just swallowed it.

A year later Mumford & Sons was huge. They used the EP to get a big deal and hired Bright Eyes' producer to make their record. I caught up with them at a Grammys after-party at the Beverly Hills Hotel. I was there with Neil Young, who had won a Grammy for the record we made together.

Mumford & Sons were drunk out of their minds, staggering about. Marcus saw me, but it didn't click who I was until the bass player saw me and yelled, "Fuck, it's Mark Howard! Mark fucking Howard, how are you?" He turned to his mate. "This guy showed up in London with the hottest fucking chick — you fucking rock!"

There was no use saying anything to them when they were so shit faced. Marcus asked if I would introduce him to Neil, so I walked him over and got Neil to say hello to him. Neil didn't know who Marcus was, but he was very nice.

I still think my recordings sounded better than what the band put out, but I guess that's my own opinion. At least I got credit for producing their first EP.

CHAPTER 29

ROBERT PLANT

WHEN I GOT THE INVITATION TO RECORD the new Robert Plant / Alison Krauss record, I was excited. Led Zeppelin was one of my favorite bands growing up, so it was a big deal for me to work with Robert Plant. Robert and Alison had already recorded the album once with producer T Bone Burnett, who had also produced *Raising Sand*, their very successful first record. They weren't content with the new album and had abandoned the material, until now.

I set up my studio in the front entranceway of Bella Vista mansion, in Silver Lake. There was a full studio downstairs in the dungeon-like basement with a Neve 8068, but I preferred to use my rig with all my GP2 BL99 custom preamps. I set up the studio facing the winding staircase. There were beautiful stained-glass windows with a scene of a forest with tall pine trees behind the stairs. The entranceway had high ceilings with hand-plastered walls. There was some echoing, but that made it great for singing, and it sounded better than the dungeon studio below.

The room makes all the difference when it comes to recording. The bottom line is if the room sounds great, then your recordings will be great. There is nothing worse than trying to get a great sound out of a bad room.

There were some complications with scheduling, so Robert and Alison couldn't make it to the studio at the same time. Robert happened to be in L.A.

seeing a new doctor. He arrived on time at noon, carrying a leather satchel and a book about William Blake, his favorite poet. Pointing to his satchel, he said, "These are all the songs of all the women I have loved and hated."

Robert Plant is a tall, thick man with a mane of hair like a lion's. He was wearing cool cowboy boots, and I asked if he'd gotten them in Spain.

His response? "No. I got them on Sunset."

I was somehow disappointed.

We started the sessions with a small crew. It was Daryl Johnson on bass and vocals, Dan on guitar, and because we had no drummer, I used drum loops that I had in my personal collection. Robert was infatuated with Africa and its rhythms. He made us watch a show he had done there with some African musicians; he said he wanted to create something like it. I used a piece of one of my rhythms and looped it so they could play on top of it. Daryl layered some hand drums on it, as well as a little string part. Dan laid a big guitar hook on it using his '50s Les Paul Goldtop guitar and his Vox AC30 amp. The song was called "Beautiful Girl."

At the time, Trixie Whitley was staying at Bella Vista. We had just completed the Black Dub album that she was the singer on. I asked her if she would sing a little on the track to model what it would be like to have Alison sing on it. It was a magical pairing between Robert's voice, Dan's band, and Trixie.

Trixie would sing a verse and Robert would sing the chorus, then they would split verses and choruses. Daryl and Robert had stacked beautiful vocal "*awws*" that I set in the background. Robert sang the chorus with the power of a Zeppelin song.

The chorus went: "The bird of the fire in the eyes of a beautiful girl, the silver and gold to the feel of a beautiful girl."

It really sounded great. I tried one of my vocal sounds on his voice, but Robert asked me to take it off.

"I don't use that Phil Collins AMS delay sound," he said. "I prefer long echoes and reverb."

I came up with a sound he loved. Because we were moving fast, I was using a handheld Shure Beta 58 microphone on his vocal, with it coming out of the speakers so he could get immediate satisfaction.

The Bella Vista sessions, with Daryl Johnson, Daniel Lanois, and Robert Plant.

On another song, I pulled out a loop that I had made with a drum beat from Brady Blade and a guitar riff from the late Chris Whitley. It was a heavy rock riff and Robert loved it. Robert went scrounging through his satchel of lyrics looking for something that would fit. He then looked through the William Blake book in which he found the line "a thousand sleepless nights." It was perfect, and Robert penned some lyrics right on the spot to complete the verses.

Robert was a little shy about singing up high like he did on the Zeppelin records. On the other Plant / Krauss record, he sang down low and never ventured out of that range, it being a safety zone for him. Toward the end of this new song, he was hitting those high notes like in the Zeppelin days. I asked him to try a track of just the high parts for the end.

"I can't sing up there anymore," he insisted.

"You were just hitting them and you sounded great," I told him.

He agreed to try and pulled off an amazing ending, still able to reach those notes.

I got Trixie to sing on the chorus with Robert, and it was also a beautiful blend. It was poignant and a little haunting that her late father was playing guitar on the track.

Robert had a ballad he wanted to try, and I used another loop of Brady Blade's younger brother Brian's slowed-down drum that I called "elephant drums." It was an intimate song with a fragile-sounding vocal. The song had lyrics about Oklahoma nights and the chorus lyric was "the stranger is too perfect." It was a moving, stripped-down track with just the slow drums, a beautiful pedal steel part, and Robert's heartfelt vocal.

In our downtime, Robert told stories of being in L.A. while on tour with Zeppelin. Oddly enough, the only song he hated singing was "Stairway to Heaven." He said he really couldn't connect to the lyrics.

He told us that John Bonham was a wild man who would get all liquored up and go to the Whisky a Go Go and heckle the drummers, yelling, "You're crap!"

Robert said he did cocaine with others and by himself, and in those days the coke was so strong that his whole face was frozen most of the time. It was at this time that he received the news that his son had died, and from that point on he stopped doing all drugs. The tour was postponed while Robert went back home to grieve his son. He said the only one who came to visit him during this period was John Bonham.

Robert was concerned that Zeppelin had not been giving credit to some of the blues singers they were copying, and Jimmy Page told him not to worry about it. Later in life, they did credit some of the legendary blues artists.

Robert told us that he didn't usually go backstage to say hello to other artists, but one time he got invited backstage to meet Neil Young, so he decided he would go. He was ushered backstage to Neil's dressing room and went inside. When Neil saw him, he called out, "Richard!" and waved him over.

Robert said that he didn't correct him.

Down the line, while I was working on Neil Young's record, I mentioned the story Robert had told me, about Neil calling Robert "Richard." Eric, Neil's road manager, laughed and said, "Oh . . . that night."

"Yes, I might have been a little stoned when that happened," Neil said to me, smiling but a little embarrassed.

In the movie *This Is Spinal Tap*, there is a scene in which the band is lost under the stadium and can't find their way to the stage, and Robert told us that that really did happen to Led Zeppelin. They were down there for ages looking for the way to the stage.

Robert said a lot of the Zeppelin money went out as fast as it came in, going out the window to pay for things like limos that sat outside 24/7 waiting on them, among other money being squandered. Robert surprised us by saying that Led Zeppelin wasn't a rock band, that they were really a folk band at heart, citing their use of folk instruments like dulcimers to prove his point.

"I don't know why Page and Jonesy are doing these silly records with these bands these days," Robert sighed.

Once Bonham died, that was the end of Zeppelin. He was the sound of Zeppelin, and no one else could match it. Robert said that Bonham lived a humble life in a house in the country with his little dog and was just another regular at the local pub.

One day, I had my 1948 Vincent Rapide motorcycle parked in front of the studio, and Robert commented that his uncle used to have one. He'd looked up to his uncle like a hero.

"When he would pull up on his Vincent, it was like seeing Marlon Brando pulling up." Robert smiled. "If you had a Vincent in those days, you were like royalty."

Robert felt a Vincent was like the Aston Martin of motorcycles. He had bought a 1965 Aston Martin DB5 at the height of his career, and it was his favorite car, even to that day. In Europe, every boy dreamed of owning a Vincent. In

LISTEN UP!

North America, the Vincent is a little-known bike, but in England, it's revered. I've ridden every bike known, and riding a Vincent feels like a riding a horse. Most bikes have shocks in the back, but the Vincent has a cantilever rear suspension, and so it pivots in the center and feels like it's breathing. It was a dream come true to own one, and riding it was the pinnacle for me. At one time, Vincent was the fastest production motorcycle on the planet, and in 1948 a man named Rollie Free broke the U.S. national motorcycle speed record in Utah, riding the first Vincent Black Lightning at the Bonneville Salt Flats, doing 151 miles per hour. Every detail of the bike is perfection and made to last the test of time, not cobbled together on an assembly line.

On the table in the pool room were a bunch of photos by Paolo Roversi, an Italian fashion photographer. Roversi had shot a series of photos of a Russian model, Natalia Vodianova, naked on a couch. The photos looked timeless, and it was impossible to tell if they were old or new. I asked Robert what he thought of them. He immediately said the model was too young for him and that if he was ever seen with a women that young, he'd be a laughing stock.

"I would need to be with a woman in her thirties at least," he said.

Robert's assistant, a beautiful Welsh woman named Nicola, would come by after the sessions were over to have a listen and a drink. Like Robert, she also had a nice set of cowboy boots, but I was afraid to ask her where she got them. She drank straight vodka and handled it well. I would walk them out at the end of the night, down the driveway. One night, on the way out, Nicola asked me if the Vincent was my bike. I was surprised — and pretty impressed — that she knew what it was.

"It's only the best motorcycle in the world," she said.

We stood by the bike as Robert and Dan carried on down the drive. Dan was there at night also.

She said, "You must take me for a ride one day," and I told her I would.

Just as she was about to leave, she kissed me good night, but it turned into a little more than just a kiss. All of a sudden, I heard Robert yelling, "Hey! What you doing?"

My heart sank. I was busted for kissing the client's assistant. We stopped and laughed, and she carried on down the driveway, but I could hear Robert saying, "Nic, what are you doing?" I was afraid that she had gotten into trouble.

The next day, I sent her a message commenting on what a lovely evening we'd had.

I got a message back that read, "Yes, it was nice, and I hope you have fun with your Russian friend."

Obviously, Robert had told her about the photos I showed him and must have said something to make her leave that comment. I didn't reply to the Russian comment but later she revealed she was just taking the piss out of me.

Nicola ended up becoming Robert's manager and we still are friends. When they come through town, she always invites me to the shows. I still owe her that ride on my motorcycle.

I recorded five songs with Robert that were great. Sadly, the record didn't materialize and the Alison sessions didn't go very well. When it was time for Alison to come in, she was suffering from migraines. We had assembled a band of local musicians. I was still set up in the front entrance of Bella Vista. Steve Nistor was the drummer, and I had set him up under the stairs. To calm the drum sound a bit, I put the drums in a tent made out of Indian tapestries; it made the drums very dry and punchy.

The first record Robert and Alison had done was cover songs that T Bone had picked. They had covered one of Tom Waits's songs, "Trampled Rose," from the *Real Gone* album I'd done. Dan was offering his songs to Alison, but she didn't want to do them. He had gone out and got his own William Blake book and had pulled the line "Surely you were meant to be mine" out of it. He tried to get her to sing this new song he'd just written, but Alison said she wasn't feeling it and that she wanted to do a bluegrass song that she liked.

Dan didn't like not getting his way and sometimes reminded me of a bratty kid, and he said, "Fine."

Dan's uncomfortable behavior was making Alison feel like she didn't want to be in the studio. In the end, Dan ended up getting Trixie Whitley to sing "Surely" for the *Black Dub* record and Trixie really nailed it. Alison sang like an angel but she was insecure about her vocals, always saying she hated them. She needed a lot of reinforcement and Dan wasn't giving her any. I would tell her she was sounding great, but perhaps it was too late. Robert had mentioned that Alison was like a fragile little bird and needed reassurance. At the first show they did for the album *Raising Sand*, she didn't want to go onstage and Robert had to sit with her while she cried, and calm her down in order to convince her to do the show. I figured at that point that the record was not going to happen. Robert's sessions had gone so well I suggested to Dan that we finish the record anyway with Robert, and make it a solo record. Daniel said he had no interest.

CHAPTER 30

NEIL YOUNG

IF THERE WAS ONE ARTIST ON THE planet I had always wanted to work with, it was Neil Young. But I figured that was pretty much out of reach; he had produced his own records for twenty years and only used his own crew to make his albums.

I had made a record for a band called Black Dub that had little films that went with each song. Elliot Roberts, who is Neil's manager, was also looking after Black Dub. Elliot had shown Neil a couple of the films, and Neil really liked them and had the idea to do a record and film each song as it was being performed. That's when Elliot called about making a solo record with Neil.

This would not be another ordinary recording experience — and there were a few guidelines that needed to be followed. A main rule was that we would only record three days before the full moon. Neil felt that people are the most creative in the days leading up to the full moon, and if magic is going happen, it is at that time. Another rule was that we needed to please ourselves before playing anything for others, and it was only when we all liked a track that the record company and management could hear it.

The record was to be recorded at the Bella Vista mansion. Before Neil came to record, I did a rearrangement of my studio setup. I moved a Neve Melbourne twelve-channel console and then set a Neve BCM 10 console on each side of the Melbourne, forming a wraparound recording and mixing station. I upgraded my speaker playback system to a double stack of Dynaudio BM15 speakers with a set of eighteen-inch subwoofers on each side, making a tower of speakers that could deliver a powerful punch because all the speaker diaphragms were in line with each other, one on top of the other. I also spent a lot of time going through all the microphones, testing each one to see which sounded better. I did the same with the guitar amps; there were at least five 1950s Fender Tweed Deluxes, and I checked out each one to see which one was the strongest. I tested the best acoustic guitar pickups, from Lawrence pickups to LR Baggs, and the Baggs won, making it the one I'd use. Testing different acoustic guitars with the Baggs pickup in them, I decided the 1950s Mahogany Guild had the best sound. I felt having a solid arsenal of excellent-quality instruments and gear at my disposal was an important starting point.

With all of this preparation done, I was set to roll tape. After having bought the last of the two-inch tape in Los Angeles, I had fifty rolls of tape stacked, ready to go, and I was ready to record on an iZ Radar 24-track digital machine. I use that machine because it's rock solid, never crashes, and is, in my opinion, the best-sounding digital machine out there.

A lot of time went into setups for filming. Adam Vollick was a Canadian who had done the Black Dub films and would do Neil Young's. I helped Adam set up a little film-editing suite upstairs. I wanted to make sure that the playback system for the audio was impressive, so I stacked some Canadian Paradigm speakers together for an impressive sound. Whenever we got a take we liked, Adam would run upstairs and start rendering, and while he was doing that, I would lay down a mix and then run it up to him to layer onto the film.

The entire crew was Canadian; there were five of us on the Bella Vista team. Adam, Dan, and I were on the creative team. Ian Galloway tuned the guitars and Margaret Marissen, Daniel's manager, was in charge of the food.

A big truck showed up the day before the session with Neil's pump organ and a bunch of his amps and guitars. Mark Humphreys, the monitor engineer for Neil's live shows, was the one who delivered the gear and stayed to take care of it while Neil was recording. Mark came with a lot of knowledge about how to do things Neil's way. I listened but mostly just to assure him that we had been warned.

Neil wanted to drive one of his old Cadillacs down from Broken Arrow Ranch, where he lived. On the day Neil was to show up, we received a call that he had just driven down and was staying at the Beverly Hills Hotel, and that he would see us the following day. He was to be in at noon, but he didn't show up. We were given no reason, just told he'd be in the next day, and it felt a bit comical. The following day at around two o'clock I heard the rumble of his 1950 Cadillac Eldorado convertible coming up the driveway. Neil was with his road manager, Eric, who used to be the road manager for Pearl Jam; he was the coolest guy, always smiling and smelling like weed. Back when Pearl Jam was opening shows for Neil, Eric would run back and forth, moving luggage and busting his ass, and Neil decided that Eric was the kind of guy he always wanted, so he stole Eric from Pearl Jam.

Eric was an artist first, and he would sometimes do paintings on stage while Neil performed, then auction off the paintings after the shows and give the money to a charity. Eric was also a master of building things out of cardboard using a glue gun. I was hanging with him at the Beverly Hills Hotel in his room, and he had built a working model which was an example of abstract art. It had

Recording Neil Young's *Le Noise*.

doors and drawers that opened to other dimensions, with other boxes inside, with smaller drawers, paper birds, and other animals; it was one big puzzle of art.

Once Neil walked into the Bella Vista, he was handed a Hoergaarden beer, a Belgian beer that was the house special. We walked Neil through the house, showing him the ideas for all the setups. There was a breakfast room — a round space with marble floors and French windows that followed the curves of the round room, making it a good place for acoustic performances. Then there was the main living room, with red-stained wooden floors, which was empty except for the pump organ and the early 1900s Steinway grand piano. It would also be a good room for acoustic performances. Neil had brought Blackie, his 1950s Les Paul Goldtop, which was painted black and had a Firebird pickup in the back. This guitar was his secret weapon. It was a bitch to keep in tune, but what a tone . . .

I hit it off with Neil talking about cars and bikes, and we spent a lot of time looking at old cars on the computer. I knew Neil had ridden Harleys most of his life, so I showed him my Vincent motorcycle in the garage.

"What a beauty," he said. "You don't see that every day."

I asked him what he was riding. That's when he offered his advice: "There are two things you don't do in your fifties. One is cocaine and the other is ride motorcycles."

A lot of his friends had died on bikes, but the big concern was that once a person is past age fifty, it is a lot harder to recover if in a crash. Neil saw one of Daniel's BMW Super-moto bikes in the driveway and wasn't impressed.

"That machine will kill you. The faster you go, the faster you can die. It cuts down your reaction time to the second if you have a car or something run in front of you."

We started recording with an acoustic song. Neil owned Hank Williams Sr.'s guitar, an old Martin D-28 Neil bought from Tut Taylor. Neil played it all the time, but it had a transducer pickup system in it that didn't sound very good. Mark, Neil's live guy, swore up and down how great it sounded and that Neil would never play anything else. I handed Neil the Guild.

I had dialed it in so as soon as Neil played it, he heard an incredible sound out of the speakers. The astonishment on his face was priceless, as though he had never heard an acoustic sound like that before. Although the great sound was due to a combination of things I was doing, much of it was owing to the sub-harmonizer I had on it, which made it like a bass player was playing along.

We recorded the song "Love and War" using this sound in only one take, and it was filmed at the same time so it really is a live performance you are watching go down. I used a Sony C-37A tube vocal microphone that I had flown down from Canada. My brother-in-law, Bill Huisman, has a beautiful collection of microphones, and he let me borrow the Sony for the recording. I also used an AKG C24, a stereo mic, on the guitar. The sound of the stereo mic mixed with the sub-harmonizer was incredible, and when Neil hit the low string, the walls would shake!

The record was meant to be a collection of acoustic songs and maybe some on piano, too. Neil had a song called "Walk with Me" that he thought might work great on his Gretsch White Falcon guitar, which was a special guitar because it had stereo pickups in it but not the type of stereo one might think. The Gretsch splits the pickup in two, so the top three strings come out of one side and the bottom three strings come out of the other side. I put one side into a 1950s Fender Tweed Deluxe and the other side into another 1950s Fender Tweed Deluxe, then used an old Sennheiser MD409 microphone on each amp. I had accidentally left the sub-harmonizer powered on from the last track, so when Neil cranked it up, the thunder that roared from the speakers was earth shaking, and the walls and windows vibrated. Neil said he could feel his pant legs moving.

Neil was like a kid with a brand new toy, often smiling away like in the photo on the inner liner of the album jacket. It's pretty hard these days to invent new sounds, and for Neil to come out with yet another huge guitar sound was groundbreaking. It was performed right behind me as I recorded it. With his back to the main speaker and his amps in front of him, he was in surround sound when he played. The windows were shaking so badly I had to tape them all down. Although we recorded a couple of takes, it was the first take we went with.

For recording I'd lay a couple of dubs live onto Neil's voice and then treatments on his guitar that he would perform to. I'd trap his guitar sound and throw it back at him and he would play on top of it, each thing feeding into each other.

When the three days leading up to the full moon were spent, Neil left, planning to return in the days leading up to the next full moon.

He arrived again in his Cadillac when the moon was right, ready to move forward. Each night at the end of the session I'd roll a joint. On the first night Neil had a little puff and said, "Oh man . . . I just remembered this song called 'Hitchhiker' that I wrote in the '60s and never finished." The pot had reminded him of the song.

The first day we recorded "Peaceful Valley Boulevard," again working in the main living room. The following day Neil decided he really wanted to finish "Hitchhiker." Neil stood in the entranceway with the front doors open and his two Fender Tweed amps facing toward him. It was recorded at night so we could project clouds passing by on the ceiling. This was a song for Blackie, what most people call "Old Black." The sub didn't work so well on this track so Neil over-dubbed Moog bass pedals on the downbeat of sections. The whole of Silver Lake must have heard it all go down because it was so loud and the doors were wide open, yet no one complained.

When he left, Eric drove out down the narrow driveway in the big Cadillac, hit the curb, and peeled some of the trim off the Cadillac. Neil took it well and said, "We can fix that no problem."

While we were making the record, Neil was in the middle of building an electric car at home. It was a 1959 Lincoln Continental convertible and he'd hired engineers from NASA to build the turbine and develop a battery system. During the break waiting for the next full moon, tragedy struck when one of the stoner kids watching the car at Neil's warehouse passed out with a charger left on in the shop, only to awake to the car on fire. Most of the interior on the Cadillac was burned and also quite a lot of Neil's nostalgic car collection that was kept in the garage.

The car was rebuilt in another chassis and became the Linc Volt 1959 Lincoln Continental. It can go 400 miles before recharging. Neil drove the car from coast to coast in Canada, claiming, "If a hippy can build an electric car, then why can't big car companies?"

Toward the end of the record, tragedy would strike again, but this time it was one of the crew. Dan had been in a bad accident on his high-powered BMW motorcycle. I received a call at 7 a.m. that Dan was in emergency. I raced over and found him in the hallway of the USC hospital in downtown L.A. They had already done some x-rays and tests; Dan had a punctured lung and broken ribs. They thought he was a homeless man.

Neil called me asking for an update. He had been at the same hospital when he had his brain aneurysm, and his doctor was the best in the hospital. Neil told me to tell the nurse to call his doctor, and within an hour Dan was sent into the first class private wing of intensive care. Keisha Kalfin was the passenger with him, and she got the worst of it, with a broken arm and leg. She didn't have very good insurance and had to wait for days to have her operations.

Calls began coming in from everyone from Bono to Robert Plant, checking to see how Dan was doing. Robert said that he had almost had a head-on accident the week before. He had been texting while driving, and when he looked up, he saw a big truck coming right at him. He swerved and just missed hitting it. Robert said that was not the way he imagined dying, that he hoped he'd be on an island surrounded by goddesses.

Weeks passed and fortunately Dan was healing. We were scheduled to go out on tour with his band Black Dub, but the whole summer tour was canceled. Neil was growing impatient and wanted to finish his album. Dan was still in a wheelchair when Neil came back to complete the work. Neil had been in Hawaii trying to finish the songs, and he said it was like sitting over a rabbit hole waiting for the songs to come out. Neil had been smoking some Hawaiian weed when the song "Sign of Love" popped up out of the rabbit hole. He wrote the song while smoking a joint, which he'd put out and saved the other half of, and on which he pulled while recording the song, hoping to summon the song back out of the hole again.

One of the last songs recorded was "Someone's Going to Rescue You." Again I came up with another crazy guitar sound for Neil, a fuzz filter envelope that had a percolation sound.

Once the album was finished, we did a road trip up to Broken Arrow Ranch, and I brought a playback system with me so when we listened to the record we had the best sound. We rented a Cadillac Escalade to drive up to the ranch and reached it as darkness fell. I set the playback system up in Neil's kitchen and we watched the film. Pegi, Neil's wife, was there, and she cried during one of the songs about a friend who had just died.

We were put up in the band house that had been dubbed "the white house." I woke up early and was snooping around outside when I discovered a 1950s black Caddy limo, decked out with velvet interior. In the garage to the white house there was a red 1959 Jensen 541, sporting a fiberglass body and a straight inline 6 Austin motor. I wanted this car but it had problems, so I had never pursued getting it. The next day, Neil showed us around the property and we visited his car museum. He had all kinds of beautiful Caddys, a Woodie, and cool '50s Ford pickups.

Behind all the cars was a wall full of every amp from the '30s to the '60s, which in and of itself could have been a museum. There was also a building that housed his huge train set. Neil took over Lionel Trains, the toy-train company, so he had the biggest train set I have ever seen. Afterward, he showed us Redwood Digital, his recording studio. It wasn't very big, but he had lots of nice classic gear.

We left Broken Arrow and took the Pacific Coast Highway home, stopping in Big Sur for dinner. I mastered the record at Bernie Grundman Mastering and cut the vinyl lacquer.

The album was originally meant to be called *The Hitchhiker* but the name was changed because of a running joke. Dan's last name, Lanois, was hard to pronounce, and most people made it sound like "le noise." Whenever Neil would text Daniel, he would write "le noise." When they were doing the album cover, Neil changed the name to *Le Noise* as a private joke.

Neil booked a solo tour and asked if I could come out on the road and show his live-sound guy, Tim, how to get the same sounds as on the record. He rented the Wiltern Theatre in L.A. to do some rehearsals and try out a new sound system. I talked to the head tech, and I asked him to bring in a couple of pieces of gear for me so I could reproduce the album's sounds live. When I showed up at the Wiltern, everything was already there. Tim had just switched over from a Midas analog console to the new Digico digital console. It was all new for him, and the guy from Digico was showing him the ropes. Neil tried out a couple of songs from the record and I dialed up the sounds I'd put on his guitar. The sound system was underpowered in the sub department for me, and I told them that I wanted sixteen subs each side of the sound system to get the bottom I was looking for. They laughed at me and said, "It's an acoustic show, not a rock concert!"

Regardless, by the first show in Washington, I had the sixteen per side I wanted, and they couldn't believe the sound I got off just Neil's guitar. The whole arena was shaking! Neil could feel it from the stage. Afterward, I heard people walking past say how amazing the sound was.

Neil normally flew on private planes for his tours, but this time he rode the bus to save money to fund the Linc Volt. Neil's tour bus, the Silver Eagle, was an amazing custom vehicle and had two Caddys welded to the roof. Knotted-wood walls flowed throughout the interior of the bus and around the Wurlitzer piano built into one wall. Neil rode alone on the bus with just his driver, Mikey. I traveled on the management bus with Eric. There was also a crew bus behind us, and riding on it was Ian Galloway, whom Neil had snapped up from the recording sessions to be his new guitar tech. On board that bus were also Tim (the sound man), the lighting guy, Alaska (the chef), and the trainer. At the end of this entourage was the shadow bus for friends like Snow Bear, who wanted to jump on the tour for a couple of shows. Then there was the transport trailer that had Neil's gym in it and all of his hockey jerseys. I was on the tour for the first five shows and then I jumped off after Buffalo, New York.

The tour had moved on to Rochester when I got a call saying Neil wanted me back immediately. The sound guy hadn't got things right quite yet. They sent a car to pick me up within the hour and I was taken to the airport on Toronto Island to be flown in a private jet, a Gulfstream G550 fourteen-seater, to New York City. The plane had leather seats and a bar, and I was the only passenger. When I landed, a Lincoln Town Car took me to straight to the venue in time for the sound check. I walked up to Neil to see what was going on.

"Oh, I'm so happy you're back. He don't got it — I can't feel it like when you mix."

I promised I could get it right for him.

After the show I went onto Neil's bus. It's like his private home, so not many people ever get to go onto it. There are guys who have been on tour with him for years who have never been on board.

When I got on the bus Neil was freaking out.

"Who the fuck put plastic on my blueberries?"

He'd had them flown in from Oregon fresh and didn't want plastic touching his food.

"Where the fuck is Alaska?" he yelled, looking for the chef. "How did this happen?"

Alaska was in charge of flying in the wild Alaskan salmon and the organic blueberries fresh every day. Neil finally calmed down and sat down at the table and offered me the contaminated blueberries.

I ate one. "Not bad for touching plastic," I said, and that made him laugh.

I suspect he realized he'd overreacted a bit.

"Thanks, it felt so good tonight," he told me. "Whatever you're doing, you got to drill it into Tim. You got me hooked on this sound. I feel like a one-man band."

He was right — it was a big sound for one guy. I finally got Tim to push the sound more so Neil could feel it.

When I mix, I do tend to push it to the limit, and I like that feeling of having all that power in my hands. It's a similar feeling to driving a muscle car with a lot of power that makes you just want to let it rip.

The record was nominated for three Grammys, and Neil won his first Grammy after waiting so many years, for Best Rock Song for "Angry World." At the after-party at the Beverly Hills Hotel, I went to sit with Bob Dylan and Tony Bennett at a small table at the back of the bar. Byron, who is Dylan's bodyguard and a former world champion kickboxer, told me to sit beside Dylan. Right beside Dylan was a tall black woman on a small couch. Dylan slid over so I could sit beside him.

"Hey, Mark, what's up with the disguise?" he asked.

I was sporting long hair and a beard at the time, and wore a bowler hat.

"It just kind of grew that way," I told him and he smiled.

He asked why I was there, so I told him I'd made Neil's Grammy-winning record. I asked him how the 1966 Harley was, the bike I'd found him back when we made the *Oh Mercy* album. He told me it was still his favorite bike.

Dylan had played a song at the Grammys with Mumford & Sons, which is why he was there. I told him we should do another record together one day, and he said that would be great.

Daniel had a side deal that if Neil's record won a Grammy, he would get a $50,000 bonus. He never got it because Neil won for Best Rock Song, which had to do with Neil's writing and not the production of the song.

The record had taken more than six months to make, waiting for all the full moons and waiting for Dan to recover from his accident. He had me add up all the days and food costs, my time, studio costs, and along with his fee it came to $250,000. Dan's manager handed the bill to Elliot, who just laughed at the invoice and told Daniel he must be dreaming because Warner Bros., who had been Neil's label for many years, only paid $25,000 for an acoustic record. The days of the big record budgets were long gone, and with companies not selling records anymore, they no longer paid out because they didn't get the money back. It was a reality check for Dan; the days of big payouts were over. He took the $25,000, and it was essentially the last record he produced.

Neil's album topped out at number two in Canada and number fourteen in the United States. It sold more than 10,000 records in its first week and received lots of great reviews; *Rolling Stone* gave it four out of five stars. *Uncut* called it the second-best album of 2010, and it was long-listed for the 2011 Polaris Music Prize.

A couple of months after the record was out, the record company wanted to put out an alternative version of "Sign of Love." I recorded Dave Grohl of the Foo Fighters on drums, and he laid down a big, fat rock beat on a big Ludwig drum kit I set up for him. The track sounded huge. I remixed it with the drums and it came out as a single.

CHAPTER 31

JONI MITCHELL

IN THE LATE '90S I HAD RECORDED Joni Mitchell on Brian Blade's second album, *Perceptual*. She came in to sing on one of the tracks at the Teatro Studio in Oxnard, California. I hung out with Joni a bit at a club called Bo Kaos, owned by my friends Frederic and Nicolas Meschin. Harry Dean Stanton was a regular there on Sunday nights. Joni was a nighthawk, often staying up all night guarding her property when she was convinced her neighbor was trying to sneak over. I found Joni's stories fascinating. In the dark club, I would sit beside her in the little booth beside the stage and listen to her tell stories all night while she chain-smoked.

In June 2013 I got a call from a producer at CBC Radio in Canada, and he asked me if I would be interested in helping him record Joni Mitchell for a CBC interview. The producer had seen an interview with Neil Young in which Neil talked about using an all-Canadian crew on his record and had mentioned my name, and the producer decided to do the same thing for Joni's interview.

I went up to Joni's house in Bel-Air and set up a little rig to record the interview. When I arrived, I found her sitting in her courtyard by a fountain. I asked if she remembered me.

"Yes, Mark, and I've been looking for you," she said. "Elliot was just talking about you the other day, and I want you to do some work with me."

I told her that I would love to help her out.

Joni's house was a gated Mediterranean-style villa, with a beautiful front garden surrounded by weeping trees and evergreen trees shaped like witches' hats. The courtyard and large cement fountain were at the back of the house. A large set of glass double doors in the center of the villa opened into the hall between the living room and the dining room. Terra-cotta floors led down a hallway to the grand salon, which boasted a huge wooden-beam ceiling, like an old Spanish cathedral. A big plaster fireplace with a large mirror above it faced a set of French windows that looked out on the courtyard. The walls were filled with Joni's paintings, vibrant in color. There were self-portraits along with scenes from her property in British Columbia, where she was building a new home. A large portrait by Mingus covered the wall beside the piano. A long couch sat in front of the window, along with two chairs covered with white linen. Toward the back of the room was a pool table centered in front of a library-sized bookcase, and a set of stairs went up to a loft where more books covered the walls.

Joni had become sick while living in this house and had discovered there was black mould growing in the walls, and she'd spent a couple of years trying to clear it all out. She didn't feel the mould had made her sick, but that she had Morgellons disease, a mysterious skin condition and controversial illness in which fibers appear from under the skin. Although some doctors take the illness seriously, many feel it is merely caused by the delusional belief that a person is infested with disease-causing agents, like parasites. Joni said that she had been seeing a Chinese-medicine doctor who was healing her and that she was finally feeling much better.

The interview was over two hours long. The interviewer had not done his homework and asked Joni irritating questions. She had to explain to him that she wasn't at Woodstock and that she wrote the song "Woodstock" from the point of view of a kid going there. David Geffen had actually made the decision not to take Joni to Woodstock because she was playing the *Dick Cavett Show* the next night and David felt that was more important.

While the interviewer impatiently stumbled through his questions, Joni answered him with both a somewhat sarcastic voice and also passionately, needing to clear up misconceptions about her. Once the interview was over, I sat in the kitchen with her. She spoke of wanting to do a ballet and that she was

Recording session with Joni and Brian Blade at her house in Bel-Air.

putting together a five-CD box set. She needed to rework a couple of tracks and wanted me to get a hold of Brian Blade to see if he'd put drums on them. I told Joni that I could bring my studio right to her house and we could work in her living room, and she was excited that she didn't have to leave home.

I spoke to Brian Blade and he said he had only one day he could work. He was flying in to do another session and asked if I could find a kit for him to use. I made a call to another drummer friend of mine, Jimmy Paxson, who played drums for Stevie Nicks. He had just bought a 1950s black-and-gold Gretsch

Duco kit that was just like Brian's, and he was kind enough to loan it for the Joni recordings.

It was late August 2013 when I set up my studio installation in the salon of Joni's house. I put my console facing the fireplace so my speakers were facing the couch and she would have great sound sitting behind me. I set up the Gretsch kit on a rug beside the couch so Joni could have a sight line to Brian. I gave Joni a set of headphones so she could hear the track closely.

I was working off a stereo mix of the master of one of her songs, "A Strange Boy," and it only had percussion on it. Brian played a couple of takes until he had the arrangement down, then Joni came in to listen. She had an idea that Brian should play low in a couple of areas. Brian had a take she was happy with, then we took a break. Joni must have talked for an hour. She spoke of first coming to California, and how Neil Young, David Crosby, and Graham Nash basically abandoned her, leaving her all alone.

It was getting late and I pushed to try the next track, a song called "Love Puts On a New Face." Brian struggled with that one. He was using brushes, but the arrangement was very complicated, and Joni was trying to direct him, which didn't work, so we ended up abandoning it. Brian had a session early the next day, so I got him out of there before Joni jumped into more stories we couldn't bear to not hear.

Joni said she wanted to try a bass on "A Strange Boy," more of a Jaco Pastorius part. My friend Hal Cragin, who'd played bass on the Iggy Pop records I'd made, was a Jaco fan and had studied his style. I told Joni about Hal, so she asked if he could come in and try a part. When I phoned Hal the next day, he thought I was joking. He was the biggest fan of Joni, so being asked to play on one of her songs was a dream come true.

Hal came in around four o'clock the next day, and I played him the track and plugged him in. He started out with the Jaco thing quite heavy, and Joni said to him, "You're thinking too hard. Let it breathe, man."

Hal asked Joni about Jaco, and it sent us into a good hour of how Jaco was the only guy who understood Joni's music and that he had a way to play around her odd chords. She said she was responsible for creating her own chord that no one else had heard before, and even Charles Mingus was impressed. She was a little bitter that men wouldn't listen to her. She said that she didn't even own any

LISTEN UP!

of her own records. After her last divorce from Larry Klein, Larry ended up with Joni's whole record collection.

Hal went back at it and Joni directed him, stopping him and saying, "You're not listening to me. You're playing on top of the beat and you need to lay back, not be so rushed."

I got Hal to turn around so his back was to the speakers, and I had him play the part again. Because he wasn't facing the speakers, there was a slight delay, which was just enough to sink him back into the pocket of the groove. Hal was a trouper and got the part down the way Joni liked.

I felt that Joni was ready to try recording a new song, but I would have to ease it out of her. She had gone to Toronto to do a show at Massey Hall. It was a tribute to her, and although she didn't want to sing, she did and sounded great. I tried to encourage her to sing a new song but she said that her singing voice was gone because of smoking, vocal nodes, and ill health. I told her that she had a wonderful singing voice, and although it was now lower, it was still beautiful.

Joni also wanted to remix her debut record, called *Song to a Seagull*. She said that David Crosby had produced it and that he "mis-produced it." David had her double all the guitar parts and because of that, she'd always hated the album. It had been mainly recorded on a 4-track with two songs done on an 8-track. She asked if I could find the original multitrack tapes to remix and I said I'd try. I made several calls and then found a guy in Santa Monica who had the tapes. The songs were on reels along with Crosby, Stills, Nash & Young, and I met the guy who had them and picked them up.

The biggest hurdle was finding a studio with both 4-track and 8-track machines, as no studios had both, so I headed to Warner Bros. studio to transfer the 4-track reels and then went to Capitol Studios to transfer the 8-track. I then transferred all the songs to my iZ Radar digital 24-track machine.

I went back up to Joni's house to mix them, and she told me to just go ahead and she would listen to them later. When I was finished, I gave her a CD. Shortly after, I got a strange call from her saying that she'd listened to them on her TV and that "it sounded different on the Dolby surround setting than the cinema setting."

I told her it wasn't a great place to listen, but she said she liked the way it sounded on the Dolby setting. I asked her if she would listen in the kitchen on her little Bose system, but she was adamant about listening on her TV. I went back and forth with her perfecting the mixes until she liked them.

I was scheduled to start another record with Lukas Nelson, Willie Nelson's son, and I had to pull my studio out of Joni's house. It took a week before I could get a hold of her. She'd fallen ill and stayed in her room. The only phone was in the kitchen and couldn't be heard from the bedroom, and it was only by chance that she was in the kitchen and picked up her phone. I went right over to retrieve my gear. She'd gotten bad news that the ballet wouldn't be happening and she was in a bad mood. She'd put so much time and energy into it that it knocked the wind out of her. She decided to go up to Canada, and our work got put on hold. It wasn't until April 2015 that she called me back asking if I knew where the multitrack tapes were. I told her I'd left them on the pool table in her salon; Joni had looked for them but couldn't find them.

I was in the middle of doing a test mastering on a couple of the songs for her to hear when the news came that she had been hospitalized. She had collapsed in her house and was discovered unconscious on the floor. She'd been rushed to hospital and it was discovered she'd suffered a brain aneurysm. Joni is a strong woman, and despite chain-smoking, she seemed very healthy and together and has made a good recovery. She ended up putting out a CD box set of all the songs that had been meant for the ballet, but the tracks I worked on never made it to the collection. Perhaps one day.

CHAPTER 32

RICKIE LEE JONES

I FIRST WORKED WITH RICKIE LEE JONES at the Teatro in the late '90s, when she was living in Ojai, California. She wanted to make a record like the English band Portishead, using drum loops and strange sounds. There was only Rickie and me in the studio. I'd play her some of the loops I had in my personal collection, and she always liked the more unusual ones, such as the "Kalimba" loop that had a bass line built into it. Rickie had bits of lyrics she'd sing over the loops. She was breaking new ground, and I really thought we were onto a new sound for her. Her voice ranted like Miles Davis's trumpet on "Bitches Brew." Many of her songs felt like they were pulled out of movies, and her haunting, little-girl voice layered over these tracks seemed to be futuristic jazz. In fact, there seemed to me no other description for this work other than "futuristic."

Rickie left the Teatro with a sketch of several tracks that I thought would lead to a brilliant record. She ended up working with Rick Boston and made an album called *Ghostyhead*. I thought it was good but not as groundbreaking as what we had done together.

In 2003 Rickie called and asked if I'd mix three songs on her new record, *The Evening of My Best Day*. The record was produced by David Kalish, Steve Berlin, and Rickie. I was working out of the Paramour Estate at that time. I was handed the song files, and there were over a hundred tracks on some of the songs — three different drum kits for different sections, forty tracks of guitars, twenty vocals, and none of it was organized or edited. It was left in my hands to pick out all the best parts. Nothing was labeled, so I had to listen to everything in order to make sense of it. Once I was done mixing each track, Rickie would show up and listen, and right away she loved it. She was known for being hard on her producers and engineers, but I found her to be an absolute angel.

The last track was a song called "Sailor Song." David Kalish was at the studio when she came in to listen. I got about two words into the verse when she asked me to stop.

"That's not the right vocal take," she said. "David, where is the new vocal? You should have known that wasn't the right vocal — where is it?"

Up until then, I had only seen the sweet side of Rickie, but she wants things right and right away. She grilled David and didn't let up, and although he was a big dude with tattoos, she had him in tears. He finally found the right vocal, and I put it in the mix and Rickie was content.

Rickie packed up her life and moved to New Orleans. In the fall of 2014, I was there producing a record for Anders Osborne. I mentioned to Anders that Rickie had moved to New Orleans. He was a big fan of Rickie's and asked if I thought she might sing on one of his tracks. I called Rickie up to see how she was doing and invited her over to the studio. She was looking for a place to make her next album, and this was a new studio she hadn't seen yet. On the day she came over, I only intended to show her the studio, not ask her to sing. She liked the vibe of the place and I played her one of Anders's tracks. She liked it and I think it won her over and gave me license to ask her if she would sing on one of his songs. She said that she would, and we already had a song picked out for her. I handed her a mic and played the track, and she nailed it on the first take. During the playback she and Anders cried, both affected by her emotional vocals. Anders couldn't thank her enough.

When I walked Rickie out, she asked me if I could help with her record, and I said I'd love to. I didn't hear from her for a couple of months, then she texted asking me to produce a couple of tracks. She had gone into the studio with another producer but they weren't getting along, and she needed at least three more tracks to finish her record.

Rickie Lee Jones at Esplanade Studio, New Orleans.

When I first flew to New Orleans on this particular job for Anders Osbourne, I wanted to work at a new studio called Esplanade Studios, located in a big, old church on Esplanade Avenue. They'd just installed a new Neve console and I ended up being the first to use it. I set up the piano and mic, then set up a vocal mic, too. I ran some tests to be sure everything was working. Rickie called from outside the studio looking for the way to get in, so I went out to fetch her. She walked into the large church room with a big grand piano sitting in the middle and said, "Wow, this place is cool."

Without blinking an eye, she sat down at the piano and said, "I want to record a song I just wrote. Can we record it right now?"

The control room was upstairs, like at Abbey Road, with a glass window overlooking the studio. I ran up there as fast as I could and pushed the record button. One pass through and that was it — we had the first song down. She had an old guitar with her that was strung with four strings in a banjo tuning, and she wanted to record the next song with that guitar.

Not wanting to burn out in the studio, Rickie only wanted to work short days and have her evenings off. Not having to work, I went for walks in the French Quarter. The Kingsway house that I'd lived in back in the early '90s had been bought by Nicolas Cage and then lost to the IRS for tax evasion. A real-estate company got hold of it and turned it into a house for events, so no one lived there. As I was walking through the French Quarter one night, I noticed a party in the building. I walked by and they had security on all the doors, only allowing people with a pass to get in. I got something to eat and then walked by again. The party was over and they were loading all the catering out, the door left wide open, so I walked right in. I hadn't been in the house for over sixteen years, and it was strange to be inside again. They had remodeled the whole kitchen and had new appliances — all polished aluminum, stark and cold. The main front rooms were the same, but brand-new tasteless chandeliers hung from the ceiling and the mirrors over the fireplace were modern and looked out of place. The original pool table was still there with the purple cloth top.

I walked up the center staircase to the second floor where there used to be four bedroom suites. My old room was gone. They had opened up the whole front of the upstairs and made it into a lounge that led onto the balcony. The Mexican Room was still intact with the green tin ceiling that Joel Ford had put in; across the hall, the New Orleans Room was all there but with a new big bathroom with a modern tub.

I walked up to the third floor and found changes there, too; they had put in a new bathroom with white subway tile, although the roof deck was the same, as was the main bedroom. It amazed me how someone with money but poor taste could take beautiful architecture and destroy it. Some things belong to certain periods, and mixing them shouldn't happen, and if it does, the modern elements should be incorporated with taste.

I walked out to the side yard, and although the Roman bath was still there, the garage that housed all the motorcycles was gone. All the beautiful banana and palm trees had been replaced with cement and stones, the oasis that had once existed there utterly destroyed. While walking around, I ran into the woman who was looking after the house and in charge of renting it out. I explained to her who I was, and she said she'd heard all the stories from when I lived there.

Back at the studio with Rickie the next day, we were finishing off the last track, called "Charlotte's Web," when she mentioned her daughter, Charlotte, was flying in. I'd met little Charlotte and her dad, Pascal, up in Ojai when she was about four. Her dad was always trying to please her. If she said, "Daddy, I want a bird, I want a bird right now!" Pascal, in his thick French accent, would say, "Yes, Charlotte, I'll get you a bird right now."

Rickie had played me a song a teenaged Charlotte had written and performed and it was breathtaking — she sounded just like a young Rickie. I thought it incredible how it all gets passed down. We finished by putting tuba on the last track, and Rickie was happy with everything and thanked me for making it a fun recording experience.

Once I arrived home, I got a call from Charlotte asking if I would help her record her own songs. I love a family affair when it comes full circle.

While sitting in Heathrow Airport waiting for my Virgin Atlantic flight to L.A., I picked up a copy of *Mojo* magazine. I came across an article about Rickie Lee Jones, and it said the songs we'd recorded were some of her finest. The song "Jimmy Choos" was also getting radio play nationwide, and I was honored to have helped an artist like Rickie.

EPILOGUE

I FEEL PRIVILEGED TO HAVE PLAYED A part in bringing so many important albums into the world and to have worked with so many of the revolutionary, pioneering, gifted artists of our time.

What stands out for me is what a gift creation is — to be in a beautiful space, connecting artists with each other, and artists with their art. So often in studios everyone is watching a screen and not listening. I don't use screens when I record, and the musicians don't either. We are all engaged with one another, going deeper together, lifting one another up. Some musicians have certain phrasings they can't get beyond, and by making them engage with each other, I take them out of their comfort zone and up to a new level. I think back to Vic Chestnutt, one of the great American songwriters. When I brought in the best musicians, he wanted to impress them, and each person excelled individually, propelled by each other, Vic included. Connection is everything.

An album is a tapestry, fibers of creativity woven together to make a beautiful whole. I think not pursuing a higher education in music was the right choice for me, and I've used it to my advantage. If I was on the same level musically as the most gifted musicians, I'd end up pushing ideas on them, rather than pulling from them their own brilliance. All the records would sound the same.

Reflecting back on the albums I've made, it occurred to me that each artistic endeavor had its own drama, whether it was Emmylou Harris's turbulent relationship with her boyfriend, Bob Dylan fighting with Dan, or Marianne Faithfull's crippling self-doubt. I wonder if the brilliant albums would have been the same, if they would have expressed the human condition, without those storms of emotions. Perhaps art does require angst; perhaps personality clashes and meltdowns and challenging circumstances all feed into it. To work successfully in the music business you need to be willing to ride those waves of turmoil to get to the masterpiece waiting on the beach.

Every time I make a record it feels like joining a family, whether I'm working with a band or a solo artist. No matter how long we are together — one month or one week — I grow really close to the artists and care about them deeply. Making an album is a shared experience. It happens on tours as well. We laugh and share intimacies and are together nonstop, but then everything is finished and people go their own ways and separation anxiety ensues. You're back at home and go through a breakup. Some people need to gradually fit back into their family life. Sometimes I have to start another project right away and don't have time for the aftereffects of leaving the group I've been working with. People who haven't experienced deep collaboration on a project night and day can't understand how it feels. I love working with people again because you already know each other and you just fall into it, picking up where you left off. You don't need to gain trust or figure out each other's idiosyncrasies.

I was lucky to have an interest outside of music. I found clarity on my bikes — they were always my escape, my meditation, and I'm sure the extra oxygen from the speed of the bike fed my brain and gave me answers to questions I had on certain projects.

It's been a ride up to this point — one I wouldn't change. Listen up: when you sing, dance, or play music, your soul is at its best.

ACKNOWLEDGMENTS

Christen Shepherd for additional writing on the prologue and epilogue, and Naomi Huisman for additional editing.

Thanks also to:
Rob Cohen and Christine Roth,
Gregory Butler,
Michael Holmes and all the ECW Press team.

LISTEN UP!

SELECTED DISCOGRAPHY

Alexz Johnson, *A Stranger Time* (Laydee Spencer Music)

All the Pretty Horses soundtrack (Sony)

Amy Correia, *Lakeville* (Nettwerk America)

Arid, *At the Close of Every Day* (Sony Music Benelux)

Augie March, *Moo, You Bloody Choir* (Sony BMG Music)

Avril Lavigne, "Complicated," "Sk8er Boi" and "I'm With You" from *Let Go* (Arista)

Bastard Sons of Johnny Cash, *Bastard Sons Of Johnny Cash* (Ultimatum Music)

Bob Dylan, *Oh Mercy* (Columbia)

Bob Dylan, *Time Out of Mind* (Columbia)

Brian Blade, *Fellowship* (Blue Note)

Chris Whitley, *Living with the Law* (Columbia)

Chris Whitley, *Terra Incognita* (Work Group)

Colin James, *Traveler* (Warner Canada)

Crash Vegas, *Red Earth* (Sony)

Daniel Lanois, *Acadie* (Warner Bros)

Daniel Lanois, *For the Beauty of Wynona* (Warner Bros)

Daryl Johnson, *Shake* (Real World)

Diane Tell, *Tout de Diane* (BMG International)

Eddie Vedder, "You've Got to Hide Your Love Away" from the *I Am Sam* soundtrack (V2)

Emmylou Harris, *Wrecking Ball* (Asylum)

Harold Budd, *By the Dawn's Early Light* (Opal)

Ian Moore, *Modernday Folklore* (Capricorn)

Ian Thornley, *Secrets* (Anthem)

Iggy Pop, *American Caesar* (Virgin)

Iggy Pop, *Avenue B* (Virgin)

k.d. Lang, *Anywhere but Here* soundtrack (Atlantic)

Kaizers Orchestra, *Maskineri* (Constanze DA)

Lisa Germano, *Happiness* (4AD)

Lucinda Williams, *World Without Tears* (Lost Highway)

Luscious Jackson, *Fever In Fever Out* (Capitol)

Marianne Faithfull, *Vagabond Ways* (Virgin)

Natalie Imbruglia, *White Lilies Island* (BMG)

Neil Young, *Le Noise* (Warner)

Peter Gabriel, *Us* (Geffen)

R.E.M., *Automatic for the People* (I.R.S.)

R.E.M., *Monster* (Warner Bros)

Red Hot Chili Peppers, *Californication* singles (Warner Bros)

Rickie Lee Jones, *The Other Side of Desire* (Thirty Tigers)

Rickie Lee Jones, three tracks on *The Evening of My Best Day* (V2)

Robbie Robertson, *Storyville* (Geffen)

Scott Weiland, *12 Bar Blues* (Atlantic)

Shannon McNally, *Jukebox Sparrows* (Capitol)

Sharon Little, *Perfect Time for a Breakdown* (CBS Records)

Sling Blade soundtrack (Island)

The Neville Brothers, *Brother's Keeper* (A&M)

The Tragically Hip, *Day for Night* (MCA)

The Waifs, *Up All Night* (Jarrah)

The Wailin' Jennys, *Bright Morning Stars* (Red House Records)

Tim Gibbons, *Shylingo* (Real Records)

Tom Waits, *Real Gone* (Epitaph)

Tom Waits, various tracks from *Orphans* (Anti)

U2, "Ground Beneath Her Feet" from *The Million Dollar Hotel* soundtrack (Island)

U2, *All That You Can't Leave Behind* (Interscope)

Vic Chesnutt, *Silver Lake* (New West)

Victoria Williams, *Musings of a Creek Dipper* (Atlantic)

Willie Nelson, *Teatro* (Island)

LISTEN UP!

Born in Manchester, England, **Mark Howard** is a Canadian record producer, engineer, and mixer. He has worked with Neil Young, R.E.M., Willie Nelson, Peter Gabriel, U2, the Neville Brothers, Tom Waits, Lucinda Williams, Marianne Faithfull, and the Tragically Hip, among many others. His brother, Chris Howard, is an author and painter.